Socialism in
Theological Perspective

American Academy of Religion
Dissertation Series

edited by
Mark C. Taylor

Number 21

Socialism in Theological Perspective:
A Study of Paul Tillich
by
John R. Stumme

John R. Stumme

Socialism in Theological Perspective

A Study of Paul Tillich, 1918 – 1933

Scholars Press

Distributed by
Scholars Press
PO Box 5207
Missoula, Montana 59806

Socialism in Theological Perspective:
A Study of Paul Tillich

John R. Stumme

Copyright © 1978
American Academy of Religion

Library of Congress Cataloging in Publication Data

Stumme, John R   1942–
   Socialism in theological perspective.

   (AAR dissertation series ; 21 ISSN 0145-272X)
   Originally presented as the author's thesis, Union Theological Seminary.
   Vita.
   Bibliography: p.
   1. Tillich, Paul, 1886–1965. 2. Socialism, Christian.
I. Title. II. Series: American Academy of Religion.
Dissertation series – American Academy of Religion ; 21.
BX4827.T53S78 1978   230'.092'4   78-3675
ISBN 0-89130-232-8

Printed in the United States of America

1   2   3   4   5

Edwards Brothers, Inc.
Ann Arbor, MI 48104

TABLE OF CONTENTS

	Page
PREFACE	1
ABBREVIATIONS	3
CHAPTER I. INTRODUCTION	5
CHAPTER II. THE CONTEXT	15
The Background, 1886-1914	16
The Turning Point, 1914-1918	19
The Beginning, 1918-1919	21
The Kairos Circle, 1920-1924	32
Within Socialism, 1925-1931	38
Socialism or Barbarism, 1932-1933	47
CHAPTER III. THE MEANING OF SOCIALISM	71
Socialism as an Expression of the Proletarian Situation	71
Socialism as a Religious Phenomenon	75
Socialism as a Prophetic Movement	85
The Symbol of Socialism: Expectation	92
Socialism as a Living Reality	104
CHAPTER IV. TRANSFORMING HISTORICAL MATERIALISM	119
Materialism: The "Matter" of Change	119
The Unity of Being and Consciousness	127
The Spirit, Ideology, and the Protestant Principle	139
The Validity of Marx's Analysis	148
Summary	152
CHAPTER V. TRANSFORMING HISTORICAL DIALECTIC	163
Dialectical Change	164
The Unity of Freedom and Necessity	170
Historical Dialectic as Expectation	178
History's Future	187
Summary	198
CHAPTER VI. THE THEOLOGICAL PERSPECTIVE	209
A Theology of Politics	210
A Critique of the Lutheran Ethic	217
Barth's Challenge	225
The Coming of the Kingdom	234
A Proleptic Model	241
The Later Years, 1933-1945	250
BIBLIOGRAPHY	271
PRECIS	295
VITA	297

PREFACE

Even a dissertation can be rooted in life. As one who came to maturity in America during the 1960's, I became convinced that profound social and religious change is required in my society. A budding theologian, I began to search for theological answers that were responsive to this imperative. In the process I experienced a deep-seated conflict between the individualism and the conservative predilection of my own religious tradition and the optimistic confidence and often one-dimensional "flatness" of those actively involved in seeking change. Therefore, it was with great interest and excitement that I discovered a first-rate theologian, nurtured within the Lutheran tradition, who had struggled with the problems of radical change in the modern world. From the beginning of my graduate study, I was intent on exploring whatever may lie hidden in Paul Tillich's religious socialism. My searching continues, but I have found Tillich to be a stimulating teacher with whom to be involved during the first part of the 1970's.

I owe a debt of gratitude to countless people for help along the way. Only a few will be named. My teacher and friend, Dr. Carl E. Braaten, Lutheran School of Theology in Chicago, first introduced me to Tillich and his theology of history. Dr. Roger L. Shinn, whom I am honored to call my *Doktorvater,* gave me always wise counsel and guidance. Dr. James Luther Adams encouraged me in this venture and in his enjoyable anecdotal manner gladly shared his rich knowledge of Tillich. Especially do I thank Dr. Adolph Lowe for his willingness to be interviewed and for his vivid recollection of Tillich and the religious socialism of which he was an important but often forgotten part. Dr. Helmut Gollwitzer, Freie Universität Berlin, added a new dimension to my study by making real the encounter between Christian faith and Marxist thought in contemporary Germany. My hope is that the following pages, with all their blemishes, show that their knowledge and their example have borne some fruit.

I express my appreciation also to others who have assisted

in the research and preparation of this study. The archivists of the Tillich archives at Harvard and in Goettingen, Dr. Maria Grossmann and Frau Gertraut Stoeber, respectively, were gracious in their aid to me, as was Frau Renate Albrecht. I thank Ms. Katherine Eklund for proofreading the entire manuscript and Ms. Frances Kirchner for typing the final draft. Finally, I am grateful to the Lutheran World Federation for having made it possible for me to pursue my investigations in the geographical setting from which Tillich's early writings came.

Except where noted, I have done the translating from German. During the later part of my writing, parts of a translation of *Die sozialistische Entscheidung*, prepared by Franklin Sherman and Roy Enquist, were available to me. While I have utilized this translation, the one in the text is my own. Also, it should be noted, the words "man" and "he," when they do not refer to an individual, are intended to include all people, male and female.

ABBREVIATIONS

"Answer"	"Answer to an Inquiry of the Protestant Consistory of Brandenburg"
"Basic Principles"	"Basic Principles of Religous Socialism"
Blaetter	Blaetter fuer religioesen Sozialismus
"Cl. St."	"Klassenkampf und religioeser Sozialismus"
GW	Gesammelte Werke
IH	The Interpretation of History
Kirchenfrage	Der Sozialismus als Kirchenfrage
Neue Blaetter	Neue Blaetter fuer den Sozialismus
PE	The Protestant Era
Pol. Exp.	Political Expectation
PPPS	Protestantisches Prinzip und proletarische Situation
Rel. Sit.	The Religious Situation
"RS (I)"	"Religioeser Sozialismus I" (in GW)
"RS (II)"	"Religious Socialism" (in Pol. Exp.)
RV	Religioese Verwirklichung
SD	Die sozialistische Entscheidung
"Th. of Cul."	"On the Idea of a Theology of Culture"
"Die Theologie des Kairos"	"Die Theologie des Kairos und die gegenwaertige geistige Lage. Offener Brief an Emanual Hirsch"
Das System	Das System der Wissenschaften nach Gegenstaendigen und Methoden. Ein Entwurf.
"Weiterbildung"	"Die religioese und philosophische Weiterbildung des Sozialismus"
WR?	What is Religion?

CHAPTER 1

INTRODUCTION

Paul Tillich is widely recognized as one of the most important Christian theologians in the twentieth century. It is not so well known, however, that for a good part of his life he was also an active socialist. During the years from 1918 to 1933, Tillich was a member of one, possibly two, socialist parties; he was the head of a circle of intellectuals whose focus was the proletarian movement, and he participated in other groups of critical socialists; he authored numerous articles and a major book on socialism; he was a founder and an editor of a socialist journal; and in 1933 he lost his professorship because of his political activities. Socialism for Tillich was a vital practical and theoretical concern.

This dissertation probes the interaction between the Christian and socialist realities in Tillich's early life and thought. It explores what Tillich said to both Protestant Christianity and Marxist socialism from his distinctive vantage point within both traditions. What for him were their meaning and their relationship, their points of conflict and agreement? In embracing socialism as a Christian, what did Tillich intend to do, and how did he seek to achieve his ends? The complex of issues in this encounter is the stimulus for approaching Tillich's thought.

Since the origin of Marxist socialism in Germany, which, for convenience, can be dated from the appearance of *The Communist Manifesto* in 1848, the involved relationship between Christianity and socialism has more often than not been characterized by political and philosophical opposition, much of which has been hostile and uncompromising. This conflict is a major part of "the modern schism"[1] and remains a powerful reality in today's world. Tillich, although aware of the deep divisions between the two, did not consider schism as history's final word on the matter, and so he worked to build bridges over this gulf and to create a new unity of the two. His stance "on the boundary between Lutheranism and socialism"[2] is a significant minority voice amidst the prevailing rift between these two notable historical forces.

Recently, in light of the poverty and inequality among the world's peoples, some Christians have once more been led back to a new consideration of Karl Marx and the structural alternative he represents. Dom Helder Camara, Archbishop of Recife, Brazil, is one who has articulated this renewed concern. In a lecture presented at the University of Chicago in October 1974 in celebration of the Seventh Centenary of St. Thomas Aquinas, Dom Helder appealed to the University "to try, today, to do with Karl Marx what St. Thomas, in his day, did with Aristotle." Just as Thomas "had the courage to deal with Aristotle who, in those days, was regarded as a pagan, a materialist, a dangerous and cursed sinner," so today, he remarked, Marx "challenges our courage because he is a materialist, a militant atheist, an agitator, a subversive, and anti-Christian." In his encounter with Aristotle, Thomas was able to incorporate "authentic reasoning" into Christian theology and to rediscover "Christian values that had been tainted, for instance, by certain aspects of platonism." In drawing the parallel to today, Dom Helder insisted that there are values in Marx's system that "are able to benefit the development of human thought." Moreover, he believed Marx deserves to be studied because he has "become the inspiration for life and for death of a great part of humanity." Dom Helder considered that the task of finding Christian values in Marx's system is one that "will require many years of patient research and creativeness on the level of the Thomist Summas."[3]

Dom Helder's appeal indicates that the relationship between Christ and Marx is again an open question. The optimism and the euphoria of the early "Christian-Marxist" dialogue of the 1960's are gone; nevertheless, this dialogue did open up long-closed avenues of exchange.[4] In the oppressive conditions of Latin America, of which Dom Helder's speech is an expression, theologians of liberation are searching for new ways of integrating faith and critical social thinking, and a movement called "Christians for Socialism" has emerged.[5] In Europe some theologians are beginning to ask if a truly human society and world is possible within the structures of capitalism, and in

America the "taboo" on socialism is being challenged.[6] Marxism can no longer be considered a monolithic bloc, and its various expressions embody diverse responses to religion.[7] Western Marxist intellectuals are demonstrating the continuing vitality of their tradition by raising self-critical questions and by re-evaluating the meaning of religion.[8] The tangled relationship between socialism and Christian faith is at points more fluid today than at any time since the 1930's.

The global economic and class situation, the concern with Marx and socialism among Christians, and the pluralism within Marxism make a new study of Tillich's efforts to relate the two worlds both fitting and inviting. New contexts in the present require fresh looks at the past, and today's context offers the possibility of gaining a deeper appreciation of Tillich's experience with religion and radical politics a half-century ago. The reader might also discover that a close look at Tillich's "religious socialism" can give historical perspective to similar contemporary efforts.

In spite of the centrality it had for his early thought, Tillich's socialism has been neglected in studies about him. This is especially true for his interpreters in North America where a book-length treatment of his religious socialism has never been published.[9] Passing references to it frequently convey the impression that his socialist commitment and theory were secondary and disposable to his "real" interests, or they indicate an ignorance or misunderstanding of its nature.[10] In the continuing process of assessing and reassessing Tillich's life and thought since his death a decade ago, his religious socialism has not received its proper recognition. A hoped-for consequence of this study is to demonstrate the significance it did have for Tillich from 1919 to 1933.

Several factors help account for this gap in Tillich studies. Historical events seemed to establish the obsolescence of Tillich's project. The defeat of religious socialism at the hands of Adolf Hitler, the preoccupation with a second world war, the disappointment of Russian Communism and the inhumanities of Stalinism, the Cold War and the antisocialist sentiment in America, the success of the New Deal--all these events contributed to the conviction that Tillich's religious socialism

belonged to the dustbin of history. Charles West expressed the
belief of probably most Christian thinkers in the West (including Tillich) during the post-war decades when he wrote, "The
time when Marxism and Christianity could be considered as basically humanist philosophies at war, or in conversation about
the best ideal for human society, is past."[11]

Moreover, after World War II, Tillich concentrated on his
Systematic Theology, and students of Tillich turned their attention to this his magnum opus. But Tillich's *Systematic Theology* no longer embodied his concrete socialist decision, and
therefore, when he and his interpreters studied the issues related to his religious socialism, their interest was usually
directed to the general categories of his philosophy of history.
Not surprisingly, the idea became widespread that the viability
of his earlier social theory and philosophy of history depended
on its severance from socialism.[12]

Such a separation, however, does violence to Tillich's religious socialism, undercutting its concreteness and destroying
its unity. Today, in light of the experience reflected in Dom
Helder's appeal, the value of Tillich's early "theology of politics" might well lie precisely in the dialectical relationship
of its religious and Marxist elements. This dissertation analyzes his thought at this juncture, believing Tillich provides
an early, elaborate, and provocative example of a Christian
thinker who viewed socialism from a theological perspective.

In previous studies, Tillich's religious socialism has
been interpreted from a variety of viewpoints, many of which
were critical of different aspects of his thought. The focus,
direction, and source of the most important of these criticisms
need to be briefly outlined.

1) For many, Tillich's theological perspective, considered on the basis of Christian norms, was unsound. Karl Barth
was the fountainhead of this criticism, and West has developed
it at greatest length. For West Tillich's ontology kept him
from doing justice to God's revelation in Christ as well as from
understanding Marxism on its own terms.[13] Likewise from a theological point of view, Eduard Heimann, Tillich's old religious
socialist colleague, later objected to his idea of the secondary
kairos because its relation to the unique kairos in the

appearance of the Christ was not clarified.[14]

2) For others, Tillich's understanding and appropriation of Marx and Marxism was erroneous. Contra Tillich, Hans Beyer contended that it was impossible to embrace both religion and historical and dialectical materialism. He made it clear that for the orthodox Marxist-Leninist there can be no conceptual agreement between religion and Marxism.[15] Renate Breipohl has argued that Tillich, like other religious socialists, misconstrued Marx by placing him within a conceptual framework of irrationalism. In her interpretation bourgeois vitalism prevailed over the rationalism of Marxism, and she doubted if Tillich's religious socialism was really socialism.[16] While Breipohl thought that Tillich had not gone far enough in adopting Marxism, Heimann believed he had gone too far in accommodating his thought to it. Rejecting his attempt to combine Christianity and Marxism, Heimann criticized Tillich for his "faulty appraisal of the facts of the Marxist doctrine," especially the doctrine of man which for Heimann "denies the glory and the misery of man's essential freedom."[17]

3) Some interpreters found Tillich's social analysis incorrect. Eberhard Amelung, drawing upon the thought of functionalism, has developed the most extensive criticism of Tillich at this point. He called his religious socialism an "ideology" since it gave a distorted view of reality, overemphasizing the role of the economy and neglecting (among other things) the differentiation of functions in modern society.[18] James Luther Adams and Clark A. Kucheman have also challenged the adequacy and accuracy of Tillich's Marxist analysis.[19]

4) For others, Tillich's ontological approach was ill-suited for understanding history and for guiding praxis. Thomas Ulrich saw in Tillich's thought an unsuccessful attempt to mediate theory and praxis by developing a theological ontology. He failed, concluded Ulrich, because his theory was not originally related to social praxis and developed from its necessity.[20] Erich Schwerdtfeger found Tillich's religious socialism to be largely an unhistorical elaboration of postulates derived from his theological and ontological presuppositions. What Tillich considered to be the unavoidable ambiguity of life belonged for Schwerdtfeger only to his own age.[21] In a similar vein,

Friedrich-Martin Balzer believed Tillich's model for relating Christianity and Marxism was undesirable because its theoretical character was divorced from the praxis of the class struggle.[22]

These criticisms, which of course could be expanded and refined, indicate the scope and thrust of a large part of the secondary material on Tillich's religious socialism. Throughout this study the validity of these critical interpretations will be tested, and some will be found to be largely on target, some will be modified, and others will be challenged. In contrast to these studies, this dissertation wants to offer a more sympathetic view of Tillich's theological interpretation of socialism, while remaining critically aware of its limits.

The time span of this treatise is limited to the years from 1918 to 1933, that is, to the time of the German republic, which originated with the overthrow of the emperor in the November Revolution of 1918 and which ended with Hitler's coming to power in 1933. Tillich's socialist and political interests did not stop with the victory of National Socialism--this "break" occurred later in 1945--but the context and social presuppositions of his thinking were then gone; moreover, Tillich was no longer in Germany. Therefore, in order to understand Tillich in terms of the situation that his religious socialism addressed, this study has been restricted to the years of the Weimar Republic.

The following interpretation of Tillich's early thought is both narrow and broad. It is narrow because the focus remains on socialism and the theological perspective by which he viewed it; it is broad in that other facets of his thought necessarily enter into the examination. This dissertation is not directly a study of Tillich's philosophy of history, his philosophy of religion and culture, his anthropology or his ontology; yet all these are involved in his religious socialism.[23] While cognizant of the interconnections of his systematic approach to reality, the following pages continually return to Tillich's concern with socialism.

Tillich considered the scope of his religious socialism to be universal. If he did not touch on everything, he did explore many areas which are beyond the parameters of this writing. Important and related issues such as Tillich's view of power, of nature, and of technology deserve greater attention than given here but in order to keep this work within manageable bounds, it has been decided not to give separate treatment to these and other themes.

The title describes both the intention of Tillich's efforts and the concern of this dissertation. The label "religious socialism" has been omitted (Tillich also dropped the phrase) because it is an ambiguous combination of words foreign to contemporary ears. Tillich's work was distinctive in that it viewed socialism from a perspective that made the relationship of the Unconditional and the conditioned, God and man, the decisive issue. The aim of what follows is to unravel the meaning of this attempt. This study is a theological and ethical investigation, done from within the Christian tradition, of a Christian thinker who dealt seriously and creatively with the theoretical issues posed by socialism. Its purpose is to understand and interpret Tillich's socialist concept as an important episode in the history of the encounter of Christianity and Marxism. Its secondary purpose is to consider in a preliminary fashion what might be learned--in terms of its insights, problems, and limits--from Tillich's model for relating the two realities.

In order to appreciate Tillich's religious socialism on its own terms, to enter into the dilemnas he confronted and the opportunities he envisioned, the dissertation sets out by exploring the biographical and historical context from which it emerged. In Chapter 2 Tillich is placed in the web of relationships and events which shaped him and to which he responded. The importance that socialism had for him will become evident here.

The systematic probing of Tillich's theological-political theory begins in Chapter 3 where his interpretation of socialism is developed. This chapter is also crucial for comprehending Tillich's theological perspective.

In Chapters 4 and 5 Tillich's view of socialism is elaborated by a detailed discussion of his critical adaptation of socialist theory. Chapter 4 examines Tillich's position on historical materialism, and the next chapter looks at his affirmation, criticism, and transformation of socialism's dialectical view of change. In both chapters the mutual penetration of socialist and religious, Marxist and prophetic, themes is of paramount importance.

Attention turns directly to Tillich's theological perspective in the final chapter. His principles for understanding the relationship between religion and politics are presented and appraised. This discussion is followed by a comparison of Tilloch's attitude to those of Karl Barth and his own Lutheran tradition. Eschatology, an especially significant theological topic in his religious socialism, is singled out for special consideration and criticism. Then, in a summary section, his socialist concept and his theological perspective are brought together once again, and some of the value and shortcomings of Tillich's religious socialism is pinpointed. The dissertation concludes with a brief survey of Tillich's relationship to socialism after 1933, in order to set the time span studied here in the perspective of his whole life.

CHAPTER 1

NOTES

[1] The phrase is Martin E. Marty's. See his book, *The Modern Schism* (New York: Harper and Row, 1969), esp. pp. 36-58.

[2] *On the Boundary* (New York: Charles Scribner's Sons, 1966), pp. 74-81. Tillich's stance was of course not unique but was part of a religious socialist movement in Germany, as will become evident in Chapter 2. Religious socialism in Germany and Switzerland had parallel movements in England and America. For a discussion of efforts to relate Christianity and socialism in a positive way in the West before 1950 see Roger Shinn, *Christianity and the Problem of History* (New York: Charles Scribner's Sons, 1953), Ch. V, pp. 131-57.

[3] "What Would St. Thomas Aquinas, the Aristotle Commentator, Do if Faced with Karl Marx?" (unpublished manuscript of lecture given on October 29, 1975).

[4] See *Openings for Marxist-Christian Dialogue*, ed. by Thomas W. Ogletree (Nashville: Abingdon Press, 1968); *The Christian Marxist Dialogue,* ed. by Paul Oestreicher (London: The Macmillan Company, 1969); Ans J. Van der Bent, *The Christian Marxist Dialogue: An Annotated Bibliography* (Geneva: World Council of Churches, 1969).

[5] Two prominent representatives of the theology of liberation are Juan Luis Segundo and Gustavo Gutierrez. See especially G. Gutierrez, *A Theology of Liberation*, trans. and ed. by Sister Caridad Inda and John Eagleson (Maryknoll, New York: Orbis Books, 1973). Phillip E. Berryman has given a helpful survey of this movement, "Latin American Liberation Theology," *Theological Studies*, Vol. 34, No. 3 (September, 1973), pp. 357-95. For documentation on "Christians for Socialism," see *Christians and Socialism*, ed. by John Eagleson (Maryknoll, New York: Orbis Books, 1975).

[6] The German theologians Helmut Gollwitzer and Friedrich-Wilhelm Marquardt deserve mention. The existence of the "Subgroup of Socialism, Group on Social Ethics, American Academy of Religion" indicates the renewed interest in socialism among some North American theologians. Also see the chapter entitled "The American Taboo on Socialism" in Robert N. Bellah's *The Broken Covenant* (New York: A Crossroad Book, 1975), pp. 112-38.

[7] Cf. Per Frostin, "Modern Marxist Critique of Religion--A Survey," *Lutheran World*, Vol. 22, No. 2 (1973), pp. 141-54.

[8] Such intellectuals with varying ties to Marx include Ernst Bloch, Milan Machovec, Lesek Kolakowski, Vitezslav Gardavsky, Roger Garaudy, Max Horkheimer, Theodor Adorno, and Juergen Habermas.

[9] See the Bibliography for a listing of secondary sources on Tillich's religious socialism.

[10] For example, Alexander J. Mckelway's study mentions

Tillich's religious socialism only once and then in a footnote where he calls it "quietistic." *The Systematic Theology of Paul Tillich* (Richmond, Virginia: John Knox Press, 1964), p. 223.

[11] *Communism and the Theologians* (New York: The Macmillan Company, 1958), p. 13.

[12] James Luther Adams, "Paul Tillich's Dialectical Analysis" (unpublished manuscript of lecture given at the American Theological Society, Midwest Division, April 22, 1955), p. 3.

[13] Op. cit., pp. 78-111, esp. pp. 107-11, 346-47. In addition to Barth, Bonhoeffer's emphasis on the secular is also present in West and provides another point of opposition to Tillich.

[14] "Tillich's Doctrine of Religious Socialism," *The Theology of Paul Tillich* (New York: The Macmillan Company, 1961), pp. 312-25, esp. pp. 316-20.

[15] "Der 'religioese Sozialismus' in der Weimarer Republik," *Deutsche Zeitschrift fuer Philosophie*, VII, 11/12 (1960), pp. 1464-82, esp. pp. 1475-76.

[16] *Religioeser Sozialismus und buergerliches Geschichtsbewusstsein zur Zeit der Weimarer Republik* (Zurich: Theologischer Verlag, 1971), pp. 167-224, esp. pp. 167-168, 194. For a further discussion of secondary literature see her footnotes, pp. 167-71.

[17] Op. cit., pp. 320-24. See Tillich's reply, "Answer," p. 346.

[18] "Religious Socialism as an Ideology: A Study of the 'Kairos-Circle' in Germany Between 1919-1933" (unpublished Doctor's dissertation, Harvard Divinity School, 1962), esp. p. 216 ff.

[19] Adams, op. cit.; Clark A. Kucheman, "Professor Tillich: Justice and the Economic Order," *The Journal of Religion*, XLVI, 1, Pt. II (January, 1966), pp. 165-83. Note Tillich's reply to Kucheman, pp. 189-91.

[20] *Ontologie, Theologie, gesellschaftliche Praxis* (Zurich: Theologischer Verlag, 1971), esp. pp. 175-205, 477-78. See my review of Ulrich's book, *Lutheran World*, XX, 2 (1973), p. 210.

[21] "Die Politische Theorie in der Theologie Paul Tillichs" (Doctor's dissertation, Marburg, 1969), esp. pp. 263-68.

[22] "Zur Geschichte der religioes-sozialistischen Stroemungen in der Weimarer Republik," *Internationale Dialog Zeitschrift*, V, 1 (1972), pp. 37-41.

[23] For studies of other aspects of Tillich's thought during this period see the following three books: James Luther Adams, *Paul Tillich's Philosophy of Culture, Science, and Religion* (New York: Harper and Row, Publishers, 1964). Kenneth Schedler, *Natur und Gnade. Das sakramentale Denken in der fruehen Theologie Paul Tillichs (1919-1935)* (Stuttgart, 1970). Eberhard Amelung, *Die Gestalt Der Liebe Paul Tillichs Theologie der Kulter* (Guetesloh: Gerd Mohn, 1972).

CHAPTER 2

THE CONTEXT

Paul Tillich's religious socialism was enmeshed in a complex historical matrix. He formulated it at a definite time and place in response to concrete social developments and political events. He came from a particular religious tradition and entered a specific socialist movement. As his several autobiographical sketches attest, his theology grew out of his experiences.[1] Tillich's theological interpretation of socialism is not fully understood without an awareness of the historical and biographical circumstances from which it emerged.

This chapter places Tillich in the context of his times and draws a profile of him as a religious socialist. The background, the people, the events, the issues, and the ideas important to him are introduced. The chapter will help clarify the integral connection between his life and his theoretical concepts to be discussed in the following chapters.

The major portion of the chapter is devoted to the Weimar period, 1918-1933, the setting for Tillich's activities as a religious socialist. The opening two sections, however, trace his previous life from his birth in 1886 to the Revolution of 1918. The first describes his early religious environment, in which he first learned of socialism, and the second shows how his experience in World War I affected his socio-political attitudes. The following four sections sketch his intense political involvement during the years of the German republic, from his initial plunge into religious socialism after his return from the War until his forced exile after the victory of National Socialism. In the concluding chapter of this study, the historical-biographical theme will be picked up once more, and a short interpretation of Tillich's relationship to religious socialism from 1933 until his death in 1965 will be given in order to understand the period studied here in the perspective of his whole life.

This chapter is not, of course, a complete biography of Tillich's complex life.[2] The focus is rather on the two

traditions, the Protestant and the socialist, that came together
in his life and thought during this period. Nor is it merely a
summary of Tillich's own autobiographical writings. Instead, by
relying upon contemporaneous writings by him and others (some of
which have only recently been published) as well as upon pertinent secondary sources, it is meant to provide a more detailed
picture of Tillich, the religious socialist, than now exists.

The Background, 1886-1914

The Social Democrat August Bebel aptly conveyed the nature
of the relationship between Christianity and socialism in the
decades before the Weimar Republic with the simple simile that
the two were "opposed like fire and water."[3] 1848, the year
of revolution, was "the year of decision."[4] That year Karl
Marx and Friedrich Engels gave the proletariat their revolutionary charter and "at Wittenberg, over the grave of Luther,
[J. H.] Wichern made the Protestant reply to *The Communist
Manifesto*."[5] With his counter-revolutionary "Protestant Manifesto," Wichern succeeded in making "Inner Mission" the major
ecclesiastical response to "the social question, that crisis of
human existence provoked by industrialism," but his program of
charity was "a very weak defense against the slumbering forces
of proletarian discontent."[6] "After 1848 German Protestantism
gradually lost its power to reach and stir the masses; their
world and their life became increasingly alien."[7] The church
became the ally of Prussian Conservatism.

> Its monarchical and authoritarian institutions, sod-
> den with antipathy for mass movements and democratic pol-
> tics, were steadfastly revered by orthodox and church-
> going Protestants throughout the period of German history
> which lasted until 1918.[8]

The attempt of the court chaplain Adolf Stoecker to win the
workers for a conservative, anti-Marxist Christian socialism
in 1878 and later was futile.[9]

The proletariat instead found in an anti-clerical, Marxist-
shaped socialism its source of hope and power. In 1863 Ferdi-
nand Lassale began the modern labor movement in Germany, and,
in spite of Bismarck's Anti-Socialist Law of 1878, the Social
Democratic Party (SPD) grew rapidly from an "illegal sect to a
mass party."[10] During this classical, heroic period, Engels
and Karl Kautsky, building upon the work of Marx, gave the

movement its ideology in "orthodox Marxism" or "scientific socialism."[11] It was an ideology that rejected religion or, at most, restricted it to the private sphere. When, for the first time, two Evangelical pastors joined the party at the turn of the century, both were ousted from their pastorates.[12] On the eve of the World War, the largest Protestant church in the world[13] and the strongest branch of socialism in the world were, as they had been since at least 1848, politically and ideologically opposed.

Hardly surprisingly, Paul Tillich, the son of an Evangelical pastor in a small, walled, feudal-like town in east-Elbian Prussia, spent his early life in a thoroughly anti-socialist atmosphere. Born in 1886, three years after Marx's death and at a time when the SPD was proscribed, Paulus internalized the deeply religious and politically conservative ethos of his childhood. His early world was "authoritarian without being totalitarian." A paternalistic home, a strict sense of discipline and duty, a deep devotion to a symbolically powerful army, and a patriotic adherence to the King of Prussia, the German emperor, were all part of his taken-for-granted reality.[14] He absorbed the fire-water relationship of Christianity and socialism. Later he wrote:

> The existence of a parliament, democratic forces, socialist movements, and a strong criticism of the emperor and the army did not affect the conservative Lutheran groups of the East among whom I lived. All these democratic elements were rejected, distortedly represented, and characterized as revolutionary, which meant criminal.[15]

Tillich's life in Berlin after 1900 and his later theological and philosophical education in Berlin, Tuebingen, and Halle broadened his horizons, but they did not fundamentally alter his social and political attitudes. As a young man he was convinced by his father's argument that socialism was incompatible with the Lutheran ethic of compassion.[16] Political questions were not a prominent feature of his theological education;[17] it was a time for reading Kierkegaard but not yet Marx.[18] Tillich was First Officer of the Wingolf Fraternity, a Christian student group with nationalistic learnings.[19] In his two dissertations on Schelling, he kept aloof from the social question.[20] His work as "apologist for Berlin" immediately before the war was non-political. The only reference to social issues in his pre-war writings was an indirect one. In a lengthy paper on his apologetic program, he endorsed "Inner Mission" by drawing a favorable analogy between it and his program.[21] Ernst Troeltsch wrote at the time that "down to the present time, the Lutheran church has never advanced farther than the renewed idea of charity; it has never made any effort to initiate a real social transformation at all."[22] Nor did Tillich show the slightest inclination to do so. The evidence supports his autobiographical statement that "like most German intellectuals before 1914, I had been rather indifferent to politics."[23] This indifference meant a largely uncritical acceptance of the church's conservative, nationalistic, and quietistic position. His readiness in 1914 to serve in the Kaiser's army bore out his continuing loyalty to throne and altar.

There were, of course, many factors in Tillich's first twenty-eight years that would play a positive role in his religious socialism. He did not, after all, abdicate his religious background in becoming a socialist; his Protestant tradition remained one source of his religious socialism. His early experiences were, for one thing, a motivating influence for his later social concern. "The deep impression of the words of the prophets against injustice and the words of Jesus against the rich" helped prompt his identification with the proletariat.[24] Perhaps, as he later suggested, the story of his grandmother building barricades in the Revolution of 1848 influenced his own affirmation of the Revolution of 1918.[25] As a child, the conflict of belonging to the privileged class but having his best friends among the "commoners" aroused a "consciousness of social guilt."[26] His early taste of the simple beauty of the past was perhaps a source of his discontent with bourgeois society and of his longing for a new, unified society, a longing sometimes tinged with romantic elements. What Tillich learned in theology and philosophy also had a significant impact on his political-theological thinking. A belief in the centrality of justification by faith, a realistic view of human nature, a discovery of the continuing vitality of Protestant theology, an appreciation for the achievements of liberal theology, a recognition of the importance of ontology, and a high estimation of German Idealism were first affirmed in these years and remained basic to his thinking.[27]

But before these influences could become operative in religious socialism, they had to be freed from the pervasive conservative milieu that determined Tillich's pre-war life. Because of the historical opposition between Christianity and socialism in Germany, because of the inability of the Protestant church to respond creatively to the social question, and because Tillich belonged to his time and church, he had to overcome some difficult barriers before he could affirm socialism. "By way of Lutheranism, the road to socialism is very difficult."[28]

What was this road for Tillich? Why was it that Paul Tillich, politically indifferent and conservative in 1914, had in 1918 become a socialist and made the social question the focal point of his theology?

The Turning Point, 1914-1918

Shortly after the outbreak of war in August, 1914, Tillich, confident of quick victory, volunteered for service in the German Imperial Army. Like most of his compatriots, he was caught up in the nationalistic fervor of the moment.[29] Imbued from childhood with a spirit of loyalty, he was now eager in a time of crisis to aid his "fatherland." In September 1914, Tillich was assigned as a chaplain to the Western front where he was to serve for four years.

Tillich's original enthusiasm for the war was evident in his first report to his superiors.[30] He wrote as a willing officer, conscientiously performing his duty. A year later, however, the problematic nature of the war was evident. In a personal letter of October 15, 1915, he spoke of "the worst battle of this war," the Battle of Champagne: "Blood flows daily here, a great deal of blood in this arid chalk. . . . And the war is without prospect [of end]."[31] In an official report, dated December 1915, Tillich wrote:

> In the first days of November there was nothing but burials, the most shattering that I have yet encountered in the war. Some of our best officers with whom I had been personally close through long months, a leading member of the division staff and so forth. . . . An inner grimness filled me when I flung from my hand the sticky

> loam of Champagne onto the casket of a man who possessed
> the most flourishing energy and who belonged in all re-
> spects to what is best and most valuable.
>
> I was no less affected by the mass burials of the
> ranks, [who were buried] without caskets, one next to the
> other, mutilated parts of their bodies stretching out from
> under the tarps, with often nothing but the grave shovel
> accompanying them. When this happened three times a day,
> one could not become apathetic; there had to come a time
> when one was broken within.[32]

He reported that bitterness and disenchantment with a war whose end "lies in the totally unforeseeable future" were growing among the troops.[33] Perhaps this experience of "being broken within" refers to that "one moment in the war, in the middle of a terrible battle, which I would always call a kairos in my life."[34]

Horror replaced Tillich's original enthusiasm; death's constant presence revealed life's abyss. His most poignant contemporaneous expression of the War's meaning for him is found in a letter written on November 27, 1916:

> I always have the strongest and most immediate feeling
> that I am really no longer a part of life. Therefore I
> don't consider it [life] important. . . . Life itself
> is certainly no ground that is able to bear life. Not only
> that one can die any day, but that everything is dying,
> *really* dying, this unheard of fact that is now a daily
> experience. And then the suffering of the men--I am the
> purest eschatologist; not that I would have childish
> phantasies of world destruction (*Weltuntergang*), but rather
> I am living through the actual world destruction of this
> time. I preach the end almost exclusively. You don't
> want the end yet. I don't either, but I must want it be-
> cause it is here. You haven't walked over fields of
> corpses, actual and spiritual. We want to feel something
> of the New Testament experience and wait on the "end" with
> gladness, and be convinced that the world lies in hopeless-
> ness and that our citizenship is in heaven. This is the
> "dominate" of my psychology.[35]

The everyday encounter with the "unheard of fact" of dying and suffering jarred the stability of his world. For the first time he considered the War to mark the end of an historical epoch, and he turned to the New Testament preaching of the end as consolation in a time of destruction.

Tillich's war experience signaled a decisive turning point in his life. Such phrases as "being broken within," "no longer being a part of life," "living through the end," express the meaning of these years. The terror of war had shattered his old world; the security of the past was gone. He could no longer go home.

> For half a decade the fate of death stood over an entire generation, remelted its soul, ripped its spirit loose from the spirit of the old, threw it into nothingness, and let it rise anew out of nothingness. Whoever has experienced this knows the building of the nineteenth century is destroyed, impossible to bring back; for him there is only change and new building.[36]

Both at the time and later Tillich knew his experience on the bloody Western front signified a "break" in his life and thought.[37]

Tillich recognized that the old was no longer possible or adequate, but he had not yet found an alternative. In 1917 his search drew him to Nietzsche who made a "tremendous impression" on him.[38] His wrestling with the idea of justification led him to "the paradox of 'faith without God.'"[39] He returned to a defeated Germany in September 1918, a changed but not yet a politically-committed person. But with the outbreak of revolution in November, Tillich for the first time "became very much alive to the political situation."[40] During the war he had come into personal contact with the proletariat and discovered for himself the "socialist bitterness" among the troops.[41] He had learned "that the nation was split into classes, and that the industrial masses considered the Church as an unquestioned ally of the ruling groups."[42] One might safely speculate that the Russian Revolution of October 1917 had not escaped his attention. Tillich's war experiences had prepared him to affirm the Revolution. Together the War and the Revolution "politicized" an unlikely subject, Paul Tillich, doctor of philosophy, Prussian Evangelical pastor, chaplain in the Imperial Army.[43] Tillich, who four years earlier had eagerly come to the defense of the old reich, now just as eagerly welcomed its demise and affirmed the possibility of building a socialist, democratic republic.

The Beginning, 1918-1919

In the crisis years of 1918-1919 Tillich began to chart his course as a religious socialist. This time marked his entry into political engagement and indicated the direction he would pursue. In the same way that his later *Systematic Theology* can be summarized as a correlation of questions and answers, his religious socialism can be characterized as a response to the socio-political predicament caused by war and revolution. The focus in this section is on the point where crisis and response first intersected. A close look at these years is therefore important to understand how Tillich initially framed the issues he encountered and to see how he situated himself within the available theological and political alternatives.

The Revolution of November 1918 swiftly and unexpectedly dethroned the Kaiser. On November 9, the Social Democrat Philipp Scheidemann proclaimed "the German Republic": two days later the revolutionary government signed an armistice ending the World War. Peace had come and the socialists were in power. Despite the chaotic conditions of a defeated nation, the spirit of a new beginning burst forth.[44]

There were some ominous signs on the horizon. Fighting in the streets continued well into 1919, and the new government used the old army to put down radical workers. The Spartacist leaders Rosa Luxemburg and Karl Liebknecht were murdered in January, 1919. The left was divided and old powers were slowly reappearing. The Versailles Treaty with its "war guilt clause" brought a new and heavy burden to the young republic. Nevertheless, a constitution was adopted in 1919 and the Weimar Republic was launched. The results of the Revolution were ambiguous, but the most significant reality was the sudden existence of a democratic republic in which the Social Democrats were the leading power.[45]

Tillich, who had returned to Berlin from the War in September, 1918, experienced the turmoil and excitement that swept through the capital city during these chaotic months.[46] He responded to the Revolution and its democratic and socialist promise by becoming a religious socialist.[47] With this decision he was aligning himself with a definite political direction. He broke through his conservative past, identified himself with the political cause of the proletariat, and accepted responsibility to work for a socialist society. Socialism was a vague notion in his first writings, but in endorsing it, Tillich was making a clear-cut political decision in a revolutionary, polarized situation.

The crisis of war and revolution soon came to signify for Tillich a decisive turning point for Germany and Europe. He perceived the moment in epochal terms, and he intuited the beginning of a remarkable new age. "We stand in . . . a period of dissolution. A new age of unity is arising."[48] He spoke of "the new, unifying culture springing from socialist soil."[49] "Will not a third period of Christianity beyond Catholicism and Protestantism arise? Is not this the meaning of the 'turning of the world' (*Weltenwende*) which the World War and the Revolution have brought us?" he asked rhetorically.[50] Without yet using the word, Tillich was grasped by the consciousness of a "kairos," a moment pregnant with significance, a qualitative time.[51] Arising from the rubble of defeat and chaos would be a new socialist-Christian era. This awareness of the kairos shaped Tillich's political convictions at the deepest level.

The number of German protestants who, like Tillich, affirmed the Revolution was not large, even in socialist Berlin.[52] Prior to the war there had been no religious movement in Germany.[53] Christoph Blumhardt's support of socialism in Wuerttemberg had had little direct impact on the German church, although it had influenced Hermann Kutter and Leonhard Ragaz who had begun a religious socialist movement in Switzerland. But in Germany religious socialism was a post-war phenomenon. Called forth by the Revolution, it began and continued as a small, marginal movement on the edge of the church's life.[54]

Shortly after the Revolution Tillich met with a few other church people, principally clergy, to discuss the relationship between Christianity and socialism.[55] His entry into the religious socialist--at first more properly called "christian socialist"[56]--movement was through a small group that had been instigated by Siegmund-Schultze's *Soziale Arbeitsgemeinschaft (SAG)*, a settlement-house-type organization in east Berlin.[57] One participant, "the proletarian pastor" Guenther Dehn, described this circle which gathered around Pastor Friedrich Rittelmeyer:

> We came together once a week in the afternoon. Mostly young men, theologians, were there, but also others from the academic world, workers only occasionally. The problem that came up for debate again and again was the question of the relationship of the church and the workers. Once I reported on Ragaz on the basis of his

essays in the "*Neue Wege*," which was now again available. Karl Mennicke developed his thoughts on the *Volkskirche*. Paul Tillich, at the beginning still in his chaplain's uniform with the *EK* I, sketched his theological ideas which stood thoroughly in relationship to socialism. Rittelmeyer was totally distant from his thought world. He himself was politically close to [Fredrich] Naumann. Once [Ernst] Troeltsch was present. He sat there with a fearful face, listened to what was said, but did not let out a sound. Soon Rittelmeyer drew more and more upon anthroposophist ideas, and so our discussion ceased after a few months.[58]

This unassuming gathering, which was Tillich's first contact with religious socialists, seems to have continued in some form throughout 1919. The group evolved, losing some of its clear theological coloring when a greater number of laity were drawn to it. Tillich's friendship and working-alliance with Karl Mennicke grew as these two came to play a more and more prominent role in the circle. Eventually they cut themselves off from the *SAG*, and the Rittelmeyer circle became the circle around Tillich and Mennicke. When the first issue of the *Blaetter fuer religioesen Sozialismus* appeared on Easter, 1920, the circle was decisively stamped by these two men.[59]

In the post-Revolution situation, the SPD was no longer an opposition party, as it had been up to 1918, but was now a governing party. Although it never held a majority in Weimar, it frequently had a voice in the government. Committed to the democratic process and reformist policies, the SPD was willing to tone down its socialist demands and form coalitions with the bourgeois parties. Also, for the first time, the Social Democrats faced a challenge from the left. Even before the Revolution some members of the SPD had broken with the majority, opposed war appropriations, and, on April 6, 1917, formed the Independent Social Democratic Party (USPD). The Russian Revolution encouraged radical Marxists in Germany to want a state based on the Soviet model. On December 30, 1918, the Spartacist wing of the USPD formed the German Communist Party (KPD) to oppose the SPD and to pursue the Revolution further. During the ensuing years the strength of the parties would vary, but the split was lasting and would finally cripple socialism's possibilities in Weimar.[60]

Not much is known about Tillich's early relationship with the parties, although he did move within the sphere of Social

Democracy. His first party-related activity seems to have been with the USPD. One example of this is a lecture he gave to a group of Independent Social Democrats in Berlin-Zehlendorf in early 1919.[61] He might have been a member of this party, but this is uncertain.[62] One can surmise that its political position was probably more congenial with Tillich's than that of either the ruling Social Democrats or the militant Communists. Standing to the left of the former and to the right of the latter, the USPD opposed both accommodation to bourgeois interests and the surrender of democratic means and goals. It "was the only party which had opposed the war and supported the Revolution with any enthusiasm."[63] Tillich's first comments on the socialist parties were apologetic in tone and critical but hopeful in content.[64]

The Revolution also threw the church into a new, unexpected, and unwelcomed situation. The loss of the emperor, the supreme bishop of the church; the inauguration of a non-Christian state; the separation of church and state; and the political gains of the Social Democrats shocked the traditional church.[65] The church resented its loss and longed for the past.[66] The Protestant church in Weimar was not receptive to religious socialist ideas; indeed, the attitude towards socialism was, according to Dehn, more hostile than before the war.[67]

As might be expected, Tillich's entry into the socialist movement brought him into conflict with his ecclesiastical superiors. On May 16, 1919, the Evangelical Consistory of Brandenburg, the church agency which had approved Tillich's theological examinations in 1909 and 1911 and had certified him for ordination in 1912, inquired about his political activity. The probe was prompted by his lecture to the USDP. In the opening lines of his reply, Tillich noted that from the inquiry "it is not possible to learn what viewpoints are supposed to be decisive for an answer," but that he assumed the issue "is not a question of political activity in general but rather of activity in a particular party."[68] This episode was, as far as I can determine, the only direct confrontation he had with church authorities over his religious socialism. And what, if anything, the Consistory said in reply to Tillich's answer is unknown. But the mere fact of the inquiry symbolizes the spirit of mistrust and opposition that religious socialism encountered within the church.

Tillich's reply to the Consistory constitutes his first statement on Christianity and socialism. The little pamphlet "Socialism as a Question for the Church" is largely a reworking of Tillich's "Answer."[69] Both versions were a strong attack on capitalism, nationalism, and militarism, and an argument for the compatibility of the Christian ethic of love and the socialist ideal. "The spirit of Christian love accuses a social order which consciously and in principle is built upon economic and political egoism, and it demands a new order in which the feeling of community (*Gemeinschaft*) is the foundation of the social structure."[70] Tillich was at this time an "idealistic socialist" who made his point largely on the basis of moral values, especially the value of community.[71]

In his appeal for the church to take a positive position towards Social Democracy, Tillich rejected the traditional social policy of the Protestant churches. "Christian social reform" (works of charity and social legislation) is, he stated, a "means for the maintenance in principle of the capitalist form of society through cutting out its worst excrescences."[72] Nor did he see it as a proper goal "*to win the workers for the present church.*" The workers view the church as an ally of the capitalist state, and, argued Tillich, to impose the bourgeois law of life on them is similar to the attempt to impose the Jewish ceremonial law on non-Jewish Christians in the early church.[73] Clearly, he was embarking on a new journey.

Tillich did not expect the church leadership suddenly to reverse its position, and so his final counsel was moderate. He asked that they "place no hindrance in the way" of those Christians who enter into the socialist movement. They should not only tolerate but welcome a "Christian socialist movement," for "the further development of this movement is of decisive importance for the future of the German Evangelical churches." He urged that no one be excluded from the life and leadership of the church because of socialist thinking, "otherwise the Christian socialist movement will be forced from the beginning into paths hostile to the church."[74]

Tillich's initial political writings came out of an ecclesiastical context, but when his simple appeal--that the position of Christian socialism be recognized as a valid Christian attitude--was in practice rejected, he was driven "into paths hostile to the church." He would remain in the church, would continue to address it in the prophetic manner of these statements, but he would become increasingly alienated from it. The result was that, for the most part, he developed his religious socialism in a non-ecclesiastical setting, a change of location that had repercussions in his theology. Tillich's "para-position," as it might be called, was a realistic choice for a politically involved theologian facing a non-responsive church. Long before the Nazi Reich his stance vis-à-vis the church was a judgment on its failure to address the social question.[75]

In his first writing Tillich encouraged "representatives of Christianity and the church who stand on socialist soil to enter into the socialist movement in order to pave the way for a future union of Christianity and the socialisty social order." He had already set out on what he called "this difficult, unknown, important way" and would continue along it.[76] He became a socialist as a Christian and as a socialist he remained a Christian. In embracing both of these heretofore antagonistic traditions, Tillich encountered the basic problem of his religious socialism. This problem was not the relationship of party and church, nor the relationship of the workers to the church. Nor was the crucial issue for him the question of personal allegiance, that is, whether it was possible to be both a Christian and a socialist. The problem was rather the overcoming of the static opposition between the two philosophies so that they could fruitfully interact in the creation of a new society. Tillich's concern was the future social order, one he believed and hoped would be structured according to socialist principles and empowered with the meaning-giving import of Christianity. Therefore, in anticipation of this development, he incorporated into the dynamic of his own life and thought the tension between the two and sought to give them unity. In light of this vision he participated in the socialist movement as a Christian, seeking to interpret, criticize, and transform socialism from a theological perspective. This was the unchartered way he began to explore in 1919.

Between the radical religious socialists and the conservative church authorities stood the liberal Evangelical Social Congress.[77] The Congress, a forum for the study of social problems, was critical of the conservative church but was not socialist. Tillich considered its liberal reformism to be "too deeply immersed in the spirit of capitalism to be able to go beyond it."[78] In July, 1919, in his first book review, a lengthy discussion of an anthology *Revolution and the Church,* written by progressives in the Social Congress tradition, Tillich indicated his agreement and disagreement with this position.[79] He found in the book "a spirit that says 'yes' to the new developments and necessities, nowhere a yearning glance back to the past." He applauded the authors' criticisms of the church and of the "war theologians," and he agreed with many of their detailed reform proposals.[80] But he questioned whether they had penetrated to the deeper meaning of their theme. He characterized the present culture, especially among the young, as "'coming to mysticism' (Hammacher)." "But if this is the case, does not the earth shake under any proposal for renewal and constitutional change?" Will not a third period of Christianity arise? Are we not at a turning point in history? Tillich wrote that he raised these questions to show that the "final depths" of "revolution and church" were not yet touched. He stated, "The spirit that creates forms must precede all reform and creation of structure (*Gestaltung*). What will this spirit be? Only the future can answer!"[81] For the "ecstatic" Tillich a reformist spirit was too prosaic, too unattentive to the significance of the moment; an alternative had to be found.

Tillich's relationship to the social philosophy of Ernst Troeltsch is rightly seen in this light. His debt to Troeltsch was clear in four articles he wrote on Troeltsch in 1923-1924, at the time of the latter's death.[82] Tillich never heard his lectures and had little personal contact with him (once, it seems, in the Rittelmeyer circle), but, he wrote, he had felt the influence of his creations for two decades. He considered Troeltsch's work as "the negative presupposition for every future construction." His social philosophy as well as his philosophy of religion and philosophy of history were important for Tillich. He called the effects on him of Troeltsch's *The Social Teaching of the Christian Churches*--"whose impression on me at my first reading will remain unforgettable"--as "extraordinary."[83] After the war Troeltsch too recognized a crisis, but he rejected both socialism and Christian socialism in favor of a democratic liberalism. But this was not enough for Tillich.

> The liberal individualism and the basically optimistic cultural philosophy [of his position] prevented a complete experience of the enormous social and political crisis of Europe. Troeltsch did not see the shattering of his ideal of humanity in the crisis of the World War and the Revolution. Therefore he did not find the saving word either as a social philosopher or as a politician.[84]

Tillich's socialist commitment and his kairos-consciousness separated him from Troeltsch.

When Tillich asked what the spirit of the future would be, he was not expecting the spirit that blew at Tambach in Thueringia, a spirit that soon took the theological initiative. From September 23 to 25, 1919, religious socialists of all types --"the church-revolutionary crowd," as Dehn called them--came together from all over Germany for the first time to discuss their mutual concerns. About one hundred people were present, including Dehn and Mennicke from Berlin, but not Tillich. The Germans, eager to learn from Switzerland's experience, invited Ragaz, but he was unable to attend. In his place came a virtually unknown follower of Ragaz, Karl Barth, pastor in Safenwil in Aargau. Having expected to hear a sharp attack on capitalism and an urgent call for socialism, those present were shocked to hear Barth reject all "*Bindestrich-christentum*," all hyphenated forms of Christianity, including religious socialism, as a secularized version of faith that dishonored God. The world was profane, said Barth, and God was totally other.[85] Barth's speech immediately became a major topic of concern for the Berlin circle. According to Mennicke, they agreed that the Swiss position was not and could not be theirs, but they recognized that Barth had raised some problems that should not be avoided.[86]

Tillich continued this discussion on November 10, in a report entitled "The Principal Foundations and the Next Tasks of our Movement."[87] According to Mennicke, Tillich understood

Barth as representing a reformed, Calvinist view of God. This view sought to blot out all human traces from history and thereby demonstrate the one, great track of God. Barth rejected, said Tillich, the appeal to any kind of subjective human experience as a source for decisive religious insights, wanting rather to see the guiding power and lordship of God recognized in its absolute reality and unimpeachability, not entangled with anything human. Tillich considered such a concept of God an "enormous abstraction," heteronomous, and divorced from human experience. He insisted that the concept of God must remain free from every abstraction which separates God from the process of life and which makes God a special reality above other objects in the world. "The experience of God for present-day people can only take place in the sense of *autonomy*, that is, only in the sense that the deepest powers which people reach or which reach them . . . become inward." And, already in 1919, in reply to Barth he spoke of the "absolute paradox."

With this criticism of Barth, Tillich began one of the most interesting and important theological discussions in the twentieth century.[88] The decisive question was the nature of God; the context was religious socialism and its legitimacy. The difference between the two were already evident. Tillich, for example, defined his task as that of a theologian of culture whose object was religion;[89] Barth was a theologian of the church whose concern was the Gospel. Tillich understood the problem of theology in relation to autonomy; Barth saw it in relationship to the preaching of the Word of God. Tillich was sympathetic to mystical influences and did not consider it essential that Christ be in the center of religious consciousness;[90] Barth was equally anti-mystical and Christological. Tillich the Lutheran stressed the immanence of God. Tillich had studied post-Kantian Idealists appreciatively; Barth had been influenced by neo-Kantianism. Tillich was only beginning to move into religious socialism; Barth had left it behind. These differences as well as the challenge of Barth's protest, especially as expressed in the second edition of *The Epistle to the Romans*, were a spur to his own theological development.

Tillich, it is worth recalling pursued, in 1919 and later, his religious socialist activities from the locus of the university. He was not and never had been a pastor in a proletarian parish as Barth had been. Nor was he ever a revolutionary like Marx, and neither did he become a politician like Troeltsch. After spending a brief time in church administrative work immediately after the War,[91] Tillich, at the age of thirty-two, re-entered the academic world as a privatdozent in the theology faculty at the University of Berlin in the spring semester of 1919. At this time, on April 16, he began his public professional career at the Berlin branch of the *Kantgesellschaft* with the lecture "On the Idea of a Theology of Culture."[92] In this lecture too he spoke as a socialist, calling upon socialism "to complete its own development" by recognizing the need for an all-embracing religious substance to give meaning and unity to the new society.[93]

Significantly, Tillich's first series of lectures at the University of Berlin, the first of his teaching career, were on the political theme. The course was entitled "Christianity and the Present Social Problem."[94] In it Tillich used his theology of culture to analyze the relationship of conservatism, liberalism, socialism, and communism to the new social situation.[95] A successful teacher and scholar, Tillich advanced in rank and standing. In 1924 he left Berlin to become Professor of Theology at Marburg. From there he went to Dresden and Leipzig, and in 1929 he was selected for the important position of Professor of Philosophy at the University of Frankfurt.[96] From 1919 until the spring of 1933 when the National Socialists deprived him of his chair at Frankfurt, Tillich was located in a German university.

Tillich's earliest religious socialism was not untouched by idealistic and romantic impulses. His mysticism and his overenthusiasm about the historical moment illustrated his mood. In a similar vein, Tillich's first socialist thinking was influenced by anarchism. A theological student, present at his first lectures and deeply impressed, wrote at the time in a personal letter that "there is only one thing I don't like--that Tillich sees the only salvation in Landauer's federalist anarchism."[97] In "On the Idea of Theology of Culture," he advocated an "idealistic 'anarchism,'" that shatters the autonomous form of the state "in favor of a theonomy built up from communities themselves and their spiritual substance."[98] These elements in Tillich's thought soon were toned down, or they disappeared, but in 1919 they served to free Tillich from the restrictions of the past and allowed him to envision new possibilities.

Thus, the years 1918-1919 represent the beginning of Tillich's religious socialism. Impelled by the crisis of his society, Tillich eagerly focused his life and thought on the political arena; among his friends he was even known as the "Red Socialist."[99] He entered the small, amorphous religious socialist movement and began to map his way amidst the various options present in the church and parties. His position was less Marxist than it would later be, but his basic direction was set. His mood would change, but the end would remain. This end, decisively shaped by his awareness of the kairos, was a "future union of Christianity and the socialist social order."

> We stand in . . . a period of dissolution. A new age of unity is arising. Socialism will form its economic and social foundation. And Christianity stands before the task to convey to this development its moral and religious powers and thereby to initiate a new great synthesis of religion and social structure.[100]

The Kairos Circle, 1920-1924

The social and political situation in 1920 and after continued to be accute. Conservative reaction, difficulties over reparations, and serious inflation kept the country in turmoil and jeopardized the future of the young republic. In March 1920, the Kapp Putsch sought to initiate a counter-revolution. Three years later Adolf Hitler made another unsuccessful attempt to overthrow the government. Assassins struck, killing (among others) the Jewish Foreign Minister Walter Rathenau.[101] When Germany failed to meet its harsh reparation payments on time, France occupied the Ruhr area in 1923, heightening domestic discontent. Inflation continued to rise and reached astronomical heights by October 1923. The Social Democrats lost some power, and anti-republic parties demonstrated strength in some elections. Only in 1924 did a semblance of stability arrive.[102]

During these years, Tillich later wrote, "the political problems determined our whole existence; even after revolution and inflation they were matters of life and death."[103] By 1920 the original group in which he had participated had evolved into "the circle around Tillich and Mennicke," or as it was also called, "the circle around the *Blaetter fuer religioesen Sozialismus*," or "the Berlin Circle," or "the Kairos Circle." In the give-and-take of this small *Arbeitsgemeinschaft*, Tillich forged his religious socialist ideas until 1924, when he left Berlin for Marburg. The group was not large and its life-span relatively brief, but it was crucially important for Tillich's development.

Dehn once again has given a valuable first-hand account of this working-community:

> For some months after the war I also took part in the meetings of the so-called Kairos Circle. Kairos means time in a qualified sense, a time of decision and nearing fulfillment. The spiritual presupposition of our convictions was that through socialism a new age would arise for which one must prepare in fundamental reflection on its genuine gestalt. It sought to ground it not only sociologically but also philosophically and theologically. For all its recognition of the significance of Marx, it was not Marxist. It was a highly intellectual circle, and sometimes the reports and discussions were over my head. The church question played no role here. I name from the participants (their number never went over ten or twelve): Paul Tillich, Alexander Ruestow, Karl Mennicke, Eduard Heimann, [Adolf] Lowe, Karl-Ludwig Schmidt. They all became professors, and some of their names have a world-famous ring today. Because they were called away, the majority of participants left Berlin, and out of necessity the circle disbanded.[104]

A common kairos awareness, rather than a fixed platform, gave the circle its identity.

> This circle never was a closed movement with a uniform program to which everyone could or should be bound; it was rather a society for exchanging ideas on the basis of a general religious responsibility for the economy and society, in which everyone held to his own ideas.[105]

In "Basic Principles of Religious Socialism," Tillich wrote that he was seeking "to present a systematic summary of our convictions," but he recognized his work as "an individual creation."[106] Reaction to his statement demonstrated that there was no unanimity on these principles.[107]

The circle was not restricted by confessional allegiance. Tillich "considered himself thoroughly an evangelical-Lutheran Christian," who knew exactly how all his ideas and views were determined from this religious perspective. He nevertheless argued that the group should be open to non-Christians; each person was to speak out of his own autonomous experience.[108] The circle was thus religious, not Christian, socialist. Clergy and laity (indeed, more laity than clergy), Christians (Protestants but not Catholics) and Jews, believers and non-believers were a part of the circle. Mennicke once caught its unorthodox character in jokingly remarking that it was composed of "'three Jews and three pagans.'"[109] In spite of its diversity, the "Protestant spirit" was, according to Tillich, "strong enough in it to make the question about the realization in time of decisive importance."[110]

Nor was membership limited only to those who belonged to the workers' parties.[111] Other voices were heard, although the circle was overwhelmingly socialist, as Dehn, too, recalled. The socialists themselves represented a variety of views, from Social Democracy to Communism. The Kairos Circle was not bound by a charter document, confessional test, or party membership but by the sense of common responsibility in a kairotic movement.

The Kairos Circle as a loosely-structured association met for intense discussion every week or two in an apartment or cafe.[112] At times the participants exchanged ideas on current events. After the Kapp Putsch, for example, they discussed the use of force. Tillich was inclined to take up arms in solidarity with the proletariat if the "reaction" should again seek forcefully to suppress the workers.[113] But their primary concern centered on theoretical questions, social and political as well as theological ones. Most of the people were in government or in academia, and their discussions were indeed "highly intellectual," often focusing on Tillich's terminology.[114] Others quite readily charged the group with "intellectualism."[115] According to Mennicke's last review of the circle's activities in 1927, four questions played a predominant role in their discussions: (1) Barth's theology and the relationship between the eternal and the historical situation; (2) Marxism, especially the question of class struggle and its relationship to ethical and religious considerations; (3) solidarity with the proletariat and pedagogical responsibility for their formation; and (4) socialist realization or the nature of the coming socialist society.[116]

The most important participants in the circle were Tillich, Mennicke, Eduard Heimann, Adolf Lowe, Alexander Ruestow, and Arnold Wolfers. Others connected with the group, but less intensely or for a shorter time, were Dehn, Karl-Ludwig Schmidt, Wilhelm Loew, Hans Hartmann, and Trude Bez-Mennicke.[117] Schmidt was a New Testament scholar and editor of *Theologische Blaetter*. Loew and Hartmann were pastors, and Bez-Mennicke, the daughter of a pastor and Mennicke's wife, had been active in the youth movement. These people, like Tillich and Mennicke, came from a religious background to socialism. Heimann, Lowe, Ruestow, and Wolfers were socialists who were concerned about the ethical and religious basis of socialism.

"*Carl Mennicke* was the heart of the circle just as indisputably as Tillich was the head."[118] He too was an ordained minister, had been a chaplain in the War, and was at the time a member of the SPD. He was especially interested in pedagogy and did more than the others to maintain contact with proletarian communities. Like Ruestow and Wolfers, he was connected with the *Deutsche Hochschule fuer Politik* as a lecturer in sociology. Later Mennicke was at the University of Frankfurt with Tillich but was by that time no longer active in religious socialism.[119]

Heimann and Lowe, both economists, provided the "substructure" of Tillich's religious socialism. Heimann,

> . . . the son of one of the leading and generally respected Social-Democratic politicians of the German Empire, . . . began his professional career as secretary to the so-called Sozialisierungskommission, a body of experts to whom the revolutionary government in 1918 entrusted the socialist reconstruction of the German economy.[120]

Already in the early 1920's he was considered an important socialist economist.[121] Dissatisfied with the vulgar Marxism of the party, Heimann reported that he entered the "free German youth movement in search of clarification of final questions" and from there was attracted to the circle by Tillich's kairos doctrine.[122] In 1922 he left Berlin for a post at the University of Freiburg and in 1925 became a professor at the University of Hamburg where he remained until 1922.[123] Lowe, who met Tillich at his *Kantgesellschaft* lecture in 1919, was a civil servant in the Ministries of Demobilization, Labor and Economy from 1918 to 1924. From Berlin he went to the University of

Kiel, and then in 1931 he joined Tillich in Frankfurt as Professor of Economics. Like Heimann, he was a Social Democrat and a Jew, attuned to the prophetic element of his tradition. Throughout the Weimar period Tillich, Heimann, and Lowe continued their common efforts and later in America remained close friends.

According to Heimann, Ruestow and Wolfers were at first members of the Communist Party but were soon "bailed out" by the circle. Ruestow, a sociologist, was Tillich's rival. "His discussions with Tillich were doubtless the highpoint of our meetings." He was a "free thinker and atheist" and an opponent of Tillich's theological views. Later he became "a rather radical liberal-democrat" and a famous sociologist in Heidelberg.[124] Wolfers, an attorney from Switzerland, who provided financial support for the group, had come to Berlin after the War. He specialized in international relations and political science and was director of the *Hochschule fuer Politik*, a new school which represented a "radical departure" in German education.[125] Through Wolfers, the circle under Tillich's leadership sponsored a series of nine lectures at the Academy in the Winter Semester of 1922-1923 with the title "The Renewal of Socialism."[126] After 1927 Wolfers and Ruestow did not play a role in Tillich's religious socialism.

The circle issued a small publication, *Blaetter fuer religioesen Sozialismus*, from 1920 to 1927. Until 1925, the *Blaetter* was a four-page journal, published monthly in small print on newspaper-type paper. From 1925 to 1927, when many from the circle had left Berlin, it was longer and neater and appeared either monthly or quarterly. The periodical was not designed for wide public consumption, and its circulation was never large. "This . . . intends in a very strict sense, without the least propaganda, to further the *Auseinandersetzung* in our circle, to strengthen and clarify its spirit," explained Mennicke in the first issue.[127] As editor Mennicke did most of the writing for the *Blaetter*, summarizing and evaluating the discussion as it progressed. Tillich and the others in the circle contributed as did others such as the religious socialists Otto Koch, Emil Fuchs, Martin Buber, William Banning-Sneek (from Holland), Andre Philip (from France), and Herman Schafft; Erich

Foerster, a representative of the Evangelical Social Congress; Felix Stoessinger, editor of *Freiheit*, the organ of the USPD, and others. In October 1927, the journal was discontinued with the intention of beginning a new journal when the resources were available.[128] During the surprisingly long life-span of the *Blaetter*, it was a focal point for the circle and gave it an identity within the religious socialist movement and beyond.

The circle around the *Blaetter* did have contact with other religious socialists. For example, they participated together in the First International Conference of Religious Socialists at Barchem, July 2-7, 1924, where Tillich gave a major lecture.[129] But, for the most part, Tillich's circle kept its distance from other groups that bore the same name. Its intellectual and non-ecclesiastical character made it distinct from the majority of religious socialists who were more practically oriented, seeking to influence church policy. By 1926 most of these groups had joined together in the "League of Religious Socialists in Germany." Tillich considered the "ecclesiastical political character" of the League as "impractical" because it sought "to reconcile socialism and the Protestant church without radically changing either."[130] For Tillich this "practical-political type of religious socialism" did not probe fundamental problems deeply enough and was therefore "unable to bring about a transformation of either religion or socialism from the deepest level."[131] Also Tillich and his circle had little in common with the "chiliastic enthusiasm" of the "Neuwerk-Kreis," which established Christian communal settlements.[132]

I have shown that in the formative years when Tillich was beginning to deepen and clarify his theological interpretation of socialism, the "handful of non-conformist intellectuals"[133] of the Kairos Circle were his primary conversation partners. With them he tested his ideas, learned about socialist theory and practice, and debated the challenge of Barth's theology. His thinking bore the imprint of these young and independent men and women, especially of Heimann and Lowe. In many ways the circle itself was a miniature of what Tillich anticipated for the whole of society: autonomous religious and socialist people working in a spirit of common responsibility to create the new society. It was not by accident that Tillich then and later identified his own efforts by reference to this *Arbeitsgemeinschaft*.

Within Socialism, 1925-1931

Following the end of inflation in 1924, the Weimar Republic began its period of greatest stability and prosperity. "By mid-1925 the 'golden twenties' had arrived."[134] The time was a conservative one; non-socialist cabinets controlled the government; extremists on the left and right generated little support. The spirit of restoration was expressed in the election of the aged Field Marshal Paul von Hindenburg, "the military father figure of the old regime," as President in 1925.[135] Relative economic growth, political calm, and foreign co-operation characterized the time. But in 1929 all this changed with the Great World Depression. The country was once again thrown into uncertainty, and a stormy period of turmoil began that would end the German experiment in democracy.[136]

In 1930 Tillich described the "rhythm" of the first decade of Weimar:

> That was the spiritual situation in the five years after the Revolution, full of passion and power, full of despair and consciousness of death, full of the mood of doom and yearning. We still feel it in our blood, but we also know that something different has come into existence since then. All who had been broken and had built anew in those years experienced a remarkable surprise; under closer examination that which they had created anew often very much resembled that which they had destroyed. The power of the old proved stronger than the five years of crisis had foreshadowed. Everywhere a reaction set in.[137]

The mood of his thinking coincided with the "rhythm" of the times. In his writings from 1925 and later Tillich articulated a new sense of realism, a "belief-ful realism," in contrast to what he called the "unrealistic enthusiasm" of the period after the Revolution.[138] Religious socialism, he wrote, was being "visibly de-romanticized."[139] "When we look upon the actual events of our time, must we not say that it seems as though a frost has fallen upon all of the things of which we have spoken? Was not all of this romanticism, intoxication, utopianism?" he painfully asked.[140]

At the beginning of this "breathing spell,"[141] Tillich moved from Berlin to Marburg, bringing to an end his bi-weekly conversations with the Kairos Circle. Scattered throughout

Germany, the members continued to communicate with one another but in different modes--through their journal and other publications, through the exchange of letters and the occasional meeting at conferences. And now, after a phase of self-clarification, they turned their attention more directly outward, seeking new allies and a wider forum for their ideas. Both Tillich and Heimann, for example, published important, popular books in 1926.[142] This movement beyond Berlin let Tillich deeper into the socialist milieu. His activity from 1925 onward is properly framed within the context of socialism as he then encountered it.

Martin Jay, an historian of the Frankfurt School, has sketched three alternatives that the "left-wing intellectuals of Germany" faced in the new situation after World War I when "the socialist center of gravity" shifted eastward after the unexpected success of the Bolshevik Revolution and the "dramatic failure" of the socialist parties in Central Europe. One choice was to "support the moderate socialists and their freshly created Weimar Republic, thus eschewing revolution and scorning the Russian experiment." A second alternative was to "accept Moscow's leadership, join the newly formed German Communist Party, and work to undermine Weimar's bourgeois compromise." A third possibility, "almost entirely a product of the radical disruption of Marxist assumptions, a disruption brought about by the war and its aftermath," was "the searching reexamination of the very foundations of Marxist theory, with the dual hope of explaining past errors and preparing for future action."[143] It is the third path that the subject of Jay's book, the "Frankfurt School" (as it came to be called), followed.

Jay's typology is helpful in understanding Tillich's relationship to the political options of his situation. As will become evident, however, Tillich does not fit neatly into any of these categories. Rather his religious socialism represents a fourth alternative, one that seeks to combine the first and third choices. A critical supporter of Social Democracy and the Weimar Republic, Tillich also worked to re-evaluate and transform the theoretical basis of Marxism. First, Tillich's place within the sphere of Social Democracy needs to be traced.

In October 1925, the Kairos Circle reassembled to sponsor

a week-long seminar called "*Akademische Arbeitswoche*."[144] The
theme was "The Present Situation and Religous Socialism," and
each member lectured and led a discussion on a separate topic.
Tillich spoke on the intellectual and religious situation, Heimann on the economic, Ruestow on the social, Lowe on the world
economic, Mennicke on the domestic political, and Wolfers on the
world political situation. The week was a greater success than
the group had anticipated.[145] August Rathmann, a participant
in the week's events and a leader in the young socialist Hofgeismar Circle, wrote a very supportive review.[146] The Hofgeismar Circle was composed of proletarian youth who challenged
the dogmatic orthodoxy of the SPD, especially at the point of
the relationship of socialism to state and nation.[147] During
this week Tillich became acquainted with Rathmann, and from
then on his involvement with socialism was tied in part to the
impulses for renewal among these young socialists and their
allies.

On pentecost weekend in 1928, Tillich along with Heimann,
Lowe, Mennicke, and Rathmann joined nearly eighty other religious socialists, young socialists, and other critical socialists for a three-day conference at Heppenheim-on-the-Bergstrasse
(near Heidelberg) to discuss "the weakening of confidence in the
life-forming power of socialist ideas in our times."[148] United
in their distress over the stagnant condition of the SPD and
eager to infuse the movement with fresh moral and religious
motives, the participants were, however, split over the meaning of a renewed socialism. One of the major speakers was Hendrik de Man, whose writings were at the center of debate in
German socialism from 1925 to 1933.[149] His *The Psychology of
Socialism* (1926) "provoked the comment of just about every socialist theoretician on the Continent, excited the attention of
academics, and made its author the center of violent controversy."[150] Tillich, too, offered a lengthy review, saying "the
book belongs to the most important appearances of socialist
literature in recent years."[151] At Heppenheim de Man presented
his ethical non-Marxist version of socialism, and in response
Heimann, the second major speaker, argued for a dialectical
socialism.[152] In the ensuing discussion Tillich supported Heimann, and insisted that their goal was "to bestow on the reality

'socialism' a new word, to struggle for a new language, a new expression for it."[153] The Heppenheim group did not meet again as it had hoped, but its direction found an outlet in a new socialist journal.

Tillich had been interested in starting a new periodical since the *Arbeitswoche* of 1925. During the next years Mennicke negotiated unsuccessfully with several publishers. De Man worked to establish an international "Young Socialism" magazine but also failed. Herman Heller also hoped to begin a publication.[154] In 1929 the publisher Alfred Protte, supported by Theodore Heuss, made 30,000 marks available for a new journal. In a letter to Rathmann on February 2, 1929, Tillich wrote that there was a push to start a magazine from two sides, from Heller and from the pedagogue Fritz Klatt. Tillich wanted to combine the two but stated that all would fail if Rathmann did not accept the position as editor. "The foundation of the magazine is, of course, socialist, but without an expressed party connection," he wrote. He suggested the title *Die Neue Stellung*.[155] Rathmann, wanting to complete his law studies, was reluctant to accept but was finally persuaded by Tillich.

> Tillich made the assent easier for me when he agreed that the spirit and the policy of the socialist movement could not be effectively influenced from the outside and declared that he wanted to become a member of the Social Democratic Party "without restrictions." How much Tillich was concerned about the success of the magazine is evident from the fact that he himself proposed that in the title the designation "religious" socialism be dispensed with since it could be misunderstood and have a chilling effect.[156]

Tillich did join the SPD at the time, however reluctantly, for practical, political reasons.[157]

The first time of what was finally called *Neue Blaetter fuer den Sozialismus* appeared in January 1930, with Tillich contributing the lead article, "Socialism."[158] Heimann wrote the second article, "Socialization," Rathmann began a two-part discussion of "National Politics," and Lowe had a shorter piece on "Reparation Policy."[159] From then on the journal was published monthly, reaching a circulation of 3,000, until June 1933 when, after repeated confiscations, the Nazis forbade its publication.[160] Each issue of the *Neue Blaetter* was approximately fifty pages, neatly printed in a small magazine format,

and contained editorials, three or four major articles, book
reviews and self announcements, and brief comments on the arts,
films, the churches, the universities, the status of women, etc.

Tillich, Heimann, Klatt, and Rathmann were listed as the
editors of the *Neue Blaetter*; Rathmann was the managing editor
and responsible for the day-to-day editorial tasks. The editorial council consisted of Trude Bez-Mennicke, Emil Blum,
Theodor Hauback, Guenter Keiser, Emil Lederer, Lowe, de Man,
Heinrich Merstens, Carl Mierendorff, Walter Pahl, Hans Plug,
Adolf Reichwein, Henry Sigerist, Hugo Sinzheimer, Wilhelm Sollman, and Erich Winkler. Most of these people were active Social
Democrats, many had come out of the Hofgeismar Circle, and some
were representatives in Parliament where they were known as
the "Young Turks." According to Hunt, because they lacked mass
support, the "Young Turks" were not really a faction within the
party, but they did have some importance for their intellectual
contributions.[161] Other contributors to the journal included
socialist intellectuals and party activists such as Heller, Gustav Radbruch, Arthur Rosenberg, Hans Simons, Hans Speier, Carl
and Hilde Landauer, Reinhols Aris, Florian Geyer, Fritz Borinski, Konrad Hebel, J. P. Mayer, and Siegfried Landshut (in 1932
the last two discovered and edited Marx's *Economic and Philosophical Manuscripts of 1844*) as well as religious socialists
like Dehn, Hermann Schafft, Harold Poelchau, Marie Hirsch, and
Walter Dirks (a Catholic).

As the sub-bitle--*Zeitschrift fuer geistige und politische
Gestaltung*--made clear, the *Neue Blaetter* had a practical intent: to reshape socialism spiritually and politically. As
Landauer has written, the journal "tried to imbue the socialist
movement with a new will to action and with a spirit that would
satisfy the heart and not merely the intellect."[162] Neither an
intellectual journal nor a party organ, the *Neue Blaetter* included within its covers complex discussions of socialist theory, careful analysis of historical trends and current problems,
and passionate appeals for new initiatives. The disturbing
events of the time--the economic depression in Germany and the
world, the rise of the radical right, the growing militancy of
the Communist Party, the ossification of the SPD, the frequent
elections, and the threat to the Weimar Constitution--stamped

the contents of the magazine. It sought a third way between the orthodoxy of the socialist party and the radicalism of the Communists.

Socialist, democratic, and independent, the people around the *Neue Blaetter* wanted to see the yearnings of youth, nationalistic impulses, and aggressive leadership placed in the service of socialism. "Above all," Hunt has stated, "they appreciated the force of irrationality, and especially irrational nationalism, in twentieth century political life."[163] Landauer (who contributed to the magazine) wrote that the need they sought to satisfy was similar to that misused by "neo-socialist" movements in Britain and France.[164] "The comparison does injustice to the Young Turks, however," Hunt has replied, "since they never moved over into the fascist camp."[165] After 1933 they maintained their socialist and democratic commitment and fought the Nazis. Some were driven into exile, some spent long years in concentration camps, and others were killed by the Nazis. Three members of the editorial board, Haubach, Reichwein, and Mierendorff, were executed for their participation in the plot against Hitler on July 20, 1944.[166]

Tillich's own involvement was crucial for the existence and the character of the *Neue Blaetter*. He was not a figurehead editor but took an active role in setting the direction of the journal. Rathmann has described his participation:

> Just as the origin of the *Neue Blaetter* was, in the last analysis, due only to the untiring, goal-conscious energy of Tillich, so also the content and level of the magazine were largely determined by him. At the somewhat regular conversations of the editors, Tillich--since 1929 at the University of Frankfurt and repeatedly inspired by Berlin--Heimann, and Lowe always participated; Klatt or for him Adolf Reichwein were there less often, and occasionally other members of the advisory board also took part. Each time we met for hours in a spirited, friendly atmosphere in which differences or disagreements could hardly arise, and in which difficult problems could also be unanimously resolved. Tillich, superior, but tolerant, and ready to accept well-grounded arguments, repeatedly surprised everyone through the crystal clarity of his ideas and his certain judgment, even in the political questions of the day. It was self-evident to him that, in accordance with the threatening development, the magazine shift its chief stress more and more to politics. His own contributions knew how to deal with the acute current crisis in a way that was fundamentally critical but at the same time positively radical; they were a model for the increasingly concerned young leadership.[167]

Rathmann's testimony points to the often forgotten practical side of Tillich's religious socialism. It is clear that his theoretical work was in contact with a lively network of socialist relationships.

The *Neue Blaetter* gave Tillich a forum for addressing political issues, a circle of allies, and an identifiable position within socialism. He was sympathetic to the ideals of the young socialists around the journal, but he was now in his midforties and belonged to another generation. Tillich saw himself and his generation as a "bridge" between the activist voluntarism of the young socialists and the calculating scientific socialism of the older party leadership. Tillich hoped to connect the two generations through a proper understanding of dialectic, a subject for Chapter 5.[168]

Tillich's relationship with the *Neue Blaetter* demonstrates his ties to Social Democracy. Although his attitude towards the SPD was critical, and his attitudes towards party membership ambivalent, he recognized (already in 1924) his commitment to socialism as "necessarily a commitment to political socialism and with it, directly or indirectly, a support for those parties that represent political socialism in reality."[169] In 1932, when the party was in grave disarray, he reaffirmed his loyalty to the SPD, even if in a qualified sense: "Therefore in the future also the fate of German socialism will be decided in the Social Democratic Party--insofar as parties can be at all determinative."[170] He was supportive of the SPD, but he stayed on its periphery; he personally knew most of the party leadership,[171] but his ideas had no discernible influence on party policies. One reason for this was his searching reexamination of the foundations of Marxist theory. His activism existed in a taut relationship with Jay's third alternative. Tillich's theoretical concerns, the content of which will be the topic for the following chapters, can be seen in his contact with the members of the Frankfurt School.

Tillich spent the final four years of the republic in the cosmopolitan city of Frankfurt as Professor of Philosophy at the city's progressive university.[172] Tillich in 1931 spoke of his "'Frankfurt Conversation'" as having "three sides": one side was an "inner-philosophical" conversation tied especially to Greek thinking. He was referring here to the philosopher and the curator of the University Kurt Rielzer and to the philosopher Walter Otto. In a second group "the common experience of the proletarian situation and socialism" stood in the center of discussion. This, I surmise, is a reference to those in Frankfurt connected with the *Neue Blaetter,* people such as Lowe, Mennicke, Sinzheimer, and de Man.[173]

> Thirdly, there is the group which first of all analyzes the situation in a reserved sociological fashion and which wants to bring all of us in the various groups into connection with our actual, real situation, and whose criticism of what happens in the other groups has become of decisive significance for me.[174]

This group was the "Kraenzcehn," a discussion circle that was composed of Max Horkheimer, Theodoro Adorno, Leo Lowenthal, and Friedrich Pollock of the Institute of Social Research; the gestalt psychologist Max Wertheimer, the sociologist Karl Mannheim, Rielzer, Lowe, Mennicke, and Tillich.[175] In 1929 Tillich had been instrumental in the creation of a new chair of "social philosophy" for Horkheimer, a position that allowed him to become director of the Institute.[176] Tillich also aided Adorno in becoming a privatdozent in 1931, thus opening the door for his participation in the Institute.[177] He was also a friend of Erich Fromm and Herbert Marcuse, two young assistants at the Institute.[178]

Tillich shared the intention of the proponents of Critical Theory to reexamine Marxist theory, even before his conversations with them began. He too was at home in Hegelian thought, recognized the barrenness of current socialist thinking, and worked on the theoretical basis of a new alternative. The purpose of *The Socialist Decision* was, for example, to offer "a fundamental reflection of socialism on itself, above all, on its unspoken assumptions"; his aim was to examine "the roots" of socialism.[179] Unlike his friends of the Frankfurt School, however, Tillich believed that one must "lay a new foundation" for a new social order by probing to the final layer of reality, to the question of the meaning of existence itself.[180] He also differed from them by incorporating a livelier tension between theory and practice than did his more detached dialogue partners who suspended their commitment to the socialist parties.

Tillich's attempt to do both, to influence socialist

politics and simultaneously to transform the theory of the movement, proved to be impossible. The paramount reason for this was the resistance of the party whose tired, entrenched leadership was captive of a closed orthodoxy and was not open to new impulses.[181] There was no room in the SPD for critical and fundamental reflection, especially if it came from a theologian.[182] A reformist party, seeking to survive in a difficult and uncertain historical situation, was not receptive to unfamiliar ideas. Such an attitude (as well as the similarly closed position of a conservative church) was in large part responsible for the ineffectiveness of Tillich's religious socialism.[183]

Although he tried, Tillich is hardly the perfect model for the uniting of theory and praxis. His social locus in academia kept him relatively isolated from the proletariat.[184] His personal character did not seem conducive to active political participation.[185] His writings at times embodied a "docetic" attitude towards the mundane world of politics, and they were remiss in not giving strategic and tactical guidelines for immediate action.[186] If these limitations helped to prevent his political effectiveness, they were, on the other hand, not without importance for his theoretical work. His relative aloofness from day-to-day political pressures and decisions was advantageous for the intellectual rigor, the sweeping perspective, and the critical edge of his religious socialism. Tillich was not a party ideologue, nor a politician, nor a "prophet to politicians," but a creative and critical theologian of politics.[187]

Finally, a brief comment is in order on Tillich's relationship to Jay's second possibility, Communism. Tillich did not eschew revolution nor did he scorn the Russian experiment, but he did consider the latter as largely irrelevant to German socialism. Although it is of greatest interest for every work on socialism, Russia, he wrote, cannot provide a model for Germany since the "rational principle" triumphed only with the Russian Revolution.[188] Interestingly, he found Bolshevism the foremost representative of the "romantic" version of religious socialism, since it set itself in the place of religion, thereby overlooking the radical criticism inherent in religion.[189] In 1934 he assured Emanuel Hirsch that his religious socialism had never been "religious Bolshevism."[190] Tillich's attitude toward the KPD, especially its intellectuals, was very negative. Some of his strongest attacks were directed at adherents of "the dogmatic rigidity of Communism." Their rejection of all ideas but their own as bourgeois ideology, the subordination of their own thinking to a party-line, and the sacrifice of their own autonomy were features of the communist ideologues that Tillich vehemently opposed.[191] Distressed by the communist-socialist split, Tillich tried in *The Socialist Decision* dialectically to appropriate some of the revolutionary impulses of communism, but he naively hoped that a theoretical clarification of their differences would "soften the sharp opposition among the socialist parties."[192]

Neither a typical Social Democrat nor a totally reserved intellectual, Tillich during the years after 1925 entered deeply into the socialist movement in order critically to transform its theoretical roots. The culmination of his activity came in 1932 in a last, desperate attempt to resist the onslaught of National Socialism.

Socialism or Barbarism, 1932-1933

In the ominous situation of 1932 Tillich wrote his most extensive and most significant work on socialism, *The Socialist Decision*. Violent clashes among Nazis, Communists, and Social Democrats brought the country to the brink of civil war. Chancellor Heinrich Bruening, who proved to be the last "great coalition" chancellor supported by the SPD, resigned on May 30 and was replaced by the reactionary Franz von Papen. On July 20 von Papen seized control of the Prussian government, the last stronghold of Social Democracy, and the socialists reacted passively. Eleven days later the Nazis scored a stunning electoral victory. The situation was still fluid, but the Social Democrats were in a very weakened situation, the "conservative political romantics" (to use Tillich's terminology) were still in power, and the "revolutionary political romantics" were making impressive gains.[193]

In *The Socialist Decision* Tillich foresaw that the future might well be one of "barbarism." Already in 1932 he recognized the possibility of war. If the militaristic, nationalistic right were victorious, insisted Tillich, "a self-annihilating struggle of the European peoples will be inevitable."[194] He believed, however, that socialism, a renewed and transformed socialism, still offered a possibility for averting this future. "*The salvation of European society from a return to barbarism lies in the hands of socialism.*"[195] The book's mood was not the excitement of new possibilities but determined resolution in the face of impending disaster. Its attitude was that of "sober expectation" or "a realism of expectation." "*Only expectation,*" wrote Tillich in the last lines of the book, "*can triumph over the death now threatening Western civilization through the resurgence of the myth of origin. And expectation is the symbol of socialism.*"[196] Tillich was appealing for "the socialist decision" while Germany was "deciding" for Nazism.

A product of his experiences both with his co-workers around the *Neue Blaetter* and with his socialist friends in Frankfurt, *The Socialist Decision* began as a lecture at the *Hochschule fuer Politik* in October 1931.[197] He wrote the bulk of the book during the summer of 1932 in the mountains of Sils Maria, Switzerland, where he was vacationing with his wife Hannah and his friends Adolf Grimme, Mannheim, and Lowe.[198] Grimme was a religious socialist who had been the Prussian Minister of Education from 1930 until the coup of July 20, 1932. In the morning Tillich would go into the woods and write, and in the afternoon he and Lowe would discuss what he had written.[199] He signed the Foreword on November 9 (the fourteenth and last anniversary of the "German Republic"), and he issued his announcement of the book in the December issue of the *Neue Blaetter*.[200] It was published in 1933, appearing as part of the series *Die sozialistische Aktion,*" sponsored by the *Neue Blaetter.*

But it was too late. Historical events foreclosed any genuine socialist decision. On January 30, 1933, Adolf Hitler took power and the barbaric future began. *The Socialist Decision* was suppressed and all the socialist literature of Alfred Protte was confiscated. Later, the remaining copies of the work were destroyed when the Protte warehouse in Potsdam was levelled by Allied bombs.[201] The book's public existence thus was extremely short-lived, and no reviews of it were printed.

Although the book never achieved its deserved recognition, it was important for Tillich and his friends. On April 13, 1933, Tillich's name appeared on the first list of intellectuals to be "purged," and, along with Mannheim, Lowe, Horkheimer, Heller, Sinzheimer, and others, he was dismissed from his teaching position.[202] The immediate cause of the dismissal was Tillich's defense of some students attacked by Nazi "Brown Shirts," and his insistence that the latter be punished. Jobless, no longer a party member,[203] but eager to remain in Germany in order to influence the political situation, Tillich traveled throughout the country to confer with his friends. He wanted to write for the underground press, but his friends told him that his style was too easily recognizable and that therefore he would be a greater liability than a help. In witnessing the Jewish boycott, a book-burning celebration, forced arrests, and the desperation of his friends, and upon being nearly taken by the Gestapo, he recognized that he would have to go into exile.[204] Before leaving in the fall, he visited an official of the Nazi Ministry of Education who had requested to see him. During their conversation, the official, according to Dr. Lowe, asked Tillich to revoke *The Socialist Decision* in exchange for a prestigious chair in theology at the University of Berlin. Tillich's reply was to laugh in his face.[205]

This episode took on the significance of a prophetic encounter for Tillich's socialist friends, and the book became for them a symbol of courage and resistance. During the next dozen years of terror and war, the few surviving copies of the book were quietly passed from hand to hand among these people, "contributing to their resolve to resist the Hitler absurdity."[206]

During the summer of 1933 Reinhold Niebuhr and Horace Friess invited Tillich to New York to join the faculty of Union Theological Seminary and to lecture at Columbia University. When he decided for exile, he accepted the offer and departed for America. On November 4, 1933, Tillich, now 47, landed in New York to begin a new life in a strange land.[207] Emigration, a reality in his own life, became a new theme in his writings.[208] Tillich's arrival in America represents the end of the German phase of his religious socialism, the subject of this study. In 1934-1935 Tillich fought a rear-guard battle against his old friend and political foe, Emanuel Hirsch, who had used Tillich's categories to justify Hitler's take-over.[209] His attention continued to be consumed by the tragic drama on the continent, although now the context in which and for he had developed his theological interpretation of socialism was gone. The future had not brought socialism but barbarism.

Summary

As I have described, Paul Tillich's religious socialism was embedded in the unforeseen and ill-fated course of German society in the first third of the twentieth century. Tillich was shaped by the events of his time, especially the experience of war and revolution, and in becoming a religious socialist in 1918, he sought to help shape his society's future.

Tillich responded by attacking the social question "at the point of greatest social tension," the conflict between the bourgeoisie and the proletariat.[210] He did so as a religious socialist, that is, as one who embraced both Protestantism and socialism and tried to reconcile the tension between the religious and the political, the pessimistic and the utopian, the conservative and the radical poles that these opposing alternatives implied. Tillich's relationship to church and party, and to the theological and socialist currents of thought of the day, have been outlined. Although he thought that the possibility of success of his efforts was "highly questionable," he did not doubt the crucial importance of what he was doing.[211]

Throughout the Weimar years Tillich kept faith with his intention of 1919, to enter into the socialist movement in order to pave the way for a future union of Christianity and the socialist social order." In contextualizing the "difficult, unknown and important way" he followed, I have noted certain developments in his religious socialism. His mood changed from enthusiasm to a sobriety needed for a long journey, and his thinking became less idealistic, more realistic, and Marxist. He moved steadily more deeply into socialism, altering his self-identification from Christian, to religious, to simply socialist (a change, however, that does not mean a surrender of his theological concerns). He matured as did his conversational partners. New terminology emerged, and older concepts became latent. Different people, situations, and ideas called forth new responses. His religious socialism developed, but there were no "breaks" in it. Its continuity is more impressive than any discontinuity.[212] Throughout these years Tillich's aim was constant: to transform fundamentally the theoretical foundations of socialism and Protestantism for the sake of a new society.

CHAPTER 2

NOTES

¹*On the Boundary* (hereafter *OB*). Originally published in 1936 as part of *The Interpretation of History*, trans. by Rasetski and Talmey (New York: Charles Scribner's Sons, 1936) (*IH*). "Author's Introduction," *The Protestant Era* (Chicago: University of Chicago Press, 1948), pp. ix-xxix (*PE*). "Autobiographical Reflections," *The Theology of Paul Tillich*, eds. Charles W. Kegley and Robert W. Bretall (New York: The Macmillan Co., 1952), pp. 3-21. Tillich's European diary from 1936 illustrates how his life and thought were intertwined. *My Travel Diary: 1936*, edited with an Introduction by Jerald C. Brauer (New York: Harper and Row, Publishers, 1970). Throughout Tillich's writings there are numerous references to personal experiences.

²There is yet no biography of Tillich. Dr. and Mrs. Wilhelm Pauck are completing what promises to be the definitive biography of Tillich. Rolly May has written a brief "reminiscences of a friendship." *Paulus* (New York: Harper and Row, Publishers, 1973). Tillich's second wife Hannah has published her memoirs which, of course, contain material about her husband. *From Time to Time* (New York: Stein and Day, Publishers, 1973).

³"Christentum und Sozialismus stehen sich gegenueber wie Feuer und Wasser." Bebel's remark comes from 1873-1874. Quoted from Kurt Kaiser's *Materialien ueber den religioesen Sozialismus in Deutschland aus der Zeit bon 1918-1933* (Doctor's dissertation, University of Basel, Switzerland; 1962), p. 8.

⁴Theodor Strohm, *Kirche und Democratischer Sozialismus* (Munich: Chr. Kaiser Verlag, 1968), p. 20. Cf. Theodore E. Bachmann, "The Church and the Rise of Modern Society, 1830-1914," *Christian Social Responsibility*, ed. Harold C. Letts (Philadelphia: Muhlenberg Press, 1957), pp. 89-137. Marty, *The Modern Schism*, pp. 36-58.

⁵William O. Shanhan, *German Protestants Face the Social Question*, Vol. I, *The Conservative Phase 1815-1871* (Notre Dame, Indiana: University of Notre Dame Press, 1954), p. 205. Cf. Gerald Christianson, "J. H. Wichern and the Rise of the Lutheran Social Institution," *The Lutheran Quarterly*, XIX, 4 (November 1967), pp. 357-70; and Shanahan, pp. 208-27.

⁶Ibid., p. ix, p. 225.

⁷Ibid., p. 193.

⁸Ibid.

⁹See Carl Landauer in collaboration with Elizabeth Kridl Valkenier and Hilde Stein Landauer, *European Socialism*, Two Vols. (Berkeley and Los Angeles: University of California Press, 1959), pp. 23-24, 279-83. See also Ronald L. Massanari, "Christian Socialism: Adolf Stoecker's Formulation for Social Change for the Protestant Church in Nineteenth Century Germany," *The Lutheran Quarterly*, XXII, 5 (May, 1970), 185-98, and by the same author, "True or False Socialism: Adolf Stoecker's

Critique of Marxism from a Christian Socialist Perspective," *Church History*, Vol. 41, No. 4 (December 1972), pp. 487-96. Cf. Tillich, *The Religious Situation*, trans. by H. Richard Niebuhr (Cleveland: Meridian Books, 1956), pp. 195-96 (*Rel. Sit.*).

[10] Richard N. Hung, *German Social Democracy 1918-1933* (Chicago: Quadrangle Paperbacks, 1964), pp. 1-16. Cf. Landauer, Chs. 1-4, 6, 7, 9, 12.

[11] George Lichtheim, *Marxism* (New York: Frederick A. Praeger, Publisher, 1961), Pt. Five, Chs. 3-5.

[12] The two were Paul Goehre and Christoph Blumhardt. Only Blumhardt, "the theological father-figure" of religious socialism (Marsch), had any significance for Tillich. See Wolf-Dieter Marsch, "Theologie und Marxismus im Religioesen Sozialismus," *Internationale Dialog Zeitschrift*, I (1972), pp. 6-10. Also, "Christoph Blumhardt's Letter to His Friends," *Metonia*, III (September 1971), pp. 5-9. In an introduction James Luther Adams wrote that the letter "deserves a key position in the documents of Protestant social ethics of the past century." P.2.

[13] Andrew Landale Drummond, *German Protestantism Since Luther* (London: The Epworth Press, 1951), p. 259. According to Drummond, the United Evangelical Church of Prussia had twenty million members.

[14] Kegley and Bretall, p. 7.

[15] Ibid.

[16] Cf., "I remember how my father who was a kind of bishop in the Lutheran Church--this word did not exist at that time, he was called superintendent--but he told me once, I take care of this old woman, she is in our house everyday, but I am absolutely against the socialist movement because this movement puts something, some law, something objective between me and her, and I do not want that personal relationship to be spoiled by legal structures. This, of course, I later on recognized, was a pure romantic longing for the past, because, at the same time, there were millions of workers in the suburbs of Berlin, with whom nobody could have such personal relations, and he would not have been able to get anywhere without the political organization into which they went. But this was genuine and well meant, although mistaken, Lutheran ideology. . . . There is compassion but there is no transformation of reality. . . ." Tillich, "The Basic Ideas of Religious Socialism" *Bulletin: The International House of Japan, Inc.* (1960), p. 12. The incident is instructive in illustrating the early influences on Tillich's social attitudes.

[17] "Tillich-to-Thomas Mann Letter" (23 May 1943), *The Intellectual Legacy of Paul Tillich*, ed. James R. Lyons (Detroit: Wayne State University Press, 1969), pp. 99-107.

[18] Ibid., p. 104. Also, "Paul Tillich," in *Philosophical Interrogations*, eds. Sydney and Beatrice Rome (New York: Holt, Rinehart and Winston, 1964), p. 362. Here Tillich wrote that he first read Kierkegaard in 1905, Marx in 1920.

[19] Letter to Mann, p. 106. Cf. his "Erinnerungen an den Freund Hermann Schafft," *Gesammelte Werke*, XIII (Stuttgart: Evangelisches Verlagswerk, 1972), pp. 27-33. Tillich later

wrote sharp words against the uncritical nationalism of the Wingolf as it developed in the Weimar Republic. "Christentum, Sozialismus und Nationalismus," *GW*, XIII, pp. 161-66. "Erwiderung," *Wingolf-Blaetter,* LIII (1924), p. 27.

[20] *The Construction of the History of Religion in Schelling's Positive Philosophy: Its Presuppositions and Principles,* trans. and with an Introduction by Victor Nuovo (Lewisburg/Penn.: Bucknell University Press, 1974). *Mysticism and Guilt-Consciousness in Schelling's Philosophical Development,* trans. and with an Introduction by Victor Nuovo (Lewisburg/Penn.: Bucknell University Press, 1974).

[21] "Kirchliche Apologetik," *GW*, XIII, pp. 33-68. Originally written in 1913. "Inner Mission arose out of the recognition that the church's influence does not reach the masses of people. . . . The apologetic [program] must be born out of the recognition that the church's preaching is not reaching the educated." P. 37. In his capacity as apologist Tillich debated leading Social Democrats, including Karl Liebknecht, on the question of workers contracting out of the church. The encounter with Liebknecht, who after the war organized the German Communist Party, took place on December 12, 1913, according to Tillich's friend Maria Rhine. Ibid., p. 20.

[22] *The Social Teaching of the Christian Churches,* II, trans. Olive Wyon (New York: Harper Torchbooks, 1960), p. 568. First published in German in 1911.

[23] *Ob,* p. 32.

[24] Kegley and Bretall, p. 12.

[25] Ibid.

[26] *OB,* p. 20.

[27] Letter to Mann; *OB,* pp. 46-58; Kegley and Bretall, pp. 9-12.

[28] *OB,* p. 74.

[29] "I was grasped by the overwhelming experience of a nation-wide community. . . ." Kegley and Bretall, p. 12. Note his comments on the army in Kegley and Bretall, p. 7. Also how he "experienced" the War of 1870-1871, fifteen years before his birth; ". . . we German children lived that war. I knew every battle, the date of every battle, every army corps that fought in this or that place. Our participation was inbred." *Ultimate Concern Tillich in Dialogue,* ed. D. Mackenzie Brown (New York: Harper Colophon Books, 1965), p. 132.

[30] "Meine Taetigkeit im IV. Reserve-Korps im Oktober 1914," *GW*, XIII, pp. 71-76.

[31] From a letter to Maria Rhine, ibid., p. 70.

[32] "Bericht ueber die Monate November und Dezember 1915," ibid., pp. 77-78. In commenting on Dix's picture "War," he said, "The trenches of the First World War, of which I unfortunately have a good knowledge--and he was right." "Art and Ultimate Reality," *Cross Currents,* X, i (January 1960), p. 8.

[33] Ibid., pp. 78-79.

[34] *Ultimate Concern,* p. 153. Brown in his Introduction

spoke of this personal kairos: "During one terrible night of the battle of Champagne, in July of 1916, he witnessed the suffering and death of hundreds of casualties in the division in which he served as chaplain. The horror of the night, during which he lost some of his friends, never left him, and the whole structure of classical idealism under which the war had taken place was shattered." P. xv. Perhaps Brown received some of these details from Tillich in personal conversation. It appears from the recently published material cited here that this personal kairos did take place during the Battle of Champagne, but that the time might have been earlier, maybe in October or November, 1915. Hans Holborn writes of the "much larger scale" operations beginning on September 25, 1915. *A History of Modern Germany 1840-1945* (New York: Alfred A. Knopf, 1969), p. 440. May also notes the significance of this event for Tillich: "'That night absolutely transformed me," he used to say." P. 18.

[35] Letter to Rhine, *GW*, XIII, 70.

[36] "Die Geisteslage der Gegenwart Rueckblick und Ausblick," *GW*, X (1968), p. 113. This manuscript, coming from 1930, was first published in 1968.

[37] "World War I was disastrous for idealistic thought in general. Schelling's philosophy was also affected by this catastrophe." *OB*, p. 52. Cf. *PE*, p. xviii, and May, p. 18. David H. Hooper, however, argues for an "ontological continuity" between Tillich's early study of Schelling and his later *Systematic Theology*. *Tillich: A Theological Portrait* (New York: J. B. Lippincott Co., 1968), p. 128.

[38] *OB*, p. 53. Tillich did not follow Nietzsche's vitalism, although, he writes, "he might well have," but his thought continues to play an important if subordinate role in Tillich's writings. Cf. *Philosophical Interrogations*, p. 362.

[39] Letter to Rhine, December 5, 1917, loc. cit. Perhaps Tillich was referring to such thoughts when he wrote in *OB* (p. 33): "The tremendous pressure of the war, which had threatened to obscure the idea of God or to give it demonic coloration. . ."

[40] *OB*, p. 32.

[41] "Bericht," *GW*, XIII, 79. Dr. Adolf Lowe, in an interview on May 24, 1972, mentioned the importance of the war for putting Tillich in direct contact with the proletariat, an experience not easy to come by in pre-war Germany.

[42] Kegley and Bretall, p. 12.

[43] "It was during the collapse of imperial Germany and the revolution of the last year of World War I that I began to understand such issues as the political background of the war, the interrelation of capitalism and imperialism, the crisis of bourgeois society, and the schisms between the classes." *OB*, pp. 32-33. ". . . the experience of the German revolution of 1918 decisively redirected my concerns toward a sociologically based and politically oriented philosophy of history." Ibid., p. 54.

[44] Peter Gay, *Weimar Culture, The Outsider as Insider* (New York: Harper Torchbooks, 1970), pp. 8-9.

[45] Holborn, pp. 509-79; Ernst K. Bramsted, *Germany* (Englewood Cliffs, New Jersey: Prentice-Hall, Inc., 1972), pp. 167-75; Gay, pp. 147-55.

[46] See Hannah Tillich's description, pp. 77-78.

[47] "The tremendous pressure of the war . . . found an outlet in the discovery of the human responsibility for the war and the hope for a refashioning of human society. When the call to a religious socialist movement was sounded, I could not and would not refuse to heed it." *OB*, p. 33.

[48] Tillich, in collaboration with Dr. Carl Richard Wegener, "Der Sozialismus als Kirchenfrage," *GW,* II (1962), p. 16. ("Kirchenfrage")

[49] "On the Idea of a Theology of Culture," *What is Religion?*, trans. with an Introduction by James Luther Adams (New York: Harper and Row, Publishers, 1969), p. 180. ("Th. of Cul.") (*WR?*)

[50] "Revolution und Kirche," *GW,* XII (1971), 199. In an article in 1920 he again speaks of "a new period of Christianity." "Christentum und Sozialismus II," *GW,* II, p. 31.

[51] His first "Kairos" essay was published in *Die Tat,* XIV, 5 (August 1922), pp. 330-50. Translation in *PE,* pp. 32-51. This is, I believe, the first time he uses the word in print.

[52] Guenther Dehn, who tried to organize a group of church people friendly to socialism in Berlin and failed, writes that the reason was that there were no such people. *Die alte Zeit, die vorigen Jahre,* (Muenchen: Chr. Kaiser Verlag, 1962), p. 162.

[53] "Kirchenfrage," p. 19.

[54] For discussions of the religious socialist movement see the previously mentioned works by Kaiser and Marsch. Also, Renate Breipohl, *Religioeser Sozialismus und burgerliches Geschichtsbewusstsein zur Zeit der Weimarer Republik* (Zurich: Theologischer Verlag, 1971), esp. Ch. 1; Breipohl, ed., *Dokumente zum religioesen Sozialismus in Deutschland,* Vol. 46, *Theologische Buecherei Historische Theologie* (Muenchen: Chr. Kaiser Verlag, 1972); Johanna Gunz, *Sozialismus und Religion im Deutschland der Nachkreigszeit* (Munchen und Leipzig: Dunker und Humbolt, 1926); Gerda Soecknick, *Religioeser Sozialismus der neuren Zeit unter besonderer Beruecksichtigung Deutschlands* (Jena: Gustav Fischer, 1926). Note the encyclopedia articles on religious socialism listed in the Bibliography.

[55] The text of *OB* is incorrect when it reads: "We met shortly after the Russian Revolution of 1917 to discuss religion and socialism." P. 78. In 1917 Tillich was still on the front; moreover, the German Revolution was the decisive one for him. The German text reads only "nach der Revolution." *GW,* XII, p, 47.

[56] In 1919 Tillich spoke about "die christlich-sozialistische Bewegung," *GW,* II, p. 20. In 1920 for the first time he used "religioeser Sozialismus." "Die Jugend und die Religion," in *Die Freideutsche Jugendbewegung: Ursprung und Zukunft,* eds. A. Grabowski and W. Koch (Gotha: F. A. Perthes, 1920), p. 12.

[57] Thomas Ulrich writes that at the time Mennicke was connected with Siegmund-Schultze's *SAG*. So, erwuchs der religioessozialistische Kreis um Tillich und Mennicke aus der *SAG*. *Ontologie, Theologie, gesellschaftliche Praxis Studien zum religioesen Sozialismus Paul Tillichs und Carl Mennickes* (Zurich: Theologischer Verlag, 1971), p. 218. Cf. *Blaetter fuer relitioesen Sozialismus,* I, 1 (Easter, 1920), 1. For more on *SAG,* see Dehn, p. 139.

[58] Pp. 212-13. For a discussion of Naumann's views see Strohm, pp. 34-44.

[59] *Blaetter,* I, 1, p. 1; Ulrich, p. 218.

[60] Hunt, pp. 26-33; Landauer, Chs. 19, 20, 26, 29.

[61] "Answer to an Inquiry of the Protestant Consistory of Brandenbrug," trans. James Luther Adams, *Metonia,* III, 3 (September 1971), p. 10. ("Answer")

[62] Adams, in his "Introduction" to Tillich's *Political Expectation* (New York: Harper and Row, Publishers, 1971) (*Pol. Exp.*), writes that Tillich was a member of the USDP. P. vi. In a personal conversation he said that Dr. Pauck had indicated this was incorrect. However, while in Germany in 1973, a student of Tillich at the time assured me that he had been a member. The student was Eduard Graefe zu Baringdo.

[63] Hunt, p. 197. During 1919-1920 the USPD enjoyed "an impressive blossoming of popularity," but by 1922 it had faded as a party. See pp.193-203 for "The Short History of the USPD."

[64] "Kirchenfrage," *GW,* II, 17-18. He was critical of their ethical materialism, their atheism (both inheritances from bourgeois culture), their radical separation of religious and political life, and their postwar actions; he was hopeful that a new religious interest would enliven and change their defects. He saw that "the demand for an ethical-religious inspiration of socialism is being raised louder and louder and it is being more and more recognized that socialism is not only an economic but also above all an educational affair." Cf. "Answer," pp. 12, 9.

[65] Cf. Daniel R. Borg, "*Volkskirche,* 'Christian State,' and the Weimar Republic," *Church History,* XXXV, 2 (June 1966), pp. 186-206.

[66] Cf. Kenneth Scott Latourette, "Protestantism in Storm-Tossed Germany," *Christianity in a Revolutionary Age,* Vol. IV, *The Twentieth Century in Europe* (New York: Harper and Brothers, 1961), pp. 246-57; Arthur C. Cochrane, "Between the Times: 1917-1933," *The Church's Confession Under Hitler* (Philadelphia: The Westminster Press, 1962), 50 ff.; Landale, pp. 258-63; Otto Piper, *Recent Developments in German Protestantism* (London: Student Christian Movement Press, 1934), p. 52; Dehn, p. 211.

[67] Dehn, pp. 164-65.

[68] "Answer," p. 10. Adams' translation in 1971 was the first publication of this document. "Christentum und Sozialismus. Bericht an das Konsistorium der Mark Brandenburg," *GW,* XIII, pp. 154-60. The inquiry was made on May 16, 1919, and we may assume that Tillich's reply came soon thereafter. In the text and in the footnotes it will be referred to as "Answer."

[69]"Der Sozialismus als Kirchenfrage," was published in 1919 as a tract for the times. Dr. Wegener, who collaborated with Tillich on this pamphlet, had worked with him before the war on the church apologetic program and was now a youth pastor for the Berlin synod. According to Bruno Theek, "Kirchenfrage" grew out of numerous discussions of their circle. It was composed of thirty theses. The publication of "Answer" that exists is incomplete. Because of their historical priority, these two writings deserve more attention than is usually given to them. Cf. Theek, "Ein Kurser Gang von Paul Tillich zu Emil Fuch," *Ruf und Antwort. Festgabe fuer Emil Fuchs zum 90. Geburtstag* (Leipzig: Koehler and Amelung, 1964), pp. 90-91. In 1964 Theek was a pastor in the German Democratic Republic.

[70]"Answer," p. 11. "Kirchenfrage" speaks of "*Bewusstsein*" (consciousness) in place of "feeling: (*Gefuehl*) and only here is "*Idee des Sozialismus*" found. P. 14.

[71]The term "idealistic socialist" is Tillich's own term. "Th. of Cul.," p. 172, and in "Revolution und Kirche," *GW*, XII, 196.

[72]"Kirchenfrage," p. 18. Cf. "Answer," p. 9. Tillich is rejecting both Wichern's Inner Mission and Bismarckian social legislation as the answer to the social question. ". . . the spirit of Wichern was still alive." Landale, p. 260. Cf. Latourette, p. 252.

[73]"Kirchenfrage," p. 19. Cf. "Answer," p. 16. At this point the text of "Answer" ends.

[74]"Kirchenfrage," p. 19. Tillich recognizes that the existence of socialists in its midst will create new areas of conflict within the church, but he considers it the character of a church in contrast to a sect to bear such tensions and make them fruitful for its future development. He used the concept of "*Volkskirche*" to argue that a church cannot call itself such if it rejects socialists when nearly half of its people are socialists. But if it accepts socialists, then he says it will have secured "*the possibility to fulfill its mission in the future.*"

[75]Helmut Gollwitzer asks if the question of the early Tillich in relationship to the empirical church is not as timely now as it was then. *Reich Gottes und Sozialismus bei Karl Barth,* No. 169, *Theologische Existenz heute,* edited by Karl Gerhard Steck (Muenchen: Chr. Kaiser Verlag, 1972), pp. 49-51. The case of Rubem Alves and the Protestant church in Brazil represents a similar decision.

[76]"Kirchenfrage," p. 19.

[77]Cf. Marsch, p. 6. For a discussion of the Congress see Strohm, pp. 44-51; 55-57.

[78]*Rel. Sit.*, p. 196.

[79]*GW*, XII, pp. 194-99. The review first appeared in *Das neue Deutschland,* VIII (1918-1919), pp. 394-97. Among the contributors were Wilhelm Bousset, Otto Dibelius, Karl Heim, Rudolf Otto, Martin Rade, and Ernst Troeltsch.

[80]Ibid., pp. 194-97.

[81] Ibid., pp. 198-99.

[82] "Zum Tode von Ernst Troeltsch," *GW,* XII, pp. 175-78; "Ernst Troeltsch. Versuch einer geistesgeschichtlichen Wuerdigung," *GW,* XII, pp. 166-74; "Der Historismus und seine Probleme. Zum gleichnamigen Buch von Ernst Troeltsch," *GW,* pp. 204-11; Review, *"Der Historismus und seine Ueberwindung,"* Theologische Literaturzeitung, XLIX, 11 (1924), pp. 234-35. For an example of Troeltsch's attitude toward socialism see "The Ideas of Natural Law and Humanity in World Politics," Appendix I, Otto Gierke, *Natural Law and the Theory of Society,* trans. with an Introduction by Ernest Barker (Cambridge: University Press, 1934), pp. 220-22.

[83] "Zum Tode," pp. 175-76.

[84] Ibid., p. 177.

[85] Summarized from Dehn's description, pp. 217-21. Barth's speech, translated as "The Christian's Place in Society," is found in *The Word of God and the Word of Man,* trans. Douglas Horton (New York: Harper Torchbooks, 1957), pp. 272-327.

[86] *Blaetter,* I, 1, pp. 1-2.

[87] Ibid., pp. 203. What follows is Mennicke's summary of Tillich's talk. Perhaps parts of Tillich's last writing from 1919, "Christentum und Sozialismus I," *GW,* II, 21-28, can be seen as a reply to Barth. CF. p. 21; also, "Christentum und Sozialismus II," pp. 25-26. In the first he insisted that to affirm socialism meant also to affirm the principles on which it stood. In the second he rejected the idea that the world was essentially evil and reason corrupt so that knowledge could only come from revelation.

[88] For a convenient summary of Barth's impact during this period see Heinz Zahrnt, *The Question of God,* trans. by R. A. Wilson (New York: Harcourt, Brace and World, Inc., 1969), Ch. 1, pp. 15-54. See Hopper, Ch. II, "The Controversy with Barth," pp. 35-64, for a report on their open conflict in 1923. The appropriate articles of this dispute are found in "The Debate on the Concept of Paradox," in *The Beginnings of Dialectical Theology,* Vol. 1, ed. by James M. Robinson (Richmond, Virginia: John Knox Press, 1968), pp. 133-62. In the final chapter I will return to another, often overlooked controversy they had in 1933.

[89] In "Th. of Cul." Tillich defined the task of a theologian of culture in contrast to the church theologian, pp. 175-81. The former was "a free agent in the living cultural movement," the latter more interested in continuity. The two were complementary and the ideal was personal union. The relationship of the two was, however, unclear, and perhaps reflects the ambiguity in Tillich's own self-understanding. See James Luther Adams, *Paul Tillich's Philosophy of Culture, Science and Religion* (New York: Harper and Row, Publishers, 1965), pp. 86-89, for a discussion of the problem. A continuing problem for this definition of a theologian's task is the source of the criteria. From where do the norm or norms come by which cultural phenomena are judged?

[90] Cf. "Revolution und Kirche," pp. 198-99. Here he wrote that the formula "Jesus is Lord" had a "strong heteronomous

sound" for those who had found autonomy to be "the highest, most freeing experience." He added that autonomy drove to a mysticism in which Christ was not at the midpoint, but very often on the periphery. Because of his fear of heteronomy Tillich never had access to a Lordship Christology. A Christology was not fully developed in his early writings.

[91] *OB*, p. 32.

[92] *WR?*, pp. 155-81. Note Tillich's remarks on this essay in the "Forward" to his *Theology of Culture* (New York: Oxford University Press, 1950), p. v. Walter Leibrecht wrote of this lecture that it "made him [Tillich] well known in Europe overnight." "The Life and Mind of Paul Tillich," in *Religion and Culture Essays in Honor of Paul Tillich*, ed. Walter Leibrecht (New York: Harper and Brothers, 1959), p. 7.

[93] Ibid., p. 180.

[94] *Berlin Universitaet Verzeichnis der Vorlesungen* Sommer Semester, 1919 (April 25 - August 31), p. 81. In the Winter Semester his lectures were on the "Philosophical and Religious Foundations of the Political Schools." Margot Hahl, "Studentin bei dem Privatdozenten Paul Tillich im Nachkriegs-Berlin 1919 bis 1922," *GS*, XIII, 549.

[95] Ibid., p. 549. Hahl's recollections give an excellent view of the impression Tillich made on his students. Notice also that he opened up his lectures for discussion and also the evenings he would spend with students at his home. See also Anna Margarete Fehling's "Tillichs Berliner Zeit," ibid., pp. 550-52.

[96] Cf. comments of Tillich's former philosophy professor Fritz Medicus, "Zu Paul Tillichs Berufung nach Frankfurt," *GW*, XIII, pp. 562-64.

[97] Ibid., p. 548. Gustav Landauer was a German socialist, who, among other things, was a close friend of Martin Buber and influenced his religious socialism. Cf. Martin Buber, "XI. Landauer," *Paths in Utopia*, trans. by R. F. C. Hull (Boston: Beacon Press, 1958), pp. 46-57. Also, Landauer, p. 1154. Tillich's early relation to Landauer has not been noted.

[98] P. 173. On occasion one notes this anarchist influence in Tillich's writings as in his call for "germ cells" as the basis for the formation of community. "Die Religioese und Philosophische Weiterbildung des Sozialismus," (1924), *GW*, II, p. 128. ("Weiterbildung")

[99] Adams in his Introduction to *Pol. Exp.* wrote: "Among some of his colleagues he was spoken of as a 'Red Socialist.'" P. vi.

[100] "Kirchenfrage," p. 16. The corresponding section in "Answer" is a little different: ". . . it can therefore rightly express the conviction that the spiritual cleavage in which we stand can only be overcome through the simultaneous overcoming of the economic cleavage, and that the idea of a new religiously imbued culture of unity is realizable only on the soil of a new social and economic unity whose soul is religion. It is our conviction that we stand at the beginning of this development. It can only be sustained, and no longer hindered; Christianity, however, stands before the decision as

to whether it will enliven and lead this development or whether staying on the side it will in principle narrow and protect past social forms and social circles." P. 11.

[101] See the comments by Eduard Heimann and Max Scheler at the time of his murder, "Zur Wuerdigung Rathenaus," *Blaetter*, III, 10 (Oktober 1922), pp. 37-38. Mennicke here claimed Rathenaus as a religious socialist in their sense.

[102] Holborn, pp. 579-629; Bramsted, pp. 173-83; Gay, pp. 151-55.

[103] Kegley and Bretall, p. 13.

[104] Dehn, p. 223. Around 1923 Dehn was "lost" to the circle because of Barth's influence.

[105] Ulrich, p. 221.

[106] *Pol. Exp.*, p. 58. First published in *Blaetter*, IV, 8/10 (1923). It was an elaboration of a lecture given a year earlier. "Tillichs Antwort," *Blaetter*, V, 5/6 (Mai/Juni 1924) p. 18. Hereafter "Basic Principles."

[107] See, for example, "Zu Tillichs Systematik," *Blaetter*, V, 5/6 (Mai/Juni 1924), pp. 17-18, and "Tillichs Antwort," pp. 18-22. Eberhard Amelung's study was based on the false assumption that the participants in the circle "all share the presuppositions [of Tillich's work] and adjust their results" from their particular fields to these presuppositions (p. 11). Their religious socialism was not, as Amelung claimed it was, "a system of analytical and normative concepts" (p. 13). Their unity was not found on the conceptual level. Even Amelung's quotation from Mennicke on p. 10 to the effect that he was opposed to system building undercut his own reification of the circle's unity. Ulrich's study is important in showing the differences that existed between Mennicke and Tillich, even when they used the same terminology. Amelung, "Religious Socialism as an Ideology A Study of the 'Kairos-circle' in Germany Between 1919-1933" (unpublished Doctor's dissertation, Harvard, 1962; university microfilm).

[108] *Blaetter*, I, 1, pp. 2-3.

[109] Quoted in Ulrich, p. 221.

[110] *Rel. Sit.*, pp. 197-98.

[111] "Basic Principles," p. 88. Tillich's later comment that religious socialism "had and has sympathizers and foes on the Left as well as on the Right" tends, however, to obscure its socialist character. *PE*, p. xviii.

[112] Tillich, "Christentum, Sozialismus und Nationalismus," *GW*, XIII, 161; Heimann, "Anhang 1, Brief von Prof. Dr. Eduard Heimann und der Verfasser Ueber die einzelnen Mitglieder des Kairos-Kreises," in Eberhard Amelung, *Die Gestalt der Liebe* (Guetersloh: Guetersloher Verlagshaus Gerd Mohn, 1972), p. 217. Interviews with Adolf Lowe on October 15, 1971, and May 24, 1972, confirm this. Much of the following information in the text comes from these interviews.

[113] *Blaetter*, I, 4 (September 1920), p. 16.

[114] Hannah Tillich, p. 102.

[115] Cf. *Blaetter* (1920), pp. 3-6. Tillich at one point in this discussion wrote Mennicke the following: "Thinking can only transcend itself through itself, not through some kind of disguise of thoughtlessness, neither in prophetic, nor in political, nor in moralistic, nor, above all, in pathetic garb." I, 4 (September 1920), p. 13.

[116] *Blaetter*, VII (Januar/Maerz), pp. 1-2.

[117] Heimann, pp. 215-17; Ulrich, p. 221; Lowe interviews.

[118] Heimann, p. 215.

[119] Ulrich, pp. 213-32. See Tillich's comments on Mennicke in 1936, *My Travel Diary*, p. 82.

[120] Adolf Lowe, "In Memoriam: Eduard Heimann, 1889-1967," *Social Research*, Vol. 34, No. 4 (Winter 1967), p. 610.

[121] Lowe, p. 609. Cf. Landauer, pp. 1643-50.

[122] *Blaetter*, II, 11/12 (Dezember 1922), p. 42. Heimann briefly described his journey to religious socialism. "The decisive event was his meeting with Paul Tillich." Lowe, p. 610.

[123] See "Biographische Daten und Bibliographie Eduard Heimann," *Zur Ordnung von Wirtschaft und Gesellschaft*, Herausgeben von Heinz Dietrich Ortlieb (Tuebingen: J. C. B. Mohr, 1959), pp. 342-38.

[124] Heimann, pp. 215-16; Ulrich, p. 222. Lowe does not recall the tie of Ruestow and Wolfers to the Communist Party and doubts if it was very significant.

[125] Ibid.; Hannah Tillich, p. 103; for a description of the *Hochschule* from Gay, pp. 39-40.

[126] *Blaetter*, III, 11 (November 1922), p. 44. An advertisement of the seminar, in which all six major participants made presentations, can be found here.

[127] *Blaetter*, I, 1, p. 4.

[128] *Blaetter*, VII, p. 36.

[129] Tillich's speech was "Weiterbildung," II, pp. 121-31. Cf. Emil Fuchs, "Die erste international Konferenz der religioesen Sozialisten," *Christliche Welt*, XXXVIII, 31/32 (1924), pp. 609-14. He refers to Tillich's lecture as "a placing of Marxism in a new, living Weltanschauung." P. 614.

[130] *Rel. Sit.*, p. 197.

[131] "Religious Socialism," *Pol. Exp.*, p. 41. (Hereafter, "RS (II)".) First published as "Sozialismus: II. Religioeser Sozialismus," in *Die Religion in Geschichte und Gegenwart*, 2. Aufl., vol. 5 (Tuebingen: 1930), pp. 637-48.

[132] Ulrich, pp. 226-27; Tillich, *Rel. Sit.*, p. 179. Cf. Tillich's comments on Hermann Schafft's Christian Socialism, which appeared to be connected with a moderate wing of the "Neuwerk-Kreis." "Errinerungen an den Freund Hermann Schaftt," *GW*, XIII, 32.

[133] Lowe, "In Memorian," p. 611. Lowe here rightly notes that these "religious socialists exerted a quite disproportionately strong influence," in Germany, later in Britain and

and America and finally in the social postulates of the Ecumenical Movement.

[134] Gay, p. 156.

[135] Bramstad, p. 180.

[136] Holborn, pp. 630-92; Gay, pp. 156-61.

[137] "Der Geisteslage der Gegenwart," *GW,* X, p. 116.

[138] *Rel. Sit.,* p. 115, 21: "Kairos. Ideen zur Geisteslage der Gegenwart," *Kairos zur Geisteslage und Geisteswendung,* Herausgegeben von Paul Tillich (Darmstadt: Otto Reichl Verlag, 1926), p. 20.

[139] *Rel. Sit.,* p. 116. Cf. "Kairos," p. 20.

[140] "Kairos," p. 20.

[141] "Die geistige Welt im Jahre 1926," *GW,* X, p. 94.

[142] Tillich's book, *The Religious Situation,* was a minor best seller; Heimann's book was *Die sittliche Idee des Klassenkampfes* (Berlin: H. H. W. Dietz Nohf, 1926).

[143] *The Dialectical Imagination* (Boston: Little, Brown and Company, 1973), p. 3.

[144] Cf. schedule in *Blaetter,* VI, 2 (Juli/September 1925), p. 72. The dates were October 18-25, and the place, the *Deutsche Hochschule fuer Politik.*

[145] Mennicke, "Unsere Akademische Arbeitswoche," *Blaetter,* VI (Januar/Februar 1926), pp. 1-4. He also noted that the socialist press had taken notice. He spoke of the new words from Tillich: "glaeubigen Realismus," and "der in sich ruhenden Endlichkeit."

[146] "*Politischer Rundbrief des Hofgeismar-Kreises der Jungsozialisten,*" Nr. 5 (Januar 1926), pp. 31-32. Rathmann was impressed by the group's fullness and breadth, by its ability to break through to reality, and by its commitment to the socialist movement. He considered the Kairos Circle to be "a source of power that was not to be valued enough." He asked rhetorically, "Can the young socialists be other than students here?" Because of the difficulty of his thought, he doubted if Tillich, "who gives the circle the foundation of its thinking," could become a "prophet," but he thought the indirect potential of his ideas was very great. See the Bibliography for Rathmann's articles on Tillich.

[147] Franz Osterroth, "Der Hofgeismarkreis der Jungsozialisten," *Archiv fuer Sozialgeschichte,* IV (1964), pp. 525-69. Hendrik de Man, the legal expert Gustav Radbruch, and the political scientist Hermann Heller were among the intellectuals connected with the group.

[148] *Sozialismus aus dem Glauben* (Zurich: Rotaphel-Verlag, 1929), p. 243. The book records the discussion of the Heppenheim meeting. The quotation is from the letter of invitation sent out by Rathmann and Hugo Sinzheimer, who also led the conference. Others there included Martin Buber, and Leonard Ragaz.

[149] Rathmann, "*Ethischer oder dialektischer Sozialismus?*" (unpublished manuscript, dated September 1971), p. 6. Cf. Peter

Dodge, *Beyond Marxism: The Faith and Works of Hendrik de Man* (The Hague: Martinis Nijhoff, 1966), esp. Ch. 4. Dodge writes that "perhaps the highpoint of de Man's activities in Germany came in 1928 when he was featured along with such figures as Paul Tillich, Martin Buber, and Eduard Heimann in a meeting at Heppenheim at which a movement for the reconciliation of Western religious traditions with the socialist ideology reached significant expression." P. 67.

[150] Dodge, p. 68. *The Psychology of Socialism,* trans. and edited by Eden and Cedar Paul, 2nd German edition (New York: Henry Holt and Company, 1928).

[151] *GW,* XII, pp. 239-43. First published in *Blaetter,* VII (Oktober 1927), pp. 21-25.

[152] *Sozialismus aus dem Glauben,* pp. 13-89.

[153] Ibid., p. 101.

[154] Rathmann, *"Tillich als religioeser Sozialismus,"* (manuscript), p. 5. A shortened version of this text is found in *GW,* XIII, pp. 564-68. Hereafter "Tillich."

[155] From a letter shown to me for my use by Rathmann, July 17, 1973.

[156] "Tillich," pp. 5-6.

[157] Cf. *OB,* p. 21. Here Tillich writes that he joined the SPD "only because of the political situation of the time." Lowe also encouraged him to join because of the growing threat of National Socialism. Interview with Lowe, May 24, 1973.

[158] I, 1, pp. 1-12. "His programmatic leading essay 'Socialism' in the first issue is after the 'Communist Manifesto' perhaps the most outstanding witness of socialist thinking. . . ." Rathmann, "Tillich," *GW,* XIII, p. 567.

[159] Ibid., pp. 12-28; 29-37; 37-41.

[160] Rathmann, *"Ethischer,"* p. 17; Osterroth, p. 568; Friedrich Martin Balzer, "Zur Geschichte der religioes-sozialistischen Stroemunger in der Weimarer Republik," *Internationale Dialog Zeitschrift,* V, 1 (1972), fn 5, 39.

[161] P. 238.

[162] P. 1396.

[163] P. 238; Hunt indicates that they are difficult to classify in usual terms.

[164] P. 1396.

[165] Hunt, p. 240.

[166] Rathmann, "Einleitung," *Die sozialistische Entscheidung,* 2. Aufl. (Offenbach a. Main, 1948), p. 7. Cf. Hunt, p. 240. Hunt also notes that Kurt Schumacher, the first leader of a revived SPD in postwar Germany, came from this circle.

[167] Rathmann, "Tillich," *GW,* XIII, pp. 566-67.

[168] *Die sozialistische Entscheidung, GW,* II, pp. 221-22. First published, Potsdam: Alfred Protte, 1933. (Hereafter, *SD.)*

[169] "Christentum, *Sozialismus* und Nationalismus," *GW,* XIII, p. 162. Cf. "Basic Principles," pp. 81, 87-88.

[170] *SD, GW,* II, 222.

[171] "They [SPD] had no leaders of real spiritual power; I knew almost all of them at the time Hitler came." *Ultimate Concern,* p. 77.

[172] Cf. Hannah Tillich, pp. 142-44.

[173] "Diskussion 27 VI. 31," (unpublished manuscript B. #6 (28, 29), Tillich Archive at Harvard), pp. 4-5. Among the participants of this discussion on June 27, 1931, were Horkheimer, Mannheim, Mennicke, Polloch, Riezler, Adorno, Emil Blum, Emil Brunner, and Otto Dibelius.

[174] Ibid., p. 5.

[175] Jay, p. 24. Lowe was helpful in identifying the people in the various groups. Interview, May 24, 1973.

[176] Jay, p. 25. Cf. Comments by Horkheimer and Adorno in *Werk und Wirken Paul Tillichs: Ein Gedenkbuch* (Stuttgart: Evangelisches Verlagswerk, 1967), pp. 15-24, 24-38, 123-32. Tillich's relationship to the Frankfurt School and their Critical Theory then and later is a subject that deserves further research.

[177] Jay, p. 24. See Tillich's brief review of Adorno's *Kierkegaard, Journal of Philosophy,* XXXI, (1934), p. 640.

[178] Note Tillich's critical comments on Fromm, *SD, GW,* II, fn. 13, 289. Also, Tillich's review of Marcuse's *Reason and Revolution, Studies in Philosophy and Social Science,* IX (1942), pp. 476-78.

[179] *SD, GW,* II, p. 220, 225.

[180] "Der Geisteslage der Gegenwart," *GW,* X, pp. 119-120.

[181] Cf. Hunt, pp. 241-57. Erich Matthias, "The Social Democratic Party and Government Power," *The Path to Dictatorship 1918-1933* (Garden City, New York: Anchor Books, 1966), pp. 50-67.

[182] Landauer records the traditional hostility of the labor movement to intellectuals, pp. 486-89. Lowe remarked in aforementioned interview that the party was ready to consider their circle as "brain fools."

[183] Tillich in a discussion with Horkheimer, Pollock and Lowe in 1945 said: "Religious socialism stood hostilely opposed to reformist socialism. I sought to break the reactionary powers of the Lutheran church over the German people as the presupposition for change. Also I sought to break the reformist powers in the SPD. Church and party have always mistreated me for that." P. 3. This unpublished discussion, entitled "Theorie und Praxis" and dated January 28, 1945, spells out some differences between Critical Theory and religious socialism at that time and during the pre-Nazi days. Available in the Tillich Archive in Goettingen.

[184] See Balzer's previously mentioned article for a critical estimate of Tillich at this point. Balzer prefers the model given by Pastor Erwin Eckert, who joined the Communist Party, to that of Tillich. Esp. p. 38.

[185] Cf. "Between Theory and Practice," *OB*, pp. 30-36.

[186] See, e.g., *GW*, II, p. 28. On the latter point, see Ulrich, p. 193.

[187] The reference is to Ronald H. Stone's *Reinhold Niebuhr Prophet to Politicians* (Nashville: Abingdon Press, 1972). Tillich might have spoken to politicians prophetically but not in the direct manner of Niebuhr. One obvious difference in Tillich's writings from those of Niebuhr is the lack of references to particular political events and people that fill the pages of Niebuhr. On the other hand, Tillich was the more fundamental theologian and philosopher. Cf. Tillich, *Tillich of Culture*, p. 165.

[188] *SD, GW*, pp. 22-23. Tillich suggests that at one point there is a correspondence between Russia and the basic demand of his writing: the relationship of proletariat and peasantry in carrying through the Revolution.

[189] "IRS (II)," *Pol. Exp.*, pp. 41, 45.

[190] "Die Theologie des Kairos und die gegenwaertige geistige Lage: Offener Brief an Emanuel Hirsch," *Theologische Blaetter*, XIII, No. 11 (November 1934), p. 326. Tillich's concern was socialism not Communism. This distinction should be clear in a book entitled *Communism and the Theologians*, but it is not always so in Charles West's book. No doubt Tillich had a streak of naivete in him, and some of his political judgments in the 1930's might appear unrealistic to someone twenty years later (West, p. 109). But West's criticism that "the deepest root of Tillich's failure to come to grips with Communism as a reality, however, lies in his ontology itself" hardly follows (p. 110). Tillich was, after all, able with his ontological theology to come to grips with Nazism. West's conclusion that Tillich's ontology "made him incapable of understanding the real issues which Marxism raises for the Christian encounter as another faith, and another organizing centre in society" seems to me to miss the point of Tillich's project. Tillich did recognize Marxist-socialism as "another faith" and "another organizing centre," but he did not consider it possible that this faith might come to be seen as "the prophetic-immanent element" of the Christian faith. Otherwise, he wrote in 1935, "a life-and-death struggle should arise between the two despite the typological cohesion of Christianity and Marxism." "The Christian and the Marxist View of Man," (unpublished manuscript, December 1935), p. 16. Later, Tillich believed this was the case and reached a conclusion similar to West's, but fully in accord with his ontological assumptions: "The decision between these two life possibilities is neither economic nor political; it is religious." "Christianity and Marxism," *Pol. Exp.* (1960), p. 96. See West (New York: Mcmillan Company, 1958), pp. 78-111 for a discussion of Tillich.

[191] *SD, GW*, II, p. 220, 222; "The Critique of Dogmatic Marxism," pp. 330-32.

[192] Ibid., p. 222.

[193] Holborn, pp. 692-768; Bramstad, pp. 183-201; Gay, pp. 161-64; Karl Dietrich Bracher, *The German Dictatorship*, trans. by Jean Steinberg (New York: Praeger Publishers, 1970), esp.

Chs. IV, V, and VII.

[194] *SD, GW,* II, p. 364.

[195] Ibid.

[196] Ibid., p. 365.

[197] Ibid., p. 223. Some of the following has also been used in my "Introduction to the American Edition" which will soon be published along with the English translation of *SD*.

[198] From interview with Dr. Lowe, May 24, 1972; cf. Hannah Tillich, p. 147.

[199] Ibid. Note Tillich's expression of special gratitude to Lowe, *SD, GW,* II, p. 223. He dedicated the book to Heimann.

[200] "Selbstanzeige," III, No. 12, pp. 667-68.

[201] Rathmann, "Einleitung," p. 7.

[202] Cf. "Nazi 'Purge' of the Universities," *Manchester Guardian,* May 19, 1933, in *The Intellectual Migration Europe and America 1930-1960,* Donald Fleming and Bernard Bailyn, eds. (Cambridge, Massachusetts: Harvard University Press, 1969), p. 234.

[203] Tillich's decision to resign from the party will be discussed in Chapter 6.

[204] "Dr. Tillich Dead; Scholar was 79," *The New York Times,* October 24, 1965, p. 86; Hannah Tillich, pp. 147-56. On the impression the book burning of May 10, 1933, made on him, see *An meine Deutschen Freunde* (Stuttgart: Evangelisches Verlagswerk, 1973), pp. 41-43.

[205] Incident reported by Dr. Lowe, May 24, 1972. The book was important for Tillich in clarifying his own stance in the situation. *Ob,* p. 26. Later, Tillich commented to James Luther Adams that of his books, he was most proud of *SD*. Conversation, September 8, 1971. Lowe has called the book Tillich's "Most prophetic" as well as his "most Jewish book."

[206] Rathmann, "Einleitung," p. 7.

[207] Kegley and Bretall, pp. 16-17.

[208] Cf. "Christianity and Emigration," *Presbyterian Tribune,* LII, No. 3 (October 29, 1936), pp. 13-16; "Mind and Migration," *Social Research,* IV, No. 2 (May 1937), pp. 295-305.

[209] Article on Hirsch previously cited; also, "Um was es geht; Antwort an Emanuel Hirsch," *Theologische Blaetter,* XIV, No. 5 (May 1935), pp. 117-19. These important writings will be referred to throughout the study; Tillich's reaction to Hirsch will be looked at more carefully in the final chapter. Hopper is incorrect in calling Hirsch "an influential proponent of the views of Religious Socialism" in the 1920's. P. 69.

[210] "Christianity and Modern Society," *Pol. Exp.,* p. 8. Originally published in *The Student World,* XXI (1928), pp. 282-90.

[211] Ibid.

[212] This is the principle that will be used in interpreting Tillich's works from 1919-1932. I see them as a piece, but I am attentive to the nuances of change. For example, in 1922

"kairos" is the predominant concept, and in 1932 "expectation" takes its place. Expectation, however, cannot be understood apart from the Kairos concept. The difference is in one of accent, and does not represent a "new period" in Tillich's development. Thus, in 1934-1935 Tillich in his debate with Hirsch will again highlight the idea of Kairos. For a different view that sees "stages" in Tillich's development see Breipohl, *Religioeser Sozialismus,* pp. 167-221.

CHAPTER 3

THE MEANING OF SOCIALISM

In Chapter 2 Tillich's religious socialism was set in the context of his life and time. His religious socialism was seen as a response to the crisis of a particular historical situation, Weimar Germany, 1918-1933. His life was described as moving within and between two conflicting currents, Protestantism and socialism, and his aim was understood to be the crucial transformation of both in the search for a new social order. In light of this biographical and historical discussion, this chapter begins to explore the substance of Tillich's religious socialism.

A logical starting point is with the question, "What was the meaning of socialism for Tillich?" The answer to this question is not a neutral definition but a characterization congenial to his theological intention and dependent upon it. Tillich's unconventional interpretation of socialism is analyzed in this chapter according to the following three points: socialism as the expression of the proletarian situation, socialism as a religious phenomenon, and socialism as a prophetic movement. Together these three features offer a comprehensive view of his concept of socialism and introduce important themes of his theological understanding of this reality.

Socialism As An Expression Of The Proletarian Situation

Socialism for Tillich was the socio-political phenomenon that he encountered in Berlin and elsewhere. It was primarily for him a concern of the workers in the urban centers who were striving for economic justice. His early book *Masse und Geist* indicated his interest in the mass movement of workers.[1] Socialism for him was always irrevocably tied to the modern industrial proletariat, a link that received its clearest expression in *The Socialist Decision:*

> Socialism is the expression of the proletarian situation. Its principle is the power of the proletarian movement. . . . In socialism the proletariat has found its consciousness; through socialism the proletariat is

constituted as proletariat. For proletariat means more than a mass of people who are affected by the same fate. It means a class with consciousness of itself as a class. And socialism has given it this consciousness. . . . The proletariat is just as much a creation of socialism as socialism is a creation of the proletariat. Both are set in and with each other. Socialism is the proletariat's knowledge of itself (*um sich selbst*) and therefore its foundation as such.[2]

For Tillich, then, the proletariat and socialism are mutually dependent on each other; if they are torn apart, they both cease to exist. He believed that socialism is only understandable through the proletariat, and the proletarian situation is comprehensible only through the socialist self-consciousness which constitutes the proletariat as proletariat. It is redundant to speak of a "proletarian socialism" (Werner Sombart), remarked Tillich, for there is no non-proletarian socialism.[3]

Tillich's understanding of the proletariat parallels that of the classical Marxist concept. He described it as "that class within the capitalist society whose members are dependent exclusively upon the 'free' sale of their physical ability to work and whose social destiny is wholly dependent upon the turn of the market." This concept, he added, has "representative and typological character";[4] it is not a purely empirical but an "*ideal-typical* concept." Moreover, proletariat is an "*existential concept*," that is, it is one that can be understood only out of the proletarian situation as one of "class struggle." According to Tillich, as a class it shares a common life-situation fundamentally conditioned by the nature of capitalism and opposed to the bourgeoisie, the owners of the means of production, who are likewise conditioned. This mutual antagonism is bound to the economic factor but extends beyond the market to the whole of life, including social and psychic factors.[6] The proletariat and socialism are products of capitalism which are struggling against capitalism.

The pivotal mark of the proletarian situation for Tillich is its meaninglessness which stamps every moment of the life-processes of the proletariat in a way that cannot be covered over. "Here the question of meaning is concretely raised. . . . Even the most simple spiritual fulfillments like love, family, and vocation stand for the most part in formlessness and distortion."[7] Because of the loss of a meaningful vital mode of existence, Tillich sees the typical proletarian situation as pointing "to the threat to, and the reality of the loss of, meaningful existence."[8] He is convinced that the proletariat continually experience an inescapable social threat, a threat he outlined in terms of insecurity, exclusion from community, and hopelessness. "All these things together finally lead the proletariat to an awareness of the complete meaninglessness of its existence."[9]

The crucial significance of Marxist-socialism is its response to this situation:

> In the class struggle the proletariat wants to obtain that of which it is deprived: the meaning of human life. Every single struggle, whether it concerns a political detail or a collective bargaining, is in the final analysis a struggle for fulfillment with a richness of being and a meaning to life. . . . The struggle of the proletariat is a struggle for the overcoming of the demonic . . . [and] therefore a struggle for the kingdom of God. And through this struggle the proletariat obtains its meaning. It feels itself to be a bearer of the struggle for the kingdom of God; it feels a kind of messianic mission for itself and for the whole society. It is raised out of its insecurity and hopelessness, and in its meaninglessness a meaning is given to it: it becomes the bearer of a struggle against a situation in which human meaning is taken from people. The creation of this consciousness was the historical task of *Marxism*.[10]

The task of religious socialism is not to refute Marxism, continued Tillich, for "Marxism is primarily a reality and only then an idea. Its reality is the fact that the proletariat has been lifted from a sense of almost complete absence of meaning to a powerful consciousness of meaning." The idea behind this reality, the Marxist dialectic, is an intellectual construction (that Tillich did take seriously), but most importantly it expresses "a religious consciousness of fate."[11]

Tillich was impressed most profoundly that Marxism offered an oppressed group of people the awareness that their struggle for life made sense. More significant than its individual ideas, its scientific theories, its empirical studies, or its party organization in themselves was Marxism's achievement in providing meaning and thereby changing those who lived in society's most negative conditions. This meaning-fulfilling quality will be discussed further in a later section.

In speaking of socialism as the "expression of the proletarian situation," Tillich was not offering a clear-cut definition, but such a definition is probably not possible for a historical phenomenon whose future is not yet decided. Tillich's use of "expression" and "principle as the power of the proletarian movement" are fruitful methodological concepts for capturing the dynamic character of a historical reality whose future is still open. "A principle does not contain the abstract generality of a quantity of individual appearances, but the real possibility, the *dynamis,* the power of a historical reality." For Tillich, then, the "socialist principle" is the dynamic of the proletarian movement grasped in conceptual form and offering a basis from which it can be both understood and guided.[12]

In connecting socialism integrally to the proletariat, Tillich was focusing on "the particular side of socialism."[13] In addition, he argued, socialism has a "universal side" which intends to transcend the proletarian situation and embrace the whole society. This universal tendency expresses itself, for example, in the striving for a new form of society, "the *classless society,*" a "symbol" that bears in itself the religious and humanistic history of the West.[14]

> *Socialism has a particular and a universal side.*
> Both sides belong together and cannot be torn asunder. Whoever takes only the universal side into consideration makes socialism into a general ethical-political idea for which there are no bearing groups. Whoever considers only the particular side takes from it the possibility of overcoming the class situation and therefore proletarian existence. It degrades socialism to the resentment of a suppressed class. Socialism is therefore only understandable from the interaction of its particular and universal moments.[15]

The Socialist Decision (as well as his other socialist writings), wrote Tillich, "can be interpreted as an attempt *to work out the universal moment of socialism without surrendering its particular side.*"[16]

Tillich ancnored socialism in a particular socio-political group, the proletariat, making it the test of socialist theory and praxis. Because the proletarian situation is "the place of most complete meaninglessness," it is "the key situation" of the present.[17] The proletariat is the primary but not necessarily the exclusive bearer of socialism.[18] Furthermore, "*the proletarian movement means very much more than the political struggle for socialism,*" for it includes trade unions, cooperatives, and organizations for religious, intellectual, and educational purposes.[19] Tillich had a particular but broad understanding of socialism.

In depicting socialism as the expression of the proletarian situation, then, Tillich was excluding the possibility of defining it as a non-historical ideal. He was insisting that socialism was dependent upon real historical forces, that is, the proletariat. Tillich recognized danger in both an intellectual socialism not rooted in the proletariat as well as a narrow Marxism that made the class struggle into a revengeful war of booty. His point of departure was found in integrating a particular historical reality with a universal perspective. It was also perilous, for the proletariat might lose its socialist self-consciousness, cease to be "proletariat," and thus destroy socialism.[20]

Socialism As A Religious Phenomenon

For Tillich the genuine significance of socialism was in its meaning-fulfilling quality for the proletariat. His understanding of socialism through the concept of meaning opened access to a theological perspective on socialism. In this section I explore how Tillich interpreted socialism as a religious phenomenon.

The concept of meaning was central in all of Tillich's thought. Indeed, it has been called "the most comprehensive and characteristic of all of Tillich's concepts."[21] It was basic for his system of the spiritual sciences.[22] His philosophy of religion elaborated the notion that "every spiritual act is an act of meaning."[23] His philosophy of history took its departure from the reality of meaning: "The new which occurs whenever history occurs is meaning. . . . History exists where meaning is realized by freedom."[24] His anthropology stated that to be human was to exist in meaning, and his theology was directed to the "Unconditional," "a reality of meaning, . . . the ultimate and deepest meaning--reality that shakes the foundations of all things and builds them up anew."[25]

The concept of meaning was equally prominent in Tillich's religious socialism, which, of course, was correlated with these other dimensions of his thought. His understanding of the proletariat and of socialism, his characterization of the bourgeois era and the future hoped-for-society--to name a few topics--were all discussed in terms of meaning. At least two of his major essays on socialism were explicitly constructed around "meaning". In one he called the question about the meaning of life "the deepest and simultaneously the most encompassing question; it contains all the rest."[26] In the other, now to be discussed, he utilized the concept of meaning to interpret socialism from a religious or theological perspective.[27]

To consider a phenomenon as religious, wrote Tillich, is "to understand it as an expression of human existence in an absolute sense." The focus of religious understanding is, for him, being in itself (*Sein in sich*), being as being (*Sein als Sein*), insofar as it is given in human existence. To understand socialism as something religious means, therefore, "to understand it from this final question, to set the fulcrum at the point beyond which there is no point, at the point of being as such, viewed from human existence."[28] Characteristically, Tillich identified the religious reality with the ontological reality.

Tillich described next the nature of human being or existence (*Sein*). "Human existence is the rise of being over itself or the rise of being to freedom." In the human, being becomes "spirit", breaking loose from bondage to the immediate, unbroken processes of life. This freedom from one's self is "the human essence" which constitutes both "its greatness and its danger." Its danger is the possibility of failing to achieve being in rising above being. For Tillich the human is that creature threatened with non-being, for he has his being only in the fact that he can fail to realize it.[29]

Human freedom is freedom in meaning: "when being rises above itself, it rises to the level of *meaning*." The human fulfills himself in meaning, but he can also fail and with the loss of meaning he loses the truth of his existence. This possibility of non-being Tillich calls the "*threat*" (*Bedrohtheit*) of being human. "Freedom always stands between fulfillment of meaning and nonfulfillment of meaning, between meaning and contradiction to meaning." But where there is this cleavage, asserted Tillich, non-fulfillment and contradiction dominate.

"Freedom is in truth unfreedom. Human existence stands under the fate to be unfree in its freedom, unfree namely to answer the question and to fulfill the demand which confronts it, unfree therefore to come to the existence that it is in truth." Tillich saw no way to escape this cleavage; human fate means to be in a condition of being threatened. "Man *must* be free and with this freedom be unfree."[30]

But, continued Tillich, human existence is not only threatened; it is also supported. A major difference exists between the threat and the "*support*" (*Getragenheit*). Unlike the threat, the support arises neither from being nor freedom, but is "beyond being and freedom." He insisted that the support is primary, for only on its basis is human existence with its threat possible. And this basis itself is not human existence.[31]

Since all human acting and thinking are an expression of human existence, then, argued Tillich, the threat and the support are always expressed. They are present in either one of two ways, religiously or culturally. If they appear immediately, directly, and intentionally, then they are religious. But they also appear in forms where the intention is not directly religious, but cultural. Where this happens, these life forms are still religious—they express the threat and the support—but in a veiled and mediated way.[32]

On the basis of this description of human existence, Tillich posed a double question to socialism: "To what extent is both the human threat and the human support expressed in it? To raise these questions means to speak of socialism in a religious way. The answer to these questions is the first and basic task of religious socialism."[33] As has been shown, Tillich saw the threat of human existence in the meaninglessness of the proletarian situation and perceived in the Marxist dialectic a symbol for the faith of the proletariat, a conviction that it is fighting for a kingdom that will arrive inevitably. Here "arises the consciousness of being supported by the Unconditional, the transcendent."[34] Although they are expressed in an indirect fashion, Tillich found both the threat and the support in socialism.

> To understand socialism as a religious phenomenon means therefore to see that in it the threat of human existence is revealed, even to the point of the demonic

> "*possession*" of an entire society, and, on the other hand, to recognize that elements of a new faith in meaning, of a new support in meaning, have appeared both in reality and in symbol.[35]

As is evident from this summary, Tillich grounded his understanding of socialism as a religious reality anthropologically, that is, in the threat to and support of life which are intrinsic to human existence. These realities are expressed, he contended, in the meaninglessness and meaning disclosed in socialism, and therefore it too is a religious phenomenon. Since this is the "datum" for his interpretation, much of Tillich's religious socialism was given to "exposing" the religious element veiled in the autonomous forms of socialism.

Clearly, Tillich's concept of religion shaped his manner of viewing socialism. His religious socialism embodied the categories and conclusions of his philosophy of religion and his understanding of theology. He first set out his principles for understanding religion and theology in his earliest essay, "On the Idea of a Theology of Culture."[36] The question he confronted is the task of the theologian in an autonomous situation. He affirmed autonomy and rejected the idea of "a double truth, a double morality, and a double justice" in which one of the pair has only "an alien kind of legitimacy dictated by religion. This double existence must be abolished at all costs."[37]

Tillich believed he found his way to a new answer that respected autonomy in the concept of religion.

> Religion is directness toward the Unconditional. Through existing realities, through values, through personal life, the meaning of the unconditional reality becomes evident. This is not a new reality, alongside or above other things . . . It is not a being, nor is it the substance or totality of beings; it is—to use a mystical formula—that which is above all things which at the same time is the absolute Nothing and the absolute Something . . . But even the predicate "is" already disguises the facts of the case, since we are here dealing not with a reality of existence, but with a reality of meaning, and that indeed is the ultimate and deepest meaning—reality which shakes the foundation of all things and builds them up anew.[38]

Tillich did not assign religion to a practical, theoretical, or emotional human function but saw it as an all-embracing attitude that included and was expressed in all human functions.[39] It is hardly an optional and dispensable feature of life; instead it is, as he frequently described it, the ultimate meaning, the inner power, the life-blood, the consuming fire of all life, "the beginning and the end of all things, also the center, giving life and soul and spirit to all things."[40] Religion is an attitude directed to the "Unconditional."[41] The Unconditional is not a supernatural reality since for Tillich there is "one reality."[42] Rather it is the quality of reality that gives reality its ultimate depth and meaning. Tillich consistently spoke of this "reality of meaning, . . . the ultimate and deepest meaning," in a two-fold way, that is, as one that "shakes" and "builds" the foundation of all things. The Unconditional is the No and the Yes, the abyss and the ground, the threat and the support of all.

Religion is not for Tillich a specific sphere apart from the rest of culture (except in a narrower, subordinate sense) but an experience that is actualized through all cultural functions. Culture Tillich defined as "*directness toward the conditioned forms and their unity.*"[43] Culture is not consciously and intentionally religious; yet in every cultural act an unconditional meaning is present. Religion therefore does not stand side-by-side with other human creations but pervades them all. Likewise, there is no religion except through cultural forms.

Tillich expressed this relationship most succinctly in the now well-known formula: "Religion is the substance of culture and culture is the form of religion."[44] Substance (*Gehalt*), he stated, is not to be confused with content (*Inhalt*), "something objective in its simple existence," but is "the meaning, the spiritual substantiality, which alone gives form its significance. Substance or import is grasped by means of a form and given expression in a content. Content is accidental, substance essential, and form is the mediating element."[45] That everything real is composed for both form and import is the presupposition of his philosophy of religion and his theology.[46]

The important concepts autonomy and theonomy are an elaboration of this ontological distinction. Autonomy is grounded in the form of cultural functions, "in the laws governing their applications," whereas theonomy is grounded in their substance, "that is, in the reality which by these laws receives its expression or accomplishment." Tillich formulated a "law" to signify this: "The more the form, the greater the autonomy; the more the substance or import, the greater the theonomy. But one cannot exist without the other; a form that forms nothing is just as incomprehensible as substance without form."[47]

Tillich's theology was built upon this understanding of religion and culture. He called it "theology of culture" and defined it as "*the concrete and normative science of religion.*"[48] Its object is not God as an object among other objects, nor a supernatural revelation, nor a set of authoritative dogmas, all of which trespass the demands of autonomy; instead, theology's object is religion.[49] As a theologian of culture, Tillich sees it as his task to bring to expression "the concrete religious experiences embedded in all great cultural phenomena."[50] He outlined this assignment in three steps: first, to analyze the cultural phenomenon according to its embodiment of form and substance and according to its expression of the No and the Yes of the religious reality; secondly, to classify it along a form-import axis by means of an historical-philosophical typology; and thirdly, to adopt a critical, negative, and affirmative attitude toward this phenomenon on the basis of a concrete theological standpoint.[51] With the concluding call of his first essay to fight "under the banner of theonomy," Tillich established the direction he intended to follow.[52]

In his religious socialism Tillich applied this perception of religion, culture, and theology to socialism. He thought that the religious element in socialism is its ultimate power operative in it, its substance, and not something extraneous to it or imposed on it from the outside. Tillich did not want socialism to surrender its autonomous form, but he did believe its meaning-fulfilling reality is evident through its form. Tillich never did so, but one might quite properly label his religious socialism as "theology of socialism," that is, a concrete and normative science of the substance of socialism.[53] As a "theologian of socialism," he took up the three-fold assignment he laid down for a theology of culture: first, he analyzed socialism as autonomous in form and indirectly religious, and he discovered both the No and the Yes, the threat and the support, expressed in it. Secondly, he classified socialism as a prophetic movement on autonomous soil. Finally, he adopted the "prophetic attitude" as his norm for his critical and affirmative theological standpoint. This is the meaning of placing socialism in theological perspective.

Tillich called his religious socialism "*dialectical* or *dynamic*" since it attempts to overcome the static opposition between these two realities by demonstrating their mutual relationship. "It does not accept the inherited, empirical forms of religion and socialism as fixed and final, but rather attempts to understand them in their elemental roots, and thus, to transform them."[54] These "elemental roots" are their ontological grounding in human existence and the Unconditional.

Tillich attributed the beginning of this dialectical religious socialism to the Blumhardts.[55] Stated theologically:

> The decisive idea of religious socialism is that religion does not have to do with a specific religious sphere but with God's dealing with the world, and that therefore it is possible that God's activity may be more clearly seen in a profane, even anti-Christian, phenomenon like socialism than in the explicitly religious sphere of the church.[56]

This insight "into the dialectic of religion," continued Tillich, makes possible "a theological foundation for religious socialism."[57] It lays the groundwork by creating "an openness for the religious understanding of the profane." As a consequence, Tillich wrote, the secular forms of socialism are seen as an expression of the human situation and of a particular situation. "Religious socialism does not abandon the theoretical and practical forms of socialist life to their apparent secularity, but penetrates to the religious character of their basis."[58]

Tillich contrasted his religious socialism with other available types. As noted in Chapter 1, Tillich's thought differed from what he called "*the practical-political type*" by its emphasis on fundamental theoretical problems. He also drew a distinction between his own version and the "*romantic*" and "*legalistic*" types. The romantic type has been previously referred to in relationship to Bolshevism. Tillich characterized this interpretation by its attempt to give a religious consecration to the present socialist movement, since it claimed in some way that "'Socialism *is* religion.'" The romantic religious socialist rightly holds that the religious principle is not confined to a religious sphere, but "it overlooks the element of radical criticism that is inherent in every religion and which allows no actual realization of it to be exempt from criticism."[59] Tillich consistently refuted any direct identification of religion and socialism and maintained a sense of judgment, of the Unconditional No, toward socialist realities. He considered it "by far the greatest danger for the religious socialist movement" to use "'religion'. . . as a matter of strategy."[60] For Tillich religious socialism has to place socialism itself under the Unconditional, something that the romantic formulation fails to do.

According to Tillich, the legalistic type believes "socialism to be a direct consequence of the moral demands of religion, especially Christianity."[61] Tillich found such a religious socialism incompatible with the demands of autonomy, and from the beginning he rejected it as heteronomous and sectarian.[62] Moreover, the attempt to make Jesus a social revolutionary or the first socialist fails for Tillich on the evidence which shows "the fundamental indifference of early Christianity toward the social problem."[63] Tillich did agree that an historic and systematic connection exists between love and the socialist idea, but the legalists mistakenly draw the relationship in a "direct and unparadoxical way."[64]

Tillich's dialectical concept of religion was also strikingly different from socialism's traditional understanding. The predominantly negative note of socialism's attitude toward religion was struck by Marx, who dismissed it as mere ideology.[65] The SPD stated its official position in the Erfurt Program of 1891 where it considered religion a private affair. Tillich saw this as an understandable attempt to neutralize the power of socialism's ecclesiastical opponents by taking religion out of the arena of political struggle, but he disputed the concept implied in this statement since it makes religion a special sphere of life existing next to numerous others. Such a limitation, argued Tillich, means that socialism overlooks the religious element expressed in all its actions. In contrast, he maintained that "*socialism is religious, if religion means life from the roots of human existence.*" He saw in socialism a "faith" that is not a special sphere but "the power bearing and determining all spheres."[66]

Tillich added an historical analysis to his systematic claim that socialism is religious in an indirect way. Considered historically, socialism, a product of the entire spiritual development of the West, was found to be a humanism whose background is Christian. Tillich understood humanism to be an attitude in which man attempts to become entirely self-sufficient, to find the fulfillment of life's meaning in existence itself, and to reject all transcendent orientation.[67] Humanism in its primary form is for Tillich a reaction against the demonic tendency of religion, a defense against the destructive erruptions of the transcendent that threaten the integrity of human nature. According to Tillich, however, such a reaction remains dependent on the religious substance whose perversions it is combating; there is no such thing as humanism in general, but only one living from a specific religious tradition. "Therefore," he concluded in reference to socialism, "post-Christian humanism is a phase in the development of Christianity."[68]

In spite of the fact that socialism is composed of Christian and humanistic elements, Tillich recognized that "the sharpest *opposition has arisen between Christianity and socialism*." Tillich thought the reasons for this were that, on the one hand, socialism rejected all transcendent orientation and thus opened itself to anti-Christian elements, and, on the other hand, the churches became fixated upon prehumanistic forms, accommodated themselves to profane humanism, and were infiltrated by an anti-Christian spirit. Because of these historical developments, the relationship between religion and socialism is not one of simple opposition or correlation, but an ambiguous one accessible only to "dialectical analysis."[69]

Tillich found the "bearer of Christian humanism" to be bourgeois society. "Its decisive negative characteristic," he wrote, "is its disavowal of any feudal-hierarchical obligations. Its decisive positive characteristic is its intention to achieve a rational understanding and control of nature and society."[70] Socialism emerged as a revolutionary countermovement in a late stage of the development of bourgeois society, observed Tillich.

> It was decisive for the history of socialism, particularly of German socialism, that it achieved its particular form simultaneously with its opposition to the idealistic interpretation of bourgeois society and also with its opposition to the romantic struggle against

the bourgeois spirit: that is, it realized its form in Marxism.[71] Therefore socialism adopted the materialistic, revolutionary element of bourgeois society and became opposed to religion which had adopted the idealistic-progressive as well as the romantic-revolutionary conceptions of religion. In order for their opposition to be overcome, concluded Tillich, both have to free themselves from their interpretations of religion.[72]

Socialism, like bourgeois society in general, represented a profane humanism that was cut off from its religious background. This humanistic tradition had broken the power of religious demonry, but it also lost any "relation to a transcendent, unconditionally meaningful, and creative principle." Thus "man is forced into ego-centric loneliness and surrounded by an infinite emptiness. In all his struggle for meaning there presses down upon him an icy covering of meaninglessness which makes him more and more torpid."[73] Because of its particular historical development, socialism was for Tillich heir to the Christian tradition and to an autonomous humanism, a combination that was the source of both its difficulty and potential.

For both systematic and historical reasons, Tillich believed that present in socialism was a religious substance that deserved his confidence and loyalty. The decision to put his faith in the power of socialism was not made, he stated, on the basis of questionable scientific or political opinion but "on the basis of being unconditionally grasped by what is finally-meant in socialism." He understood the finally-meant as that which was expressed in socialism's "symbols" (not only scientific concepts to be proved or refuted), symbols such as the classless society, the history of humankind that would follow its prehistory, the demand for a coming justice, freedom, or community.[74] Such a hope, from our point in history, appears to me to be one of Tillich's more optimistic. Yet such a hope was essential for his attempt to interpret and shape socialism anew on the basis of its religious power.

Tillich's contention that socialism is religious and its implications for his theological understanding of socialism can be summarized with these four points:

1) Because socialism expresses life's ultimate threat and support in the social sphere, it is a religious phenomenon. Its

meaning-fulfilling symbols go beyond the sphere of finite possibilities and point to the transcendent; socialism is directed to the finally-meant, to the Unconditional. Since for Tillich no reality can remain neutral in relation to God, he looks to socialism and there, as it were, discovers the presence of the divine.[76]

2) Socialism is religious in an indirect way. Because of its autonomous, humanistic form, religious symbols are rejected or limited to private life, and reference to transcendence is eliminated. The religious element is not directly intended but is hidden under forms antithetical to socialism's import.

3) This antipathy between its substance and its form is the source of much of socialism's weakness. "The deep ambiguity that adheres in all the vital utterances of socialism" results from this "peculiar dialectic."[77] It creates conflicts within socialism that threatens socialism's possibility to be a genuine alternative to bourgeois society.

4) The future of socialism depends on whether or not it recognizes the ultimate import of its own life and reconstructs its thought and action from there. Tillich works to bring this religious dimension to life, to nourish its development, and to transform socialism on the basis of its meaning-fulfilling substance. A true and adequate foundation for the socialist struggle can only be found, maintained Tillich, at the point of ultimacy: socialism must see itself in relationship to the Unconditional.

Socialism As A Prophetic Movement

Marxist-socialism has given meaning to the proletariat in its threatened life circumstances. In light of its power Tillich considered it a religious phenomenon. Furthermore--and this is a third major feature of his understanding of socialism --socialism's faith expressed a particular religious attitude, one that Tillich called prophetic or eschatological. "*Socialism is prophetism on the soil of an autonomous, self-sufficient world.*"[78] Although a secular movement, socialism embodies an attitude toward the ultimate that Tillich believed is analogous to that of the Biblical prophets.

In the mutual joining of Marx and the prophetic-early Christian expectation of the end, religious socialism endeavored to free socialist faith from its disguise and to raise it to expressiveness. Only from here is religious socialism to be understood.[79]

In this section and the next, the object of study is Tillich's understanding of the prophetic attitude, his theological norm, and his relating of it to socialism. The following pages focus on the theological meaning of his position, and the next section investigates his elaboration of prophetic in terms of expectation.

In a letter, published in part in the *Blaetter* in 1922 with the title "Toward the Clarification of the Basic Religious Attitude," Tillich stated his theological perspective in a clear manner. Continuing a discussion within the Kairos Circle, he rejected characterizing "the mystical attitude as the affirmation of the holiness of what is (*Sein*) and the prophetic as the affirmation of the holiness of what ought to be (*Sollen*)." Instead he urged that both attitudes be seen as a unity of the holiness of what is and what ought to be and that the difference be sought in the content of the ought. According to Tillich, the mystic demands the rejection of the world on the part of the individual, and the prophet demands formation of the world on the part of the community. Yet Tillich did not think that a choice has to be made only between these two since they converge into a third, an attitude--and this is the key statement--"in which the point is reached in which you seek the unity of what is and what ought to be within the concrete reality."[80]

> I call this point "breakthrough" (*Durchbruch*) or "grace." It means that the given reality stands not only under the "no" of the unconditional "is" (*Sein*) or the unconditional "ought" (*Sollen*), but that simultaneously it bears in itself a "yes" from the Unconditional, that it is not only to be judged, but also *justified*. Justification is, however, a paradox. It claims that this entity which is unconditionally denied by the unconditional demand, be it as ascetic or ethical type, is at the same time affirmed by this same Unconditional. Therefore the demand remains; it enters into the consciousness in conceivably greater sharpness; at the same time, however, the holy is experienced as graceful presence (*Gegenwaertige*) breaking through this demand. Thus is the point reached within the world in which the holiness of that which is and that which ought to be (*Seinsollen*) become one, and yet the holy remains raised over the reality of the world.[81]

"This religion of grace," as he called it, "is necessarily the inner tendency of all religious development." Prophetism, remarked Tillich from this point, "is either proclamation of the unity of grace and judgment--as the great prophets of Judaism and Christianity--or it becomes a mere proclamation of what ought to be, that is, a preaching of the law--as the secondary prophets of all times." In the latter case, he added, the unconditional demand is imposed on people as a foreign law, and since the law cannot be fulfilled, one is forced to make compromises, and a totally preliminary attitude is raised to the sphere of the holy. But, he cautioned, "the first thing in relationship to God is always God."[82]

Tillich proceeded by pointing to two dangers that threaten grace as "the synthesis of the actual presence (*Gegenwaertigkeit*) and demand." "There exists the possibility of forgetting the unconditionality of what ought to be, which is the presupposition of every breakthrough, of every experience of grace, under the impression of the present holiness." He saw this as the danger of Lutheranism and secular forms of mysticism, and for them the tension and the real depth of the idea of grace is lost. The opposite danger he envisioned in that "the actual presence of holiness in its power to overcome the law is forgotten and an idol, which takes the place of the universal (*Ueberseienden*) that rages over all being, emerges from what ought to be." Tillich found this pitfall in the pedagogy and orthodoxy of all confessions, in the Enlightenment, in NeoKantianism, and in socialism. Tillich rejected both tendencies on the basis of a religion of grace, his theological norm. "The religious value of a phenomenon can be measured in the degree that it stands closer or farther from this point."[83]

In a concluding note Tillich singled out for special criticism the attempt to insert the holy into some condition of the world that is demanded. Such a position, he protested, stands a "sun's distance" from any actual religious attitude. At this point, he wrote, "there exists for me an absolutely unbridgeable either/or. A religion in which the Unconditional cannot be experienced as that which unconditionally supports me and is present for me in every moment is no religion but law."[84]

This revealing selection demonstrates that Tillich's "basic

religious attitude" was derived from his understanding of justification.[85] In making justification his fundamental theological principle, he was drawing upon his Lutheran tradition.[86] Certain features of his theology as expressed in this letter need to be highlighted:

1) Tillich perceived the Unconditional under two aspects, *Sein* and *Sollen*, grace and judgment, gift and demand, yes and no, ground and abyss, support and threat, promise and demand, import and form, the sacramental and the rational, etc. All of these polar terms are related to his interpretation of justification. The structure of his theology is found in the contrasts of Gospel and Law, and the problem of his theology is how to distinguish and relate these contrasts.

2) Tillich asserted the pre-eminence of grace. His comments in this letter demonstrated his own sense of the gracious presence of the holy as well as his theological conviction that everything depends upon the breakthrough of grace. The gift character of the divine is not to be ignored, squandered, or subordinated.

3) For Tillich justification is the "breakthrough" of grace in which the divine *Sein* and *Sollen* are united in concrete reality. Both the Unconditional no and the Unconditional yes are paradoxically present. From this point Tillich consistently opposed an un-grace-ful legalism, a grace-conscious indifference, and a non-concrete religion.

4) Finally, Tillich's theological norm means that the Unconditional is present in the conditioned but without losing its unconditionality: "the holy remains raised over the reality of the world." The Unconditional is not separate from the finite, but it can never be identified with any finite reality. Such an understanding allowed for and necessitated a critical theological principle which Tillich would develop under the rubric of the "Protestant principle".

Tillich's basic religious attitude, which expressed the paradox of justification or "the paradoxical immanence of the transcendent,"[87] was in other places called "the prophetic attitude" or "The Inner Attitude of Religious Socialism."[88]

> The prophetic attitude is essential to religious socialism. It exists in socialism even though it is frequently distorted by reflection, rationalism, and

political strategy. Everything depends upon whether
these elements in socialism are subordinated and its
pure prophetic power becomes manifest. The fate of
the socialist movement hinges upon the success or
failure of this effort.[89]

Tillich considered the prophetic attitude as "the unity and a higher form" of two other basic tendencies, the sacramental and the rational. In a way consistent with his ontological distinction of form and import and his theological distinction of what ought to be and what is (the distinctions are parallel), Tillich defined the sacramental attitude as "a consciousness of the presence of the divine" and saw its source in sacred symbols, forms, and relationships. The opposing attitude, the rational, is derived not from the holy but from the concept of right (*Recht*). In this attitude, he wrote, "spirit is directed toward form and thereby loses the presence of the holy. It becomes separated from everything given and becomes empty and without import." This critical rational spirit is the dynamic principle of history, "the titanic world-forming will that wants to restore the lost presence of the holy through the creation of form." But, objected Tillich, "the holy that is given cannot be replaced by the holy that is demanded."[90]

As in the letter, Tillich believed both attitudes to be inadequate in themselves since the first lacks a dynamic historical consciousness, and the second lacks awareness of the presence of the holy. Having again posed the issue in terms of contrasts, he once more sought a synthesis in an attitude that corrects and unites the two.

> The demand of the holy that should be arises upon
> the ground of the holy that is given . . . . Prophetism
> grasps the coming that should be from its living connection with the present that is given. It has the holy, but only as it permeates law and form; it is free
> from sacramental indifference, but it does not succumb
> to rational purgation.[91]

He believed that this attitude is one that "persists", although it is susceptible to distortion through mantic or moralism. He further explained that prophetism radically affirms law and form, even more strongly than rationalism, but it recognizes that "the presence of the Unconditional is the *prius* of all conditional action, that the unconditioned import of meaning is the *prius* of all forms of meaning . . . ."[92] In setting out the prophetic attitude here, Tillich reaffirmed what he had written earlier: the holy that is given has priority over the holy that is demanded, but the holy demand, arising from the ground of the holy given, remains in all its intensity.

Tillich called the content of the prophetic view of history "kairos . . . a moment of time filled with unconditional meaning and demand." In the first chapter it was pointed out that Tillich used kairos to express his epochal consciousness, his political judgment about the crisis of society, but it also had a theological meaning. Kairos, Tillich wrote, does not signify a prediction nor a "mere demand or ideal"; rather,

> Kairos is the fulfilled moment of time in which the present and the future, the holy that is given and the holy that is demanded meet, and from whose concrete tensions the new creation proceeds in which sacred import is realized in necessary form. Prophetism is consciousness of Kairos in the sense of the words: "Repent: the time (*kairos*) is fulfilled and the kingdom of God is at hand."[93]

Kairos then marks the unity of the divine contrasts in time; it is, one might say, justification of an historical moment. Similarly, Tillich, on the basis of "the paradox of the Unconditional," spoke of "a *massa sancta*," or, as one might also say, justification of a collective.[94] In a special time and in a special group the holy gift and demand come together to effect a new creation, according to Tillich's development of his theological principle.

The new creation that emerges from the tensions of the kairos is a theonomous society. "Theonomy is the goal of religious socialism."[95] In Tillich's conception, theonomy is neither an other-worldly or a this-worldly utopia but "a condition in which the spiritual and social forms are filled with the import of the Unconditional as the foundation, meaning, and reality of all forms. Theonomy is the unity of sacred form and sacred import in a concrete historical situation." He considered it both a just and sacred reality, "a creative synthesis of form and import in which the eternal idea, the absolute synthesis, is revealed."[96]

Kairos, like justification, is a matter of grace. In the kairos, "the decisive element, the new breakthrough of import, is not a matter of work. Rather, it is fate and grace."[97] Grace precedes praxis; yet the paradoxical breakthrough of grace is a call to praxis. "Kairos," Tillich wrote, "is always demand and gift simultaneously. Were it only demand, then it would be only a new law. Were it only a gift, then it would be a consecration of the past power."[98] Tillich wanted neither activism nor quietism, but action in accord with grace.

The kairos concept was Tillich's attempt not only to indicate the proper relationship between Gospel and Law in the social sphere, but also to express the right tension between the Unconditional and the conditioned. In the kairos the Unconditional is present, but it does not forfeit its transcendence; the conditioned becomes a vehicle for the Unconditional, but it is itself not the Unconditional and remains under its judgment.[99] For Tillich the absolute is not so impotent as to remain separated from the relative,[100] but the cross stands as a protest against the claim of any finite form to be absolute.[101] Tillich frequently expressed this relationship with the words of Jesus that the kingdom of God is "at hand." Even though it is real, the Unconditional has not arrived in a tangible way. It is "always the coming, that which is near at hand," and therefore no one can say "'It is here or there.'"[102] Kairos, continued Tillich,

> . . . means a new breaking through of import into form, a new breaking through of grace through the law. It means a new solution of the eternal task which is given every historical period; to represent the Unconditional in the form of the conditioned, to be a symbol for the eternal ungraspable unity of ground and abyss, of form and life.[103]

On the basis of this prophetic attitude with its paradoxical understanding of transcendence, Tillich carried on "The Struggle of Religious Socialism."[104] The struggle for theonomy, he wrote, is not against the secular, but against the "demonic," the irrational antidivine power that contradicts and opposes form.[105] For Tillich this is a "two-sided conflict" which opposes both the old sacramental demonry with autonomous forms and the new demonry that moves into the empty space created by autonomous criticism.[106] "In the conflict against sacramental and natural demonry, religious socialism adopts rational, liberal, and democratic elements. In the struggle for a new import it opens itself to the theonomous elements of past and present spiritual situations."[107] In this struggle the decisive issue for Tillich is the proper relationship of form and import, of law and grace, and he opposes both an attitude oriented only to form (law) and one oriented only to import (grace) in favor of an attitude oriented toward their unity in a living breakthrough of the Unconditional into reality.

Tillich's prophetic attitude set his understanding of justification in an historical-eschatological context. He took a doctrine traditionally addressed to the individual and applied it to an historical situation, to a moment in time and to the bearers of a new order. In giving the paradox of transcendence a corporate meaning, Tillich also separated it from the Christian community, insisting that the breakthrough of grace was not dependent upon the form of the church, but was a universal phenomenon.[108] He found warrant for this historical and universal application of his theological principle in the eschatological symbols of the tradition which embrace all reality.[109] Tillich's understanding of justification and eschatology were mutually dependent; his view of the "now-not yet" eschatological tension and of the kingdom as being both "inner-temporal and concrete, and trans-temporal and unconditional" reflect the God-human relationship present in what he had called the basic religious attitude.[110] The following section will look more closely at his eschatology as he developed it in terms of expectation, the subjective counterpart to the symbol of the "at handness" of the kingdom.

Tillich's prophetic attitude, as it was discussed in this section, was the basis for his affirmative and critical theological interpretation of socialism. He claimed that this attitude is present within socialism, though in a distorted form, and he asserted that it is the true and proper attitude from which socialism should operate. What this meant for him can best be seen in *The Socialist Decision*.

The Symbol of Socialism: Expectation

Tillich's most complete and systematic discussion of the relationship between the prophetic attitude and socialism is in *The Socialist Decision*. As was noted earlier, the thesis of this book was that socialism is a prophetic movement in an autonomous, self-sufficient world. The purpose of this section is to establish the meaning of this statement. In *The Socialist Decision* the explicitly theological argument of this position drops into the background in favor of an anthropological emphasis. Tillich established the tie between prophetism and socialism on the basis of their structural similarity rooted in human existence. First, then, his anthropology will be discussed; secondly, his understanding of the prophets, where his anthropological norm was developed, will be studied; and finally, his linking of the prophets and socialism, especially in relationship to "expectation", will be discussed.

A secondary purpose of this section is to introduce *The Socialist Decision*. Although in continuity with his previous work, it is marked by its own language and logic; its scope is inclusive and its argument tightly knit. Because of its uniqueness and its importance for this study, it is necessary to become acquainted with its content and structure.

The structure of *The Socialist Decision* witnesses to the political situation of 1932. In the first part of the book, "Political Romanticism, Its Principle and Its Contradiction," Tillich analyzed and attacked the presuppositions of the political right through the category "the myth of origin." He distinguished between the "conservative form," represented by the present rulers Hindenberg and von Papen, and the "revolutionary form," represented by Hitler, but he saw both as rejecting the demand of justice.[111] In the second part, "The Principle of Capitalist Society and the Inner Conflict of Socialism," he attended to the traditional opponent of socialism. He critically interpreted the "bourgeois principle" as an attitude that viewed reality as a set of objects to be rationally controlled thereby reducing people to things and cutting them off from the creative springs of life. Moreover, he characterized the presupposition of the bourgeois era as a rational "belief in harmony," a belief, however, contradicted by the class struggle. From here he outlined the "inner conflicts" of socialism, which, on the one hand, had to struggle against the bourgeois principle but which, on the other hand, had been forced to defend it against pre-bourgeois forms.[112] In the final part of *The Socialist Decision*, "The Principle of Socialism and the Solution of its Inner Conflicts," Tillich gave his "answer" to the "predicament" with the socialist principle and applied it to socialist thought and practice.[113] Throughout the book he appealed for "the socialist decision," that is, that non-socialists (especially the revolutionary political romantics) consider genuine socialism and socialists reconsider the roots of their actions.[114]

The departure point of *The Socialist Decision* is man: "*The roots of political thinking must be sought in human existence itself.*"[115] Nature, Tillich wrote, is a life process which is entirely one with itself and which is bound to what it finds in itself and its surroundings, but, in contrast, man is

> a life process which asks about itself and its environment, which places demands on itself and its environment, which is therefore not one with itself, but has the "doubleness" to be in itself and at the same time to stand over against itself, to think itself, to know of itself.[116]

Man, unlike nature, is "the being that is 'doubled' in itself to the point of self-conscious being." This does not mean, he added, that man is composed of two independent parts, such as nature and spirit, body and soul, but that he is *one* being who is "doubled" in himself, in his unity.[117]

According to Tillich, man as a unity of consciousness and being is the source of the two roots "from which all political thinking originates."[118] The first root springs from the experience of "'being thrown'" into existence.[119] Man discovers himself and his environment, which means that he has not stemmed from himself, but that he has an "origin" (*Ursprung*) which is not himself, and that therefore he asks the question "*Woher?*", "Whence?", "From where?" In describing the origin, which allows man to arise as something new and particular but always brings us back to itself, Tillich quoted the first words of Western philosophy: "'But whence that which is arises, thither must it return again of necessity.'"[120] Everything living follows the course of birth, development and death; in being born one has to die. Tillich understood this circular law to be the them of myth: "All myth is myth of origin, an answer to the question of the whence and an expression of standing in the origin and in being bound to its power." It is the first root of political thinking: "The consciousness of the myth of origin is the root of all conservative and romantic thinking in politics."[121]

Tillich continued that man is not simply bound to the cycle of life and death, for he experiences a "demand" that loosens his boundness to the given and forces him to ask the question

"*Wozu?*," "Whither?," "For what end?" With this demand, the second root of political thinking, man is raised above the sphere of the merely living, "for the demand demands something which is not yet there, which should be, which should come to fulfillment." Tillich considered this demand "unconditional" since it is not given in the unfolding of what exists. "The whither is not enclosed in the limits of the whence. It is an unconditional new that lies beyond the new and old of mere unfolding."[122] Because of this demand, stated Tillich, man

> . . . has the possibility to go beyond (*hinausgehen ueber*) what he finds in and around himself. This is human freedom, not that he has a so-called free will, but that he is not bound to what he finds, that he stands under the demand that through him the unconditionally-new should come.[123]

Where this consciousness pervails, Tillich considered the tie to the origin to be fundamentally dissolved and the myth of origin to be fundamentally broken. "*The breaking of the myth of origin through the unconditional demand is the root of liberal, democratic, and socialist thinking in politics.*"[124]

Having distinguished the two roots of political thinking, Tillich related them in two ways: first, he grounded the demand in the origin, and secondly, he argued for the priority of the *Wozu* to the *Woher*. The unconditional demand "is not foreign" to man for then it would not concern him. He insisted that it concerns man "only because it places his own essence before him as a demand. The unconditionality, the irresistibility with which the 'ought' comes to man and must be affirmed by him rests on this alone." Because the demand is man's own essence, it is based on the origin, although what is demanded is unconditionally-new in relation to the origin. Thus, concluded Tillich, "*the origin is ambiguous*. In it there is a cleavage between the true and actual origin." The fulfillment of the origin is for Tillich what man experiences as the demand. "The *Wozu* of man is that wherein his *Wohin* is fulfilled." Tillich saw that the actual origin disguises and distorts the true origin, and therefore the true origin denies in part the actual one. The unconditional demand is for Tillich what reveals the ambiguity of the origin, but the mythical consciousness knows nothing of this ambiguity and considers it an outrage to go beyond the actual origin.[125]

In describing further the nature of the unconditional demand, the fulfillment of the true origin, Tillich makes it dependent on other people. "The demand is concrete only in the encounter of the 'I and you.'"[126] The content of this demand, he affirmed, is that the "you" be given the same "dignity" as the "I," "the dignity to be free, to be a bearer of the fulfillment of what is meant in the origin. The recognition of the 'you' as having equal dignity with the 'I' is justice."[127] In contrast to the situation where the unbroken powers of origin are in tension with one another and seek to dominate and destroy the others, a situation in which the second root of political thinking predominates has in Tillich's scheme risen above this "tragic cycle" and opposed it with the unconditional demand of justice.[128] Yet Tillich did not see merely opposition (*Entgegensetzung*) between the "is" and the "ought" but viewed justice as "*the true power of being*."[129] The result of this anthropological discussion is that Tillich insisted that the actual origin, the mere power of being, be "subordinated" to justice, and the second root of human existence and political thinking be considered "a higher range" than the first. "*The myth of origin may enter into political thinking only when it has been broken and its ambiguity revealed.*"[130]

The whole of *The Socialist Decision* was constructed from this rather abstract anthropological understanding of political thinking. The opposing and yet mutually interdependent relationship of the two roots provided the framework and the norm for his critical analysis and prescription. From here Tillich was able to comprehend and illuminate an extremely broad spectrum of political alternatives--National Socialism, aristocratic conservatism, liberalism, democracy, socialism, and communism--and he did so in relation to social, political, economic, cultural, intellectual, and religious areas of life. His uncovering of the "roots" of human existence proved to be a methodologically fruitful undertaking.

The two questions that Tillich saw as the source of all political thinking are questions of meaning. They are religious questions, that is, existential quests for ultimate meaning, and the differing answers to them represent fundamental human possibilities. In *The Socialist Decision*, too, Tillich's basic ontological polarity between import and form lie in the background. The two roots are similar to Tillich's earlier distinction between the sacramental and rational attitudes.[131] The first root, the origin[132]--a concept Tillich did not often use before and after *The Socialist Decision*--resembles the sacramental attitude of "Basic Principles," although it is broadened to include a new phenomenon, the revolutionary political romantics, who, however, like the conservatives, reject the second root, the demand for autonomy and justice. The second root with its unconditional demand, especially in its bourgeois form, corresponded closely to the rational attitude. In *The Socialist Decision*, too, Tillich sought a solution that would unite the two ontological possibilities in a new perspective, the prophetic attitude, but this time more clearly than before he makes the second root superior to the first. What this means can be seen in his description of the prophets and of expectation.

Tillich discussed the prophets in the first part of *The Socialist Decision* under the title, "The Break with the Myth of Origin in Judaism."[133] "The world historical mission of Jewish prophecy" is for him "the shattering of the myth of origin." In the prophets, he interpreted, God is free from the soil, the holy land, not because he conquers foreign lands but because he leads foreign conquerors into his own land in order to punish the "'people of his inheritance'" and to subject them to the unconditional demand. Other "powers of the origin" besides soil-- the holy aristocracy, tribal membership, and the priestly tradition--are judged from the demand for justice.[134]

Positively, Tillich saw the significance of the prophets in their view of time, for they grasp it "in its essential independence" and raise "*time over space.*"[135]

> Time acquires a direction; it moves toward something that did not exist but will exist and, once it is attained, will not be lost again. The expectation of a "new heaven and a new earth" means the expectation of a reality that is not subject to the structure of existence, that cannot be grasped ontologically. The old and the new cannot be subsumed under the same concept of being. The new being is intrinsically unontological. It cannot be derived from the original state. It goes beyond the origin in a second affirmation, as it were, an affirmation of the *new in history.*[136]

Tillich noted that in such a view of time the origin becomes "the beginning of the historical process" or "creation." In addition, time receives a "goal" and a "'center'," from which Tillich believed the meaning and direction of process are understood, and the "side-by-sideness" of space loses its significance in relation to the unity of directed time. Therefore, wrote Tillich, "polytheism is broken through the monotheism of the God who effects his will in history and of the community that is the bearer of history."[137]

The prophets signify for Tillich the decisive discovery of the second root of human existence, the direction toward the "whither." They represent a fundamentally new human attitude with their "'tension forward'" and their demand for justice. It is "the *function of the Jewish spirit*" in both Judaism and Christianity "to raise the prophetic protest . . . against every attempt to revive such bondage to the myth of origin, and to help time, the unconditional demand, and the 'whither' to be victorious over space, mere existence, and the 'whence.'"[138] Jewish prophetism shatters the dominion of the origin, but it does not deny it, since, Tillich wrote, "the father as origin remains also for the prophetic consciousness as bearer of the demand, as ruler of history, and as creator of the new." The tie to the origin is not cut off (which Tillich saw as happening first with the autonomous consciousness of the bourgeois era), but the nature of the origin is radically transformed.[139]

The remarkable passage (written at a time of growing anti-Semitism) indicates both the importance that the prophets had for Tillich and the strong eschatological thrust of his thinking, at least at this point. One wonders if the anticipation of the "unontological" eschatological reality does not strain the limits of Tillich's own ontological theology, a question that will be discussed further in Chapter 6. According to his conception, the two roots of political thinking--the "whence" and the "whither"--have with the prophets been changed into the creation and the eschaton, the beginning and the end of history, and the eschaton, "a new heaven and a new earth," is not the destruction but the completion of creation. Because this is so, it appears that the second root cannot simply be identified with the demand but includes the promise, the gift of a new future. In other words, the question "For what end?"--the eschatological question--must be answered with both Law and Gospel, demand and grace, and, therefore, as it had appeared to be in his earlier writings, grace cannot only be connected with the sacramental, the past, the already given, or the origin. When Tillich made the second root a higher order than the first, he was emphasizing the demand of justice more than he had, but he was also giving grace a greater future quality than he had before, although he was not always consistent on this latter point. Tillich's discussion of the prophets and expectation in *The Socialist Decision* should be seen as a beginning attempt to place his basic theological principles in a clear eschatological framework.

When Tillich turned to analyzing socialism with these anthropological assumptions and this interpretation of the prophets, he found an "inner conflict" in "the socialist faith."[140] Socialism, Tillich explained, shares the belief that the world can be rationalized and an economic and social order created by knowing and structuring objects. But since it does not share the bourgeois belief in a hidden "automatic harmony"--it knew from the existence of the proletariat that disharmony resulted from the free sway of productive forces--socialism directs its faith toward the future, transforming the belief in harmony into an end-expectation, a future time of harmony.[141] At this point, however, Tillich perceived an inconsistency:

> *Socialism, if it awaits a coming harmonious world, must reckon with a "leap" which in no way can be made understandable from the given reality.* But in doing this the socialist belief breaks through the bourgeois principle, the presupposition of a rational world order which is in correspondence with reality. It contains an element of the prophetic proclamation, the expectation of a new existence, but it gives this expectation an expression that is completely determined by the bourgeois principle, that is, an expression that is purely immanent.[142]

He accounted for this state of affairs historically, stating that socialism was pushed to the side of immanence (though its expectation went beyond it) because the bourgeoisie utilized the transcendent expectation as an anti-revolutionary ideology which socialism then had to unmask. This inner conflict was the source of "the continually recurring shift between hope and disappointment, between utopia and forced compromise, which fills the history of socialism."[143]

Tillich sought to resolve the inner antagonism of socialist

faith (as well as its other internal conflicts) by means of "the socialist principle" which includes three elements: "*the power of the origin, the shattering of harmony, the orientation to what is demanded.*" He elaborated that the socialist principle involves a "yes" to the power of the origin, a "yes" to the breaking of the tie to the origin by the unconditional demand, and a "no" to the belief in harmony. These are intertwined so that in saying "yes" to the unconditional demand, the bondage to the origin is broken, and in saying "no" to the belief in harmony, space is created for the powers of the origin, subordinate to the demand for justice. Tillich summarized these three elements with the concept of "expectation," which then becomes a "symbol"; "*Socialism counters the myth of origin and the belief in harmony with the symbol of expectation. It has elements of both but it transcends both.*"[144]

In summarizing the socialist principle with the symbol of expectation, Tillich is bringing socialism "into an explicit relationship with the prophetic tradition." He saw that the prophets, that is, "that historical movement in which the second root of human existence was radically grasped," also combined these three elements: "the tie to the origin, expressed in the form of patriarchal religion; the breaking of the tie to the origin by the unconditional demand; the fulfillment of the origin not in a present interpreted in terms of harmony but in a promised future." Therefore, concluded Tillich, "*the socialist principle is prophetic according to its substance*"; socialism is a "prophetic movement" but in a world where the bourgeois principle, which had cut all ties to the origin, dominates. In other words, "*Socialism is prophetism on the soil of an autonomous, self-contained world.*"[145]

As has been noted, this statement is the key thesis of *The Socialist Decision*. Tillich links socialism with the prophets because their meaning-fulfilling qualities are structurally similar. Although socialism's form is dictated by the autonomous context in which it arose, its import is, according to Tillich, prophetic; that is, it embodies an expectant attitude toward the future and stresses the second root of human existence.

"Expectation" or "anticipation" (*Erwartung*) apparently began to assume a role in Tillich's writings around 1929.[146] In "The

Protestant Principle and the Proletarian Situation" in 1931 he spoke of expectation in the context of justification, using it to describe the "transformed" person's relationship to ultimate fulfillment. Living from faith in justification means living "from the certainty that in the paradoxical overcoming of human perversion man is called to the transcendent fulfillment of his destiny." In this paradox, which he called "the positive side" of the Protestant principle, fulfillment is "ungraspable and yet real, transcendent and yet in the world, beyond man and yet for him." He summarized this dual character (beyond and actual) of fulfillment under the rubric of expectation: "expectation is neither having nor not having." In reference to the saying that the kingdom is "at hand," the "classical" formulation of expectation, he introduced the "image of nearness" as a way of expressing the converse double-sidedness of being there and not being there.[147]

> Transcendence in the sense of the Protestant principle is given in the objective symbol of nearness and the subjective symbol of expectation. In the paradox of both concepts is hidden the mystery of the end, which is not a mystery of hidden objects but the mystery of the givenness (*Gegebenheit*) of the transcendent.[148]

Expectation was clearly integral to Tillich's basic theological position and became for him an important expression of the relationship between the Unconditional and the conditioned. Whereas earlier Tillich had made kairos the paramount expression for this relationship, here and especially in *The Socialist Decision*, expectation replaced it. The former highlighted the objective pole, the sense of nearness, of the prophetic attitude, and the latter signified the subjective pole, the response on the part of the human subject.[149]

Also in this article Tillich connected expectation to the proletariat. "*Expectation is the form in which the proletariat directly experiences the relationship of its existence to transcendence (to the 'meaning' of its existence).*" He added that the expectation of the proletariat means that it has become aware of the evil of its situation and simultaneously shares in that for which it hopes, the overcoming of its situation. "Through expectation the proletariat is no longer *only* proletariat," and this fact, he commented, is the difference in the proletariat before and after it was molded by Marxism.[150]

In *The Socialist Decision* Tillich developed his nascent thinking on expectation and made it the central symbol of the book. In discussing the meaning of the socialist principle, he gave an extended description of this attitude:

> Expectation is tension, direction forward. Expectation directs itself toward what is not, but shall be, toward the unconditionally-new that has never been but is coming. The fulfillment of being is not to be sought in the unfolding of the origin between birth and death. The ambiguity of the origin prohibits this. There are no eternal laws that regulate all social existence . . . . Man is a new possibility in relation to nature. In history this new possibility is realized. But because it is realized in history, no present time can be affirmed as the fulfillment of this possibility. History tears loose from every present into the future. History is tension towards that which is to come; concretely, toward the new order of things. The prophet waits for it; the tension of socialism is directed toward it, regardless of how rationally this tension may be expressed. History, in each of its moments, points beyond itself. Only in this way can history be seen as history, as tension toward the unconditionally-new.[151]

What is most pronounced in this depiction is the priority given to the future. Expectation for Tillich is a taut (note the repetition of the important word "tension"), future-oriented posture; it is "going beyond."[152] Every present is relativized and recognized as incomplete, for the essence of human existence is the movement over any and all presents toward that which is not yet. Expectation characterizes life's *"fundamental openness,"*[153] the human creature's freedom to transcend the given and search for the new. Tillich considered expectation the "basic human attitude" and therefore anthropologically normative, and he also claimed that this prophetic attitude "belongs to the foundation of Christian faith" and is "the basic attitude of early Christianity."[154]

Expectation is directed toward the new, the unconditionally new, but how is this new to be understood? In giving an answer to what can be expected, Tillich rejected the possibility of the religious conservative political romantic, typified by Friedrich Gogarten, which adapted the prophetic element "by attempting *to refer man's final expectation to the destiny of the individual soul*, and to sever it from historical destiny, the transformation of the world." In such an expectation "the movement of history as a whole is not seriously included," and history is seen as "a circle of circles in which human suffering and divine grace contend with each other, but nothing fundamentally new happens." From this point of view any expectation whose goal is to restructure the world is disappointed since irrational powers stemming from the irrational depths of the divine hold sway over life; instead one has to subject oneself to these authorities and not rebel. For the conservative Christian, "the new lies beyond history; in history itself, it is claimed, no change is possible."[155]

In reply to this position Tillich clarified the attitude of the prophets and the socialists. Socialism also knows the frustrations of history, does not believe that history will be "miraculously transformed," and recognizes "the possibility of chaos and barbarism in the immediate or distant future." Moreover, prophetism is not to be confused with divination or prediction.[156]

> The prophetic attitude presupposes only that history as such, in each moment, is oriented toward the new, toward that which is demanded and promised. Expectation is not a subjective attitude. It is grounded in the impulse of events themselves. It *is*, so to speak, this impulse . . . .[157]

But this impulse, continued Tillich, must not be objectified and made into a utopia of a coming age of fulfillment, for fulfillment is not an empirical concept and when made such, "disappointment" always follows.[158]

> Expectation is going beyond. As such it prevails over an objectified tie to the origin ("Everything remains the same") as well as over an objectified final expectation ("Someday everything will become new"). It is a non-objectified expectation ("The new breaks into the old").[159]

In summarizing "the elements of the socialist principle," Tillich once more asserted that "socialism has prophetic character because it assumes this posture," even though it, like the prophetic attitude of all ages, is constantly threatened with deviating into false objectification and ending up in either resignation or utopianism.[160]

In his polemic against the two distorted versions of the "new," Tillich was waging one of his most persistent struggles. He rejected the transcendent individualism of a religious world view and the literal utopianism of a political world view and argued that the perversions of both could be avoided by a symbolic, non-objectified image of the future. His own picture for the new recalled his kairos concept in which what is expected breaks through or into the old as transforming power. Tillich in his concern to be non-literalistic and concrete has given the prophetic-eschatological perspective historical significance, but one might well ask if in his rejection of a final expectation, of a "new heaven and a new earth," he has not eliminated a crucial intent of the prophetic message.[161]

Tillich called expectation the "impulse" of history in order to distinguish it from an arbitrary, fanciful attitude without a basis in reality. With this metaphor Tillich was bringing expectation into conscious relationship with the socialist dialectic. In the following three sections of *The Socialist Decision* Tillich probed the meaning of expectation as a way of interpreting historical dialectic, a subject for a later chapter.[162] What he had already written about the symbol of socialism is the basis for this interpretation.

Tillich in *The Socialist Decision* drew a connection between prophetism and socialism with the concept-symbol of expectation. Historically, he argued that socialism was dependent on the Judaic-Christian eschatological tradition, a dependence that he saw running through the revolutionary Christian sects back to early Christianity and the prophets.[163] More importantly, however, he developed the idea that the two exhibited a structural "affinity,"[164] that is, socialism represented a fundamental human attitude that was analogous to that of the prophets. Tillich asserted, from the viewpoints of theology, anthropology, and socialist theory, that this attitude of expectation is the true and proper one. As shown in this section, socialism for Tillich is a prophetic movement (in the modern autonomous world) because it shares with the prophets the posture of expectation.

Socialism As A Living Reality

The concern of this chapter has been with Tillich's understanding of socialism. The distinctiveness of this understanding is that Tillich viewed socialism in terms of the ultimate, that is, he placed socialism in theological perspective. Tillich affirmed, criticized, and transformed socialism from a theological point of view. The aim of this chapter has been to demonstrate that this was the intention of his project and to show in a preliminary way what such a task meant.

"What was the meaning of socialism for Tillich?" To answer in one sentence one might say: "Socialism, the expression of the proletariat, is a religious phenomenon that embodies a prophetic attitude in an autonomous form and world." In this chapter Tillich's concept of socialism has been developed according to the three related points of this "definition." By calling socialism "the expression of the proletarian situation," Tillich made it dependent on a particular socio-political group. The other two features of his concept pointed to socialism's universal significance. As a religious phenomenon socialism expresses the threat and support of human existence and makes the ultimate available to the proletariat; all its myriad activities and ideas were seen by Tillich as giving meaning in a web of meaninglessness. Finally, socialism is a prophetic movement, incorporating in its life an attitude that Tillich found present in the Jewish prophets, but in contrast to the prophets this movement takes place in an historical condition shaped by autonomy.

With this three-part understanding Tillich had three criteria by which to evaluate socialist theory as well as Christian social thought: 1) Is it related to the situation of the proletariat? Any theory, socialist or religious, that bypasses the key significance of the proletariat is wholly inadequate. 2) Has it penetrated to the religious dimension of socialism? In Tillich's view, anyone who overlooks this element of socialism has missed its genuine meaning. 3) Does it express the meaning of the prophetic attitude, while respecting the demands of autonomy? This attitude, which has been discussed in terms both of kairos and expectation, is the foundation for understanding socialism's past errors and preparing for new tasks in the future.

Tillich's concept of socialism was composed of propositions that already carried within them the presuppositions and direction of his thought. He understood socialism in light of his own theological intent. With this in mind, it is helpful to mention briefly a few ways by which Tillich did *not* approach socialism. This should not imply that Tillich considered these aspects of socialism unimportant, but they were not his avenue of access to socialism, and/or they were not his central concern in interpreting socialism theologically.

Perhaps most frequently socialism has been perceived as a particular economic theory and arrangement.[165] Tillich certainly concurred that socialism involved a different economic structure than capitalism, but this was not his point of departure. Instead he took a flexible position in relationship to possible economic structures of the socialist society. "Socialism", he wrote, "depends neither upon a specific economic theory nor upon the realization of *one* specific form of economy." He did not accept Marx's economic theories as final but saw them as something to be surpassed. He laid down one criterion: "The only essential thing is the coming of an economy in which the lack of coordination of the forces and counterforces in capitalism is overcome, and through which the possibility of a meaningful society is given."[166] Tillich's respect for the autonomy of the sciences, his refusal to equate a theological perspective with an economic conclusion, and the influence of Heimann's critique of Marxist economics stood behind this position.

Tillich also did not identify socialism by means of a political party. Though of course necessary, political organization was not the determining factor in his understanding of socialism, and party politics remained at the periphery of his theoretical interest. Nor did Tillich set out his understanding of socialism in programmatic terms. Indeed, one can argue that there was a "programmatic lacuna" in his project since there was no agenda of action for the next political step, a task that Tillich seemed willing to leave to the politicians. Also, he did not present violent revolution as a leitmotif of socialism. These various elements were to some degree a part of his thinking, but they did not offer him his entre into the meaning of socialism. Tillich's concern was the religious meaning of socialism (and its closely connected moral values) that was expressed by this historical movement of the proletariat, a concern, he hoped, that could provide a framework for the other facets of socialism.

Tillich knew that his understanding of socialism was not that of the Marxist orthodoxy that dominated the German Social Democratic Party during this period, and in "Socialism" he spelled out an obvious but vital presupposition of his challenge to this orthodoxy. Socialism, he insisted, is alive. "To be alive is to go beyond oneself . . . . Where there is life there is a tension between 'being one with oneself' and 'separating from oneself.'" Without such a tension, wrote Tillich, a person, an historical movement, or a concept is dead. Although socialism possesses the depth and intrinsic power to maintain this tension, he saw strong forces of orthodoxy which bestow the character of "motionless idols" on the forms that once lived, and like all priests of idols, they give "*one* picture of socialism's timeless permanence," raising a fuss if this "holy of holies" is touched. "The human primordial anxiety before the new, before the venture, before the threat to fall into nothing," along with their position of power, explained Tillich, drives the orthodox to harden and idolize their position.[167]

At this point the existential character of Tillich's socialism becomes evident. Socialism, he asserted, must have the audacity to risk anew just as it had once been risked. "The venture does not cease so long as life should be. For life is a thrust into the undetermined." Socialism as venture, he stated, is the opposite of "opportunistic accomodation" that lacks the courage to risk, and it is clearly distinguishable from "radicalism" that hides its own anxiety and is "often nothing but the undertone of anxiety." To venture, however, means "to push out from the tension of the given toward what is coming." This venture also involves risking socialism's concepts which Tillich anticipated would be resisted by the orthodox who "cling to the concept as the place of least mobility." He recognized that one might deviate in two ways, either by keeping a concept in itself (*Stehenbleiben in sich*) or by separating it from itself (*Sichtrennen von sich*); a concept could be changed to such an extent that one would say, "'that is no longer socialism,'" or it could be changed so little that one would respond, "'that is only the old socialism.'" For Tillich, "anyone who makes socialism into a venture once again must constantly go between these two attacks on the word and the issue itself," and he observed, it can not be decided in advance if these attacks are right or not; otherwise it would not be a risk.[168]

Socialism, insisted Tillich, is not fully defined by its past and present and has not achieved a fixed and final shape, a state reserved for the dead. Socialism is living and like all life is a venture. In 1930 Tillich wrote that socialism is at the end of its "first heroic period" and is entering a "second period of formation: that is "externally easier, internally more difficult." In this new phase Tillich sought to find new answers that were still socialist but that pushed to "the final possible depth" and embraced "the greatest possible universality."[169] The presupposition for this was that socialism is alive, and this assumption gave his efforts to set socialism in theological perspective a dynamic, existential tone.[170]

Thus, we have seen, socialism, a living reality, was for Tillich the expression of the proletarian situation, a (indirect) religious phenomenon, and a prophetic movement on autonomous, self-sufficient soil. In addition, it was at least one more thing--a powerful complex of ideas. Tillich considered Marx's historical dialectic an original and imposing intellectual achievement. Marx for him was a scientist and a philosopher as well as a prophet and a revolutionary.[171] He was most interested in the presuppositions of Marx's thought and in the issues he raised, such as the relationship between consciousness and existence and the nature of historical change.

Although he held Marx (whom he always saw as Hegel's pupil) to be a creative person in the Western philosophical tradition, he discovered the Marxist tradition after him to be sterile. Often he used Marx against the Marxists. He welcomed the publication in 1932 of the *Economic and Philosophical Manuscripts of 1844*, which in a striking way confirmed Tillich's interpretation of Marx as an original philosopher. He wanted "*to extricate Marxism from the dogmatic narrowness into which it has fallen among the epigoni, and to restore it to the breadth which it had in the young Marx.*"[172] In the following two chapters Tillich's encounter with the theoretical aspects of Marx and Marxism will be investigated. On the basis of his understanding of socialism as presented here, the focus of the study will turn to Tillich's appropriation, criticism, and transformation of historical materialism and historical dialectic.

CHAPTER 3

NOTES

[1] (Berlin and Frankfurt a.M.: Verlag der Arbeitsgemeinschaft, 1922). *GW*, II, pp. 35-90.

[2] *GW*, II, pp. 277-78. Interestingly, Tillich said the same about Marxism: "Marxism was the way in which the proletariat grasped itself as proletariat and thereby constituted itself. In Marxism the proletariat gained its socialist self-consciousness." *GW*, II, 320. Tillich often used the two interchangeably. Socialism for Tillich was a socialism deeply influenced by Marxism.

[3] Ibid., pp. 278-79; "Sozialismus," *GW*, II, pp. 144-45; *Protestantisches Prinzip und proletarische Situation* (Bonn: Friedrich Cohen, 1931), pp. 6-7. An English translation, which is somewhat different from the German version, is found in *PE*, "The Protestant Principle and the Proletarian Situation," pp. 161-81. Cf. p. 162. Except where the rendering is exact, the German will be used, followed by reference to the English text. ("PPPS")

[4] "PPPS," *PE*, pp. 164-65; German, pp. 10-11.

[5] *SD*, *GW*, II, 278.

[6] "Klassenkampf und religioeser Sozialismus," *GW*, II, pp. 184-85. The class struggle will be discussed further in Ch. 4, Section 4. ("Cl. St.").

[7] "Sozialismus," *GW*, II, p. 144. Cf. "Weiterbildung," *GW*, V, p. 122.

[8] "RS (II),"*Pol. Exp.*, p. 47.

[9] "Cl. St.," *GW*, II, pp. 182-84.

[10] Ibid., p. 186. Note that Tillich's understanding of the significance of Marxism is similar to that given by Dom Helder who said of Marx that he has "become the inspiration for life and death of a great part of humanity."

[11] Ibid.

12 *SD*, *GW*, II, pp. 233-34; for a discussion of "Principle and Reality," see pp. 232-34; also, "PPPS," pp. 7-8, for a methodological discussion of principle in the context of the Protestant principle. Cf. *PE*, pp. 162-63. The meaning of the "socialist principle" will be spelled out in section 4. Cf. *SD*, *GW*, II, fn. p. 15, p. 249. Tillich here speaks of *"dynamis"* or "productive possibility," an Aristotelian term which contains the distinction between "actual" and "potential" being.

[13] Ibid., p. 277.

[14] Ibid., pp. 279-80.

[15] Ibid., p. 277.

[16] Ibid., p. 280. Tillich expressed a similar notion in different language in 1919: ". . . socialism is not only a matter

for the workers, but *a new ethical ideal* that has validity for all circles." "Kirchenfrage," *GW,* II, p. 19. Cf. "Sozialismus," *GW,* II, p. 144.

[17]"Sozialismus," *GW,* II, p. 145.

[18]Cf. *SD, GW,* II, pp. 332-35; see below, Ch. 4, Sec. 4.

[19]Ibid., p. 308. Cf. "Sozialismus, *GW,* II, p. 144.

[20]Tillich, of course, recognized this possibility since it was a topic very much discussed by socialists in terms of the "'*Kleinbuerger*'" development within the proletariat. He always knew socialism to be a risk. Also, he considered the question as "hypothetical" during the time of the Depression when millions were unemployed. Cf. "Sozialismus," p. 145, and below, Ch. 4, Sec. 4, and Ch. 6, Sec. 5.

[21]Adams (1965), p. 56. See Adam's book for a complete discussion of meaning in relation to Tillich's theology of culture, philosophy of religion, and system of sciences. In *OB* Tillich wrote "that there is a correspondence between reality and the human spirit which is probably expressed most adequately in the concept of 'meaning.'" P. 83.

[22]*Das System der Wissenschaften nach Gegenstaenden und Methoden, GW,* I (1959), 230 ff. Originally published in 1923.

[23]"The Philosophy of Religion," in *WR?,* p. 56. Originally published as "Religionsphilosophie," *Die Philosophie in ihren Einzelgebieten,* II, ed. Max Dessior (Berlin: Ullstein, 1925), pp. 769-835. Tillich continued here that no matter how one understood the relation of subject and object in this act, whether as "a meaning-receiving act" (realistic epistemology), or "a meaning-bestowing act" (idealistic epistemology), or with him as "a meaning-fulfilling act," "spirit is always (the medium for) the actualization of meaning (*Sinnvollzug*)," and what the spirit intended "is a systematic interconnection of meaning." He argued that all acts, theoretical and practical, scientific and aesthetic, legal and social structures, have their unity in and share the common characteristic of meaning. Ibid., pp. 56-57. Meaning therefore is not to be understood intellectualistically and identified with theory.

[24]"Eschatology and History," *IH,* p. 273. Originally published as "Eschatologie und Geschichte," *Christliche Welt,* XLI, p. 22 (November 1927), pp. 1034-42.

[25]"The. of Cul.," *WR?,* p. 163.

[26]"Sozialismus," *GW,* II, p. 143.

[27]"Cl. St.," *GW,* II, pp. 175-192.

[28]Ibid., pp. 175-76.

[29]"Cl. St.," *GW,* II, p. 176.

[30]Ibid., pp. 176-77. In *RV* Tillich footnoted this statement, saying that this is the proper meaning of "'*servum arbitrium.*'" P. 299, fn. 6. This ultimate threat to human existence is also the meaning of "the human 'boundary situation.'" Cf. "The Protestant Message and the Man of Today," *PE,* pp. 195-99. Originally published in *RV.*

[31]Ibid., p. 177.

[32]Ibid., p. 178.

³³Ibid.

³⁴Ibid., p. 186.

³⁵Ibid., p. 187. It should be underscored here that socialism represents the threat in the *social* sphere, and it does so so profoundly that it is an indication of the human situation in general. Tillich recognized that the threat is present in other areas of life but considered socialism as the deepest expression of this brokenness. Cf. p. 182.

³⁶As noted in the first chapter this essay appeared in 1919. *Religionsphilosophie der Kultur: Zwei Entwuerfe von Gustav Radbruch und Paul Tillich* ("Uber die Idee einer Theologie der Kultur,") (Berlin: Reuther und Reichard, 1919), pp. 27-52. Also in *GW*, IX (1967), pp. 68-90. For a detailed treatment of this essay see Adams, Chapter III, "The Theology of Art and Culture," pp. 65-115. Adams in his book does not deal with Tillich's religious socialism. What follows is based largely on this early essay of Tillich, but is not intended as a complete handling of it, but only as an introduction to certain features of his theology of culture directly related to his religious socialism. It should be remembered that his theology of culture and his philosophy of religion are interdependent. Cf. "The Philosophy of Religion," *WR?*, p. 33.

³⁷Ibid., p. 162.

³⁸Ibid., pp. 162-63.

³⁹Ibid., p. 160. Cf. "The Philosophy of Religion," *WR?*, pp. 101, 126. In the latter place Tillich called religion "the homeless one."

⁴⁰Ibid., p. 181. Three years later Tillich ended another essay in a way that seemed to contradict his earlier ending or at least changed the emphasis: the philosophy of religion must perceive "that God and not religion is the beginning and end, the center of all things." "The Conquest of the Concept of Religion in the Philosophy of Religion," *WR?*, p. 154.

⁴¹For a discussion of the ambiguities of this crucial condept for Tillich see Adams (1965), esp. pp. 32-55; 262-65. Karl Barth's question appears to be the point: "Is it God that is spoken of here? Why this hide-and-seek with the frosty monster 'the unconditioned'?" "Critical and Positive Paradox," *The Beginnings of Dialectic Theology*, p. 147. Tillich's reply hardly clarifies the question: " . . . it is impossible for the one who is aware of this situation to speak of God as if this word could directly convey to him its essential richness. Therefore we must speak of the *unconditioned*. Not that this is a substitute expression; it is rather a key to open for oneself and for others the closed door to the holy of holies of the name "'God.'" "Answer to Karl Barth," ibid., p. 156.

⁴²"Christentum und Sozialismus (II)," *GW*, II, p. 31. The status of a personal God is in doubt in Tillich's theology. Cf. Adams, pp. 267-69.

⁴³"The Philosophy of Religion," *WR?*, p. 59.

⁴⁴"Church and Culture," *IH*, p. 235. Originally published as *Kirche und Kultur* (Tuebingen: Mohr, 1924). Cf. "The Philosophy of Religion," *WR?*, pp. 59-62, 72-76.

⁴⁵"Th. of Cul.," pp. 165-66. The *Inhalt* or content tended

to drop from his consideration. One might note a parallel omission in his religious socialism with its paucity of references to specific political actors and events. *Gehalt* is usually translated as "substance" or "import." A free translation might be "meaning-giving power." Cf. Robert Schlarlemann, "The Scope of Systematics: An Analysis of Tillich's Two Systems," *Journal of Religion,* p. 48 (1968), esp. pp. 146-49; and Adams, pp. 77-81.

[46] "The grasping of the essential elements form and substance is the presupposition of my polar and dynamic interpretation of the world." "Antwort," *Blaetter* V, 5/6, 20. Cf. *OB*, p. 28, for a description of his discovery of these fundamental categories. One of the values of Ulrich's book is that he analyzed Tillich on the basis of this ontological polarity. E.g., p. 23.

[47] "Th. of Cul.," p. 164.

[48] Ibid., p. 157.

[49] Ibid., pp. 157, 159.

[50] Ibid., p. 164.

[51] Ibid., pp. 165-68.

[52] Ibid., p. 180.

[53] Cf. "*Religious socialism is the attempt to understand socialism from a religious point of view and to bring about socialism on the basis of this understanding. At the same time it is an attempt to relate the religious principle to the social situation and thus to give it a new form.*" "Cl. St.," *GW*, II, p. 175. Also, cf. "Weiterbildung," *GW*, II, p. 121.

[54] "RS (II)," *Pol. Exp.*, p. 41.

[55] Ibid., p. 44.

[56] Ibid. Cf. "Karl Barth," (1926), *GW,* II, p. 187.

[57] Ibid.

[58] Ibid., p. 54.

[59] Ibid., p. 41.

[60] "Kairos," *PE,* p. 50.

[61] "RS (II)," p. 40.

[62] For examples see "Christentum und Sozialismus (I)," *GW*, II, p. 25; "Christentum und Sozialismus (II), *GW*, II, p. 30; "Kairos," *PE,* p. 52; "Cl. St.," *GW*, p. 176, etc.

[63] Review of Ernst Lohmeyer, *Soziale Fragen im Urchristentum, Archiv fuer Sozialwissenschaft und Sozialpolitik,* L (1923), p. 250.

[64] "RS (II)," p. 40.

[65] See below, Ch. 4, Sec. 3.

[66] *SD, GW,* II, p. 293. Cf. ibid., pp. 293-98, 349-54. For an early discussion see "Kirchenfrage," *GW*, II, pp. 17-18.

[67] "Cl. St.," *GW*, II, p. 179. Cf. the definitions given in "Kirche und Humanistische Gesellschaft," *GW*, IX (1967), p. 47; and in "RS (II)," *Pol. Exp.*, p. 42.

[68] Ibid., p. 180. Cf. "RS (II)," *Pol. Exp.*, p. 42; "Philosophy and Fate," *PE*, p. 9. For a ten-point description of the Christian substance of humanistic society see "Kirche," *GW*, IX, pp. 50-54.

[69] "RS (II)," *Pol. Exp.*, pp. 42-43. Cf. "Cl. St.," *GW*, II, pp. 180-81.

[70] Ibid., p. 43.

[71] Ibid. Cf. "Cl. St.," *GW*, II, pp. 181-82. In *SD* Tillich described socialism as a "counter-movement" against both bourgeois and feudal society. *GW*, II, p. 225.

[72] Ibid., p. 44.

[73] "Cl. St.," *GW*, II, p. 182.

[74] "Sozialismus," *GW*, II, p. 142.

[75] Ibid., p. 143.

[76] Cf. Gogarten's remarks in contrasting his starting point with Tillich's in 1924: "I . . . am seeking in terms of Jesus Christ, yes, more precisely, in Jesus Christ, the reality of the world and of life and the knowledge of it, while Tillich seeks for the knowledge of Jesus Christ, or, as he so characteristically says, of the Spirit of Christ, in the knowledge of the world and of life." "The Intellectual Situation of the Theologian," *The Beginnings of Dialectic Theology*, p. 162.

[77] "Cl. St.," *GW*, II, p. 187. Tillich illustrated this ambiguity in reference to science, which, contrary to its nature, is an object of faith among the proletariat, and to other aspects of socialism that will be discussed below.

[78] *SD*, *GW*, II, p. 310. Tillich had written something similar already in 1921. Masse und Gesit, *GW*, II, p. 83.

[79] Ibid., p. 285.

[80] "Zur Klaerung der religioesen Grundhaltung," *Blaetter*, III, pp. 12 (Dezember 1922), 47.

[81] Ibid.

[82] Ibid.

[83] Ibid.

[84] Ibid.

[85] Cf. "Rechtfertigung und Zweifel," *GW*, VIII (1970), pp. 85-100. "*Durchbruch*," the polarities of Law and Gospel, the "nevertheless," the message of grace, and the universal significance of justification were emphasized here by Tillich in the context of his theme of "justification and doubt." See esp. pp. 86-87, 99-100. The relationship of justification to Tillich's religious socialism has not been adequately noted.

[86] Cf. Ch. 2, p. 48; *OB*, pp. 74-81. "The substance of my religion is and remains Lutheran." Pp. 74-75. Note also, Adams, "Paul Tillich on Luther," in *Interpreters of Luther*, ed. Jaroslav Pelikan (Philadelphia: Fortress Press, 1968), pp. 304-44, and Carl E. Braaten, "Paul Tillich as a Lutheran Theologian," *Chicago Lutheran Theological Seminary Record*, Vol. 67, No. 3, (August 1962), pp. 32-42.

[87] Adams (1965), pp. 155, 164-66, 239-41, etc.
[88] "Basic Principles," *Pol. Exp.*, pp. 59-61.
[89] Ibid., pp. 60-61.
[90] Ibid., pp. 59-60.
[91] Ibid., p. 60. This theological concept was important for Tillich's concept of dialectic. See below, Ch. 5, Sec. 2.
[92] Ibid., pp. 60-61.
[93] Ibid., p. 61. Cf. from here his discussion of Ritschl's view of the kingdom, "Albrecht Ritschl," *GW*, XII, p. 157.
[94] *Masse und Geist*, *GW*, II, p. 77, also 72-73. Note that the holy *Sein* and *Sollen* meet in the masses, p. 89. This was important for his view of the proletariat.
[95] "Basic Principles," p. 96.
[96] Ibid., p. 92. See below, Ch. 5, Sec. 2.
[97] Ibid., p. 86. Tillich continued: "Belief in the Kairos is the expression of the consciousness of existing in that fate and of being touched by a new breakthrough of the Unconditional. All rational work in theory and practice can have no other meaning than to give expression to this import in every sphere of life."
[98] "Weiterbildung," *GW*, II, p. 128.
[99] "Kairos," *PE*, pp. 42, 47.
[100] Ibid., p. 38.
[101] "Church and Culture," *IH*, p. 234.
[102] "Weiterbuilung," *GW*, II, p. 127.
[103] Ibid. Note the parallel of import and form, grace and law.
[104] "Basic Principles," *Pol. Exp.*, pp. 66-88. See this section for an extensive discussion of Tillich's dialectical criticism of sacramental and rational positions and of his own constructive theonomous proposals.
[105] Ibid., p. 66. Note later comment on his concept of "demonic" in this essay, "Antwort," p. 19. Cf. his later essay, "The Demonic," *IH*, pp. 77-122. Originally published as *Das Daemonische* (Tuebingen: Mohr, 1926).
[106] Ibid., p. 67.
[107] Ibid., p. 69.
[108] *Masse und Geist*, *GW*, II, p. 77.
[109] Ibid., p. 70.
[110] "The Interpretation of History and the Idea of Christ," *IH*, p. 264; "Christentum und Idealismus," *GW*, XII, p. 234.
[111] *GW*, II, pp. 234-63. Cf. his counterpart to this book, "Protestantismus und politische Romantik," *GW*, II, pp. 209-18.
[112] Ibid., pp. 264-305.
[113] Ibid., pp. 306-65.

[114] Ibid., pp. 219-20.

[115] Ibid., p. 225. In *SD,* in contrast to most of his earlier writings, Tillich highlights the category of "political."

[116] Ibid., p. 226. Characteristically, Tillich defined man in terms of his ability to make and receive demands and to raise questions, facts that show he is not one with himself. Cf. Ch. 3, p. 8; "The Protestant Message and the Man of Today," *PE,* p. 197; "Gegenwart und Religion," *Neuwerk,* XI, p. 1 (1929), 2-3; "Das Fragen," *Der Staat seid Ihr* (1931).

[117] Ibid.

[118] Ibid., p. 227.

[119] Ibid. The German word is *"Geworfensein,"* and comes from Martin Heidegger.

[120] Ibid. The words quoted are those of Anaximander as translated from the Greek by T. V. Smith in *From Thales to Plato* (Chicago, 1956), p. 6.

[121] Ibid., pp. 227-28.

[122] Ibid., p. 228.

[123] Ibid.

[124] Ibid. For the meaning of a "broken form of myth" or a non-literal view see "The Religious Symbol," *Journal of Religion,* II, p. 1 (Summer 1940), 24. The essay was originally written in 1928.

[125] Ibid., pp. 228-29.

[126] Ibid., p. 229.

[127] Ibid. Recognition for Tillich was the ground for justice and power. Cf. "RS (II)," *Pol. Exp.,* p. 53.

[128] Ibid. On the soil of the myth of origin, "'might makes right'; and this is the only possible ethic on the soil of a consistent myth of origin." P. 240.

[129] Ibid. The unconditional demand of justice is the fulfillment of being; the "ought" is not something detached and strange to human existence, but is given ontological status in the essence of man. This being, however, is not the being of empirical existence, which is ambiguous, but the true being. Thus he agrees with Plato, "'The good is beyond being.'" P. 240. In later years he will maintain the idea that value and obligation are gounded in the "is," the essence of man. Cf. Tillich, "Is a Science of Human Values Possible?," *New Knowledge in Human Values,* ed. Abraham H. Maslow (New York: Harper and Brothers, 1958), pp. 189-96. Also the discussion in *Interrogations* over the question of "Being and Value," pp. 394-99.

[130] Ibid., pp. 229-30.

[131] Tillich's description of the two roots in the companion essay to *SD,* "Protestantismus und politische Romantik," makes this relationship clearer: *"Political romanticism is more than an historically limited political theory. It is a basic political attitude, indeed a human possibility in general.* One can distinguish two basic human attitudes, the one grounded in his creatureliness, the other grounded in his humanness. The first

is the direction to the '*whence*,' the second the direction to the '*whither*.' Man knows himself *born*; and the question about the whence is the question about the bearing ground; and man knows himself *demanded*; and the question about the whither is the question about the goal set for him." *GW*, II, p. 209. Here the relationship of the whence and the whither is the same as the ontological relationship of import and form and the theological relationship of Gospel and Law. The question I raise here and in the text relates to Tillich's claim that the second root is of a "higher range" than the first. Does this mean that form and Law are elevated over import and Gospel? It seems to mean this in part, a requirement of the political situation. However, why is it that the second root has to be identified with the demand and the first root with being born? To me, this seems arbitrary to restrict the sense of being supported, of grace, to the past, to the question of whence. In the Christian message, the question of "whither" or "For what end?" is answered not only by demand but also by promise. Cannot one be carried by promise? When Tillich futurizes his categories, that seems to me to disrupt his previous divisions. Perhaps in part Tillich realized this in *SD*, although it was never clear. The concept of promise began to be more prominent at about the time expectation did. Could it have been that closer attention to this central Biblical and reformation idea might have caused a shift in some of his categories?

[132]"*Ursprung*" or "origin" has a broad meaning in *SD*. At times it refers to "powers of origin," such as soil, blood, and group expressed in "myths of origin," in other words, values of the past which have a value, but one limited by the demand of justice. At other times it refers to the vital, non-rational center of man as well as to what might be called the essence of man. Because of the prophets it also means creation. Perhaps Tillich did not use it later because of its rather all-encompassing meaning. For his discussion of this concept see esp. *SD*, *GW*, II, pp. 234-39.

[133]*SD*, *GW*, II, pp. 239-40.

[134]Ibid., p. 241.

[135]Ibid.

[136]Ibid.

[137]Ibid., pp. 241-42.

[138]Ibid., p. 242.

[139]Ibid., p. 244.

[140]Ibid., pp. 283-85. "Conflict" (*Widerstreit*) had a special meaning for Tillich and was contrasted with "contradiction" (*Widerspruch*). Political romanticism was involved in a contradiction because it sought to make the first root of political thinking the only one, but socialism was involved in an inner conflict or antagonism, that is, a tension arising from the subject itself, which could only be solved by the matter coming to a new form, not by a subjective decision for or against, as was required with the contradiction of political romanticism. P. 281.

[141]Ibid., p. 283.

[142] Ibid.

[143] Ibid., pp. 283-84.

[144] Ibid., p. 309. In this section, "The Elements of the Socialist Principle," Tillich set down his own position. Pp. 309-12.

[145] Ibid., p. 310.

[146] Cf. "Protestantism as a Critical and Creative Principle," *Pol. Exp.*, pp. 26-27 for his first discussion on expectation. First published as "Der Protestantismus als kritisches und restaltendes Prinzip," in *Kairos: II* (Darmstadt: Reichl, 1929), pp. 3-37. Also, "The State as Expectation and Demand," *Pol. Exp.*, pp. 97-98. First published, "Der Staat als Erwartung und Forderung,: in *Religioese Verwirklichung* (Berlin, 1930). Cf. "RS (II)," *Pol. Exp.*, P. 50.

[147] "PPPS," pp. 18-19 Cf. *PE*, pp. 170-71.

[148] Ibid.

[149] Ibid.

[150] Ibid., pp. 19-20. Cf. *PE*, pp. 171-72.

[151] *SD, GW,* II, pp. 310-11. Tillich's "phenomenology of expectation" has parallels in Wolfhart Pannenberg's anthropology of hope. See Pannenbert, "Openness to the World and Openness to God," *What is Man?* (Philadelphia: Fortress Press, 1970), pp. 1-13.

[152] Ibid., p. 312.

[153] Ibid., p. 319. Tillich's discussion of expectation is a discussion of freedom. In *OB* he wrote, " . . . a doctrine of man must be a philosophy of freedom . . . " Pp. 82-83. Cf. "The Idea and Ideal of Personality," *PE*, p. 116.

[154] Ibid., p. 311. Cf. pp. 242-43.

[155] Ibid. Theodor Strohm has used Tillich's concept to examine critically Gogarten's theology. See Strohn, *Theologie im Schatten politischer Romantik* (Muenchen: Chr. Kaiser Verlag, 1970).

[156] Ibid.

[157] Ibid., p. 312.

[158] Ibid.

[159] Ibid.

[160] Ibid.

[161] This question will be taken up again in Ch. 6, Sec. 4.

[162] See below, Ch. 5, esp. Sec. 2. The three sections are entitled: "Expectation and Action," "Expectation and Origin," and "The Prophetic and Rational Character of Expectation." *SD, GW,* II, pp. 312-20.

[163] *SD, GW,* II, p. 310.

[164] Tillich used the word in 1919 to suggest that the ethic of love had "a greater *affinity*" for some social orders than others. "Kirchenfrage," p. 14.

[165] Cf. Landauer, "Socialism is a system of communal (or social) ownership of the means of production, established for the purpose of making (or keeping) the distribution of income, wealth, opportunity, and economic power as nearly equal as possible." P. 5. Tillich would, I believe, accept this definition, although he would perhaps not make equality the basic value. Cf. Robert L. Heilbroner, *An Inquiry into the Human Prospect* (New York: Norton, 1974), p. 71. Joseph A. Schumpeter, *Capitalism, Socialism and Democracy,* Third Edition (New York: Harper Torchbooks, 1950), p. 167.

[166] "RS (II)," *Pol. Exp.,* p. 49. For a fuller discussion of Tillich's economic proposals see "Basic Principles," *Pol. Exp.,* pp. 78-80; and esp. *SD, GW,* II, pp. 357-63.

[167] "Sozialismus," *GW,* II, pp. 139-40. Tillich's discussion of life here reflected his concept of dialectic. See below, Ch. 5, Sec. 1.

[168] Ibid., pp. 140-41.

[169] Ibid., p. 150.

[170] The strong existential character of Tillich's religious socialism was present throughout. For a few examples, see "Christentum und Sozialismus (I)," *GW,* II, p. 21; "Christentum und Sozialismus (II)," *GW,* II, p. 29; *SD, GW,* II, p. 230. Also, note Adams' "Introduction" to *Pol. Exp.* where the social existential nature of Tillich's religious socialism is made clear. Pp. vi-xx.

[171] "Christentum, Sozialismus und Nationalismus," *GW,* XIII, pp. 162-63. Tillich wrote that "the spirit of the old Jewish prophets" appeared in Marx in the nineteenth century. "Kairos," *Kairos I* (Darmstadt: Otto Reichl Verlag, 1926), p. 4.

[172] *SD, GW,* II, p. 331.

CHAPTER 4

TRANSFORMING HISTORICAL MATERIALISM

In Chapter 3 Tillich's understanding of socialism was outlined. There it was seen that Tillich, in accord with other Marxist-influenced socialists, understood socialism to be a socio-political position whose bearer is the industrial proletariat, but, in contrast to Marx and his followers, he discerned in this movement a transcendent meaning whose import is prophetic. Tillich knew that his theological interpretation of socialism, with its elements of continuity and discontinuity with traditional understandings, had to be developed in relation to Marxism, that is, "in relation to the first and basic attempt at a conceptual exposition of socialism."[1] In this chapter and the next, Tillich's position on socialist theory will be probed.

Marxist philosophy or dialectical materialism is a unit, but for the sake of discussion it will be broken down into two parts: historical materialism and historical dialectic. In *The Socialist Decision* Tillich himself did this, calling the two "the central problems of Marxism."[2] In the present chapter Tillich's interpretation of historical materialism is studied, and in Chapter 5 historical dialectic will be the theme for consideration.

This chapter begins with a discussion of the meaning of historical materialism for Tillich and his dialectical attitude toward it, a topic that leads to a study of aspects of his anthropology that are crucial for his critical affirmation of materialistic motifs. In Section Three Tillich's understanding of the relationship between spirit and social situation, particularly in regard to the concept of ideology, is investigated further. Finally, I consider Tillich's outlook on Marx's interpretation of the modern era.

Materialism: The "Matter" of History

Karl Marx was a materialist, and since him materialism has been an integral part of socialist theory.[3] Its meaning, however, has often been unclear, even among socialists, and it has been a source of deep controversy between socialists and non- and anti-socialists, especially among church people. Moreover, Tillich found it to be a significant contribution to intellectual history and to the socialist movement. Because of its importance as well as its ambiguity, it is necessary to analyze Tillich's interpretation of Marx's materialism and his own conception of historical materialism.

Because of its various conflicting meanings, Tillich had continually to dispute its distorted forms in order to clarify what materialism actually means for socialism. A recurring theme in his writings, literally from the first to the last, is his attack on these misconceptions. One of his main targets is "ethical" or "practical" materialism, that is, a mind-set that "is turned exclusively to material things, that diverts men from all heights and ideals and leads to the substitution of the most base interests."[4] With such an attitude, he insisted, historical materialism has nothing to do.[5]

More importantly, Tillich sought to prevent historical materialism from being confused with "ontological" or "metaphysical" materialism, a task made more difficult because of the mixing of the two among socialists themselves. Socialism, he wrote, has never produced its own ontology but has taken over "the most spiritless of all ontologies, natural scientific materialism." Although "Marx's historical materialism is something entirely different from natural scientific materialism," Tillich saw Marx and especially Engels as partly responsible for its entry into socialism;[6] and the "vulgar Marxism" of recent decades, influenced by bourgeois thinkers like Ernst Haeckel, had spread it among the masses.[7]

He described mataphysical materialism as "the technical-mathematical explanation of the world by means of natural science, the rational conception of reality as a machine with eternally constant laws of movement manifest in an infinitely recurring and predictable natural process." The mentality that has created this conceptual framework, continued Tillich, has overlooked that it is a human product and has made itself a part of the machine. With this reification, warned Tillich, "the materialistically minded among the socialists," who are "heirs of a powerful philosophy of history" and "bearers of the present consciousness of history," threaten to replace the possibility of meaningful history with a meaningless natural process, since a materialistic interpretation of history in this sense is a contradiction in itself.[8]

Tillich considered vulgar Marxism to be "the shabby, decrepit garment of the bourgeois-capitalist attitude" which expresses the spirit of an age in which all reality comes to be an empty machine.[9] He doubted if any "modern man" takes it seriously as a philosophy of life, and he noted that Marx had rejected this type of materialism in his "Theses against Feuerbach."[10] He remarked that the deepest spirits in socialism had always resisted this corruption, whose spiritual death lay in the past, and then added, "Religious socialism makes direct efforts in wide circles of workers to bring to recognition its passing. In so doing it knows that it stands very much closer to the genuine spirit of Marx than the self-placed protectors of Marxism."[11] Tillich in his open letter to Hirsch in 1934 commented that his critical battle against metaphysical materialism had no parallel in Hirsch's enthusiastic endorsement of National Socialism.[12]

Socialist materialism is neither practical nor metaphysical but historical materialism. Having repudiated the former two, Tillich was prepared to assert the qualified validity of the latter.

Tillich affirmed the materialistic form of the Feuerbach-Marxist anthropology, including the use of the term "*historical materialism*," on the basis of "the seriousness of its anti-idealistic protest."[13] For Christianity, he wrote, the opposition of idealism and materialism is finally "an indifferent, non-serious matter," for God stands over the world as a whole directing both nature and spirit, matter and the ideal. Furthermore, he suggested, Marxism, in demonstrating that people are bound to material conditions, has, in spite of its poor ontology, represented "a Christian perception in opposition to idealism: the wretchedness of the actual situation, the distance of God from history."[14] Tillich considered it a judgment on idealism that it had totally denied the reality from which socialism was born, that it had not been able to gain any kind of influence in the proletarian movement in the nineteenth century, and that it is still misused by conservatives and liberals as an ideology.[15]

First of all, then, historical materialism is for Tillich a "*Kampfbegriff*," a polemical concept, developed in opposition to historical idealism and intent on exposing it as an ideology. In rejecting the notion of "a directing reason in history," and in searching for "the real causes of the historical process," historical materialism found the final cause of "human nature and its drive determinations." Marx, in contrast to Feuerbach, identified human nature "as a historical reality which is indissolubly bound to a given social and economic context," and not as a universal, supra-historical essence. Therefore, he summarized, "*The 'matter' of history, according to the materialistic conception, is therefore people who seek to satisfy their needs in common production*." The subject of history is not "an all-embracing reason" but "socially producing man."[16]

Tillich noted that how one understands the needs that are to be satisfied and the consequent direction of the common production process depends on the image of man present in the theory. Nevertheless, he agreed that every image has to reckon with the fact that "the immediate vital needs on which man's very existence depends are usually the most pressing. Were it otherwise, the survival of the human race down to the present would be inexplicable." If one calls a theory materialistic that asserts the urgency of these needs, then, proposed Tillich, every interpretation of man and history that deals with reality would have to be materialistic.[17] In stating the meaning of materialism in a broad but careful way Tillich has pointed to an obvious but important truth in it.

A doctrine becomes materialistic in an untrue and dogmatic sense, he argued, only when it denies that in many specific instances the urgency of immediate vital needs is overcome, and when it fails to see that even these needs are colored by their relationship to other needs and by the historical situation in which they come to be. Tillich found the reason for this statement in his anthropology: "*Man is always man, even in the way in which his most vital needs are expressed* . . . ." He is not to be thought of as an animal on his lowest level on which everything else is built, insisted Tillich.[18]

> The "matter" of history is man, socially producing man. But this means real man, not an artificial construct, not a combination of animality and spirituality which does not show human traits in either the one or the other dimension.[19]

Negatively, historical materialism is a well-directed protest against historical idealism; positively, it pinpoints the "material" of history, socially producing man, or, as he called it in another article, historical materialism is concerned with the "substratum" of history, the basis of historical change.[20] The proper theme of Marxist materialism is people producing socially, with emphasis on people, on activity--satisfying needs--and on its social nature--in common production.[21] In this broad sense Tillich is a materialist, but he is emphatic that the nature of the actor and the activity be properly perceived, a subject to be picked up again in the next section.

Tillich recognized that this initial description of historical materialism, though basic, is not sufficient. Marx's materialism goes further and "*asserts the primacy of the economy over other human functions. It makes the economic process the fundamental factor of historical development . . . . Materialism is economism.*" He remarked that hardly any other notion in Marxism has been so sharply attacked as this one since it appears to be a rejection of "all so-called higher values" and of "all culture and religion."[22] Although, as will be seen below, he was not satisfied with the way Marx had stated his position, he did not believe this idea led to these results. As he interpreted it, the economic interpretation of history discloses the inseparable relationship that exists between creations of the spirit and the social situation.

Already in 1919 Tillich found value in Marx's perception:

> The Marxist interpretation of history, which is rightly called economic and falsely called materialistic, contains in and of itself neither materialism nor a rejection of the life of the spirit, but rather merely asserts a causative connection between the economic basis and the spiritual construction of culture, an insight which rightly used is methodologically extremely fruitful and most rigorously must be protected from any confusion with metaphysical materialism.[23]

Throughout his writings Tillich reaffirmed this position. "If his formulations are still imperfect," he wrote, "the insight itself has become a component that cannot be lost for all deep spiritual scientitic considerations."[24] Since the time of Marx, he did not think it permissible to speak of the spiritual situation without speaking of the social situation: "The connection of the two is much too close regardless of what categories under which it is considered."[25] In his open letter Tillich criticized Hirsch for writing about the "'filth of economic materialism.'" The choice of words, responded Tillich, indicates not only Hirsch's suppression of a matter for which he is not inwardly prepared, but also shows "the simple lack of knowledge that economic materialism is a method of research" which "cannot be avoided in any deep, penetrating investigation."[26] He expressed shock that a serious scientific book on the present social sitaution could have been written without a sociological analysis of the groups and classes that bear definite tendencies. The reason for this failure, concluded Tillich, is that "sociology is one of the strongest weapons against an unbroken enthusiasm."[27]

Tillich consistently applied Marx's methodological insight to his own work. In *The Socialist Decision,* for example, he analyzed "the principle of political romanticism," "the bourgeois principle," and "the socialist principle" in relationship to the groups that carry these principles. Since the roots of political thinking are not ideas but human existence, he wrote in the "Introduction," "political thinking is a necessary expression of a political being, of a social situation," and therefore to understand political thinking one has to know the social situation from which it comes.[28] From this it is clear that Tillich's use of "expression" in describing socialism is appropriated from Marx's insight.

Tillich's appreciation of Marx's materialism was based on a "loose" reading of "economism." He found that Marx's insight demonstrates the reciprocal bond between the social situation and the spirit, but he did not follow Marxists (and in part Marx himself) in drawing a "tight" and determinative relationship between the economy and culture. Tillich's reasons for rejecting a narrow economic determinism are evident in his discussions of the well-known substructure-superstructure image which Marx on occasion used to describe the connection between the economic foundation of society and its spiritual construction.[29]

Tillich thought that the image had been distorted by the inappropriate manner (by means of bourgeois thinking) by which it had been implemented. He found it "totally erroneous" to interpret the image "to mean that an independent quantity 'spirit' is causally dependent on another independent quantity 'economy.'" He objected first to the use of causal language which he noted is inadequate both to the image--the foundation of a building does not *cause* its structure--and to the reality-- the economy does not *cause* the spirit. Moreover, he asserted, "the very positing of the two independent quantities, 'economy' and 'spirit,' must be dismissed as unthinkable." The economy was not a "think," but a "complex, infinitely variegated reality," which, according to Tillich, has to be considered in relation to the quality of needs and to the techniques, social circumstances, and aim and direction of production. Therefore he set down this requirement: "*All aspects of human existence must be considered along with it when it is to be considered.* It cannot be isolated and made the cause of that which is intrinsic to itself, and without which it cannot be conceived."[30] In other words, the economy too is spirit.

Likewise Tillich maintained that spirit can not be isolated in an undialectical fashion. It is "inherently inconceivable" to make a quantity "spirit" an effect of the economy. "*Spirit is never something in itself; it is always the spirit of something: the spirit of a being that comes to itself in spirit.*" To make being the cause and spirit the effect loses the unity of being and consciousness, a connection Marx saw "most clearly and emphasized most sharply."[31] Tillich appealed to Marx against the Marxist to support his own criterion, the human being as a unity.

On this basis Tillich found the metaphor of "reflection" to be inadequate in clarifying the relationship between the spirit and the economy, since this image assumed "that there is an entity that is what it is, quite apart from its reflection." A person is independent of the physical mirror in which he sees himself, but human existence is never independent of human consciousness, he explained. "*Social existence apart from social consciousness is a meaningless concept,* for the being of society is inseparably bound to consciousness."[32]

Tillich had in effect undercut the philosophical value of Marx's architectural image. He challenged, convincingly, I believe, the idea that the economy is the most fundamental factor in historical development in a simple and immediate fashion and that social, political, cultural, and religious life are not more than by-products of it.[33] He recognized that the intertwined realities of the economy and the spirit cannot be abstractly divorced from one another, made into discrete factors, and placed in a cause-effect relationship; the economy itself is a complex reality that is always dependent upon and being influenced by other aspects of societal life, and the spirit is not so autonomous that it can be either the cause or the effect of the economy. Tillich sought a dialectical not a causal relationship between the human and his world and among the various aspects of life, and he opposed the implicit anthropology of economism with his own conception: the subject of history is the socially producing man, but this means that creature who is always both being and consciousness.[34]

Tillich first discussed Marx's picture of the substructure-superstructure in an essay from 1924, a discussion that reveals some other of his differences with it.[35] He wrote that he would keep the image temporarily, but he wanted to change it in two ways. It is incorrect, he stated, that the economic basis, severed from the other levels, has a purely natural causal relationship to them; instead it stands in immediate relationship to the whole structure. What bears everything is the "idea of building, or better, the drive for creation (*Gestaltungstrieb*) breaking forth from the depths" which expresses itself just as much in art as in science or the economy. Therefore, in place of "mechanical causality" he substituted the notion of "gestalt," maintaining the economic as the "weighty substructure," and then carrying the image "further up and down":[36]

> Down insofar as we have the substructure and with it the whole construction rooted in the basic biological drives, in the immediate will to live, which is always simultaneously the will to power and the will to abandonment. Every gestalt comes from this mother soil of the unfathomable (*Unergruendlichen*). But it is a gestalt only because a final grasping for meaning comes to expression in it. The direct turning to this final meaning of life, the longing to grasp and to realize it, is religion, whose symbol in our image is the crowning roof, on the one hand, and, on the other hand, the tower pointing to the height that is elevated over every gestalt and every building.[37]

The right to develop Marx's ideas in this way, suggested Tillich, comes from Marx himself who went beyond the idea of an individual building to the historical dialectic, a conception that makes it obvious that the "static picture of a building" has only a preliminary right.[38]

Tillich's uneasiness with Marx's metaphor is evident also in this somewhat playful expansion of the metaphor. He recognized that his corrections and additions did not really alter the fundamental fault of the image--its static, layered view of human activity. His changes do, however, demonstrate his differences with orthodox Marxism and with Marx (in spite of his attempt to appeal to Marx). For Tillich activity directed toward satisfying economic needs is in itself too restricted to be the foundation for understanding human life and history, for it comprehends neither the depths, the will to live, nor the heights, the quest for ultimate meaning. Once again Tillich posits an opposing anthropology, one he believed more adequate in comprehending the full character of the socially producing man, and here too meaning is the decisive characteristic of human being, meaning inherently united with man's biological nature.

Tillich's socialist thinking was significantly influenced by Marx's historical materialism, but he did not accept it uncritically. He instead tried to clarify its interpretation and give it a more solid footing in a view of human activity that he believed does justice to life's fullness and complexity. In the process he said "no" to practical and metaphysical materialism, "yes" to historical materialism's protest against idealism and to its insight that the socially producing man is the "matter" of history, "yes" to its perception of the inseparable connection between the social situation and the life of the spirit, and "no" to the undialectical execution of this idea by economism, as well as "no" to the image of man present in a strict economic interpretation. As seen throughout this discussion, Tillich's understanding of human being is crucial for his perspective, and so in the next section this theme will be probed further.

The Unity of Being and Consciousness

The concern of the following pages is Tillich's understanding of man as it relates to his consideration of historical materialism. Some aspects of his anthropology have already been discussed: man's distinction from nature, the two roots of political thinking, the threat and the support of human life, and human existence in meaning. Here I am interested in

Tillich's assertion that man is a unity of being and consciousness, since from this point he "seeks a basis that lies beyond the opposition between the materialistic and the idealistic conceptions of man."[39]

In structuring his argument according to the two roots of human existence in *The Socialist Decision*, Tillich was attempting to bring a new interest in the anthropological question into a Marxist setting.[40] He believed that such an effort is essential to get below external appearances, but he recognized that anthropology is a very dubious concern for many Marxists. Their mistrust, he noted, has its origins in historical materialism, that is, in Marx's rejection of Feuerbach's "picture of 'man in general'" in favor of "the actual man determined by his social and class situation."[41] But, protested Tillich,

> Even the class-determined man is a man, that is, an essence that has a history, lives in society, can be split into classes, experiences "de-humanization" and "thingification," and can fight for a social order in which his destiny, a "real humanism," is fulfilled.[42]

To accept this statement means to presuppose "structures," structures which must be investigated since they throw light on social movements, just as every conception of man stands in closest connection with the concrete social situation. Tillich considered that there should be a "reciprocal illumination of *human existence and social situation*, and he asked that *The Socialist Decision* be understood in this light.[43]

Tillich rejected the argument that one should remain with the historical reality and not demonstrate the roots of the political thinking. Advocates of this position, wrote Tillich, consider the roots unknowable and without reality, assert that apart from the historical reality there are no independent, original elements (*Urelemente*) of human existence, and believe man is what he is in the social situation and nothing more. Tillich saw a contradiction in this attitude as soon as words like man, history, and social situation are used, since these words are to apply to the whole history of man and therefore themselves are not bound to an historical moment.[44]

> It is not necessary therefore to speak of an "eternal essence" of man. But it is necessary to conceive the encountering, historical man as a unity, for otherwise nothing at all could be said, not even about the most concrete historical appearance. Above all, every norm would be abolished in the process.[45]

Tillich did not find representatives of such "radical historical thinking" consistent. The passion with which they judge capitalism and the manner in which they evaluate all of history as a history of class struggles demonstrate that "the consciousness of a norm" has not at all disappeared but that they possess a picture of human society in which human existence comes to a better fulfillment than in the present. He saw that they too, even if they do not intend to do so, affirm "a suprahistorical moment": "human existence is one to be fulfilled."[46]

No theory, then, is without anthropological presuppositions. Anti-anthropological thinking is contradictory since an anthropology is required to deny its necessity. Even the Marxist insistence on understanding human existence in the concrete social situation does not do away with the question, "Who is man?," even if the question is raised in a different fashion. Tillich rightly acknowledged the unavoidability of at least making assumptions about man that are more than applicable to the immediate situation, and he has given some good reasons and an incisive demonstration for deliberately examining the "structures" of human being. Any answer to such an undertaking is necessarily provisional, but this recognition does not eliminate its importance.

Tillich clearly differed on this point from Marx who considered "the essence of man" to be "the ensemble of social relationships."[47] Tillich has shown that this is not enough,[48] but agreement with Tillich's criticism does not necessarily mean acceptance of his own conclusions as the answer to Marx's challenge. There are in his anthropology strong deductive, non-historical elements which tend to gloss over historical distances.[49] Is it really true that all political thinking is derived from the two roots of human existence? What historical particularities are covered over in embracing both the eighth century prophets and modern socialism under the same concept of prophetic? Tillich has revealed some striking similarities, but he has not said enough about the differences. Too often his thinking on man appears to be a sophisticated juggling of his ontological categories import and form, and anything that does not fit into one or the other disappears. This is not meant to discredit his often perceptive anthropology, but it is meant to caution that the concreteness of historical existence is not always fully appreciated.

There is one point (and there are others) where Tillich's anthropology has trans-historical and trans-sociological significance. This element is what Tillich called "the dual starting point" for his conception of man: "*the unity of that which is vital and spiritual* in man, and the simultaneous *disruption of that unity* which is the source of the threat to man's being." Man for Tillich is one, a unity of "being and meaning," "of body and soul," and therefore "the meaning of his existence cannot be separated from the meaning of his bodily existence." In this, he wrote, "religious socialism represents the original intention of the Old and New Testaments."[50] In his encounter with historical materialism Tillich is led to re-emphasize an often forgotten or corrupted Biblical notion and from there to re-evaluate the meaning of historical materialism.[51]

Standing behind Tillich's conception is the belief in the goodness of the whole created world. "Belief in creation includes the belief that matter, even earthly matter, is not something opposed to God." Since it is God's creation and perfect throughout, "it is not necessary to flee from matter in order to reach God. A resounding Yes is pronounced upon the entire creation."[52] Therefore the human being as a whole is good, and there is no need to escape from the matter he is, but there is reason to evaluate the matter and himself positively. "The victory of Christianity is the victory of the idea that the world is a divine creation over the belief in the resisting power of an eternal matter."[53]

Tillich's conception concerns the whole person. There is in man no body-soul dualism, and the disruption of his existence does not divide him into two parts. "The body is no 'prison' but rather a 'temple,' and it is not the body that struggles against the spirit but rather 'the flesh'--a term that signifies the pride of the spirit as well as the lusts of the body," wrote Tillich in reference to the Biblical teaching. This means that the whole person is under the judgment and promise of God. "The Protestant principle, which exempts no aspect of human existence form the judgment that it is involved in contradiction with itself, considers the whole man, man as a unity of body and soul, in his relationship with the transcendent."[54]

As was noted previously, this unity is important for Tillich's interpretation of the proletarian situation, a situation "in which man is radically threatened" because "the shattering of the meaning of life in the vital dimension amounts to the shattering of the meaning of life in general."[55] Quite consistently, he rejected the religious attempt to save the soul and leave the body to perdition. There is no validity, he wrote, in the demand of the church and idealism that compensation be offered in a spiritual world divorced from the meaninglessness of the bodily existence of the proletariat.[56]

The conviction that man is best understood as a unity also provides Tillich with the rationale for incorporating within his own thought a Marxist understanding of the relationship between the spirit and the social situation. Political thinking, he wrote, cannot be derived from a pure movement of ideas, from religious-moral demands, or from philosophical judgments, but it "emerges from man in his unity. It is rooted simultaneously in being and consciousness, more exactly, in their indissoluble unity." Therefore, to understand a system of political thinking one has to uncover the human and social existence in which it is based, that is, "the interaction of drives and interests, pressures and strivings which constitute social existence." This insistence, however, does not mean one can make political thinking a by-product of social existence, for "*human and social existence in each of its elements down to the most primitive impulses is formed through consciousness*." Any attempt to dissolve this connection on either the one or the other side, warned Tillich, bypasses "the first and most important essential characteristic of man," the unity of being and consciousness.[57]

Man is a unity, or as he sometimes called him, a "gestalt," a living structural whole. The human being for Tillich is a living structure "who cannot be composed from its parts but can only grow forth out of an original, creative source"' life is the presupposition for the processes which go on within it.[58] Tillich never divided man into two, but within his unity he always distinguished between being and consciousness or the vital and the spiritual. "Vitality" is a prominent feature of his anthropology, and he believed that a proper understanding of the vital center of human existence would have far-reaching consequences for socialist theory.

In his elaboration of Marx's image of the substructure-superstructure (see above, p. 154), Tillich carried the image "further down" into "the basic biological drives, in the immediate will to live, which is always simultaneously the will to power and the will to abandonment." This in brief is what Tillich meant by the vital center, by being, or by life. "Life," he wrote, "originates on a level which is 'deeper' than the Cartesian duality of *Cogitatio* and *extensio* ('thought' and 'extension')," a level for which one has to use indirect, symbolic terms.[59] The vital refers to the source of life, or, "the absolute giveness, the underivability, the inconstruability of the living structure, the non-rational ground on which this structure rests and which comes to expression in the demonic-divine polarity of conflict and social integration, of the will-to-power and love."[60] Frequently in this context Tillich spoke of *Maechtigkeit*, the "inner powerfulness" or "intrinsic power" of being.[61]

"Everything real," asserted Tillich, "is the individually creative synthesis of universal form and of the irrational ground of nature."[62] This irrational ground, "the substratum of the realization of all forms," was conceived by Tillich (as made evident in the previous paragraph) as a "duality": as love, *Eros*, "as a drive to become one with being (*das Seiende*)," "as will to abandonment"; or as power, *Macht*, "as a drive to transcend being," as "will to self-assertion." These "polar opposites" are "basically identical substrata of all creative form-giving power," and therefore they are "the bearers of divine and demonic ecstasy." For some, like Plato, mystics, and romantics, love was considered the more worthy primordial element, and for others, like voluntarists, the philosophers of nature of the Renaissance, Boehme, Schelling, Schopenhauer, and Nietzsche, the will-to-power was most clearly recognized. Tillich saw both present in every creative reality, although one usually is more clearly recognizable.[63]

According to Tillich's ontological framework, the "dominion of the pure form" wants to eliminate both love and power. "The perfected autonomy of form would create a rational reality without the erotic and the dynamic. It would be without the demonic, but also without divinity." Such a reality, however, is not possible since these two powers are "the real in every actuality, forming its ground and abyss."[64] Tillich interpreted the bourgeois era as one of the dominion of pure form and as the attempt to drive out the erotic and the dynamic, and situation that leads to the rise of new demonic elements in the emptiness of the autonomous form. This situation defined for him the "struggle of religious socialism," which both defends autonomy against sacramental demonry and seeks recognition of a sacred power and love.[65]

In *The Socialist Decision* (where the focus was more directly anthropological) Tillich's concern with the "problem of life"[66] found form in the concept of the "powers of origin." The original mythical powers of origin were described by him as the soil, blood, and the social group, all of which generate and support life.[67] These powers, which refer to the first root of political thinking, it will be recalled, are shattered in their dominion by the prophets, but only with the rise of autonomous consciousness is every tie "to the father" loosened. Although the Enlightenment suppressed these "primordial" powers which preceded rational analysis, they did not eradicate them, wrote Tillich, naming "*eros, fate,* and *death*" as psychic powers that had resisted Enlightenment rationality.[68] In its attack on all ties to the origin, the bourgeois era represented for Tillich a time of "*thingification*" (*Verdinglichung*), a time in which nature, humankind, and society are reduced to things in order to be rationally controlled.[69]

The socialist understanding of human existence was deeply influenced by the bourgeois principle's rejection of the powers of origin. "The inner conflict of the socialist conception of man," wrote Tillich, is based on the fact that socialism, in order to struggle against the pre-bourgeois concept of man which the bourgeoisie had adopted to strengthen its class rule, has to take over the bourgeois concept against which socialism also has to fight.[70]

Tillich characterized the bourgeois concept as one "constituted from reason" so that things outside and within people become "areas for the domination of reason."[71]

> In the process those layers of human existence are lost which one could characterize as the "center" and which are more original than the abstractions of subjective reason, on the one side, and of objective drive mechanisms, on the other. This center layer

between pure reason and the mere stuff of subjection is covered up by the bourgeois principle. Consciousness sees only itself and its objects, but it does not see being as being, and it does not see the creative-destructive powers from which in truth it is determined, by which it is raised or destroyed. *Being, also human being, is to be shaped on the basis of consciousness.*[72]

According to this view, continued Tillich, being is steadily being raised into consciousness, and thus people, including socialists, speak of "the most advanced consciousness."[73]

Tillich found that socialism had adopted this conception of man, but because it knows that bourgeois society is class society, it does not accept the possibility of there being reasonable people and a reasonable society in the existing order; only in the end, in the classless society, does socialism expect people to act according to reason. At this point he noted an antagonism, for the society in which reason is to rule is to be ushered in by people who are not yet determined by reason. "*Nothing mediates the jump from non-reason. An abyss lies between reality and expectation.*"[74]

The people standing in the class struggle, the only people known, are better described by Nietzsche's "will-to-power" than Lessing's "education of the human race."[75] Tillich found no answer to the question as to how it is possible that the will-to-power becomes at one point the renunciation of power, the question of how the movement from "pre-history" to history (Marx) takes place. For this reason, he commented, Marxism, in spite of its hostility to utopia, has never been able to prevent the suspicion of a hidden utopian element in itself. "If socialist theory rests on the belief that it is a change of the social situation that will change man, it bypasses the question how a changed social situation is possible without a change of man."[76] The meaning is clear: by overlooking the powers of origin in human existence socialism has an inconsistent and unrealistic view of man.

Tillich thought that this inadequate concept of man prevents socialist theory from recognizing the powers of origin operative in the proletariat. Socialists had rightly seen the situation of the proletariat as one of "thingification," but then, he asked, why do the proletariat react to this process if they are nothing but things?[77]

> Something that has become merely a thing no longer resists its being made into a thing. The reaction of the proletariat is, in contrast, the reaction of a genuine man, not man as he is presupposed in a rational system, but man as he continues to be related to the origin; he derives from the origin the power to protect himself from being totally cut off from the roots of his being . . . . *What reacts in the proletariat is the same as that which political romanticism makes the sole principle of man and society--the origin.*[78]

In understanding the proletarian situation from here, Tillich argued that it is not only interpreted economically since it is the human element that reacts against the economic; the struggle against bourgeois society emerges from the proletariat which is not "'thingified.'" As he described it, "the proletarian movement is the reaction of the human being in the proletariat against the threat of total human depersonalization because of economic depersonalization."[79]

Tillich wanted to resolve the inner conflict of the socialist conception of man on the basis of the powers of origin that he found in the proletarian movement. In conceiving human existence from its vital center, he sought to move "toward a new socialist understanding of man." He insisted, in accord with the whole argument of *The Socialist Decision,* that this effort is not to be done in a manner that "robs man of what is uniquely human, the 'doubling' of being in consciousness, but rather in the sense of the socialist principle, i.e., the subordination of the origin to the demand."[80]

"The first step" in this direction "is *the repudiation of the primitive 'drive psychology'* on which vulgar Marxism built its calculations of the future." According to this psychology, which conceived man as a mechanism driven by elementary pleasure and pain reactions, as the suffering of the masses became worse and worse, "a pain-reaction would result which would compel the revolution to begin." In addition, it foresaw a time after the revolution when there would be "a universal and uniform satisfaction of needs."[81]

Tillich considered this mechanistic construct nothing but "an extreme product of bourgeois 'thingification,'" for if man were a mechanism determined by simple pleasure and pain reactions, then he would be a thing and not a person. He agreed that there are pleasure-pain mechanisms: "but the fact that there are mechanisms at play in a living being does not make that being into a mechanism." For Tillich it is ironic that socialism, a movement against "thingification," has adopted a mechanistic psychology: "*Socialist thoery has advocated an image of man against whose practical realization the whole socialist movement is directed: man who has become a thing.*"[82]

In the search for a new image of man Tillich welcomed the efforts to form "an *alliance of Marxism and psychoanalysis*" when it incorporates Freudian-type insights.[83] Psychoanalysis is important for Marxism, declared Tillich at a time when their connection was only beginning to be explored, because it

> . . . dethrones consciousness and shatters faith in its supremacy. It points to the forces of the vital psychological center that determine consciousness, even where it believes itself to be self-sufficient and capable of making free decisions. Psychoanalysis opens up access to levels, the exposure of which profoundly threatens mechanistic psychology. Above all, it points to the connection between vital being and spiritual forms which correspond to the true Marxist view of history, undistorted by bourgeois influence.[84]

Tillich was insistent that understanding man from the vital center has important consequences for socialist theory. One area where this is so is in the scientific work of calculating the future development of capitalist society. He did not dispute the need for positivistic science to continue to establish the cause-effect relationship of the economic mechanism, stating that "*the methodological demand for rational analysis must remain unquestioned*." "A methodological requirement," however, should not be made "an ontological thesis," since being cannot be reduced to objective and calcuable components. "Since all living beings, including man, are derived from the origin, man is not determined by a fixed number of impersonal factors whose present and future combinations could be calculated." Marxist economists might accurately predict the development of the economy, he explained, but even so, "nothing has been decided concerning human reactions, neither that of the proletariat nor that of other groups." Moreover, noted Tillich, recognition of the powers of origin provide an anthropological basis "for the Marxist idea that the terminus of capitalism may be not only socialism, but also barbarism."[85]

A second consequence that Tillich drew from his conception of man concerns "the domination of the conscious mind" in the socialist struggle. While acknowledging the excellent pedagogical work done among the proletariat, Tillich attacked its failure to exhibit the authentic meaning of symbols of the origin and to demonstrate their significance for human existence and for the coming society. Therefore socialism overestimates the strength of rational appeal and neglects the ability of the non-rational to motivate people. "It is not the most enlightened, the so-called most progressive consciousness that influences history. It is the consciousness whose energies storm out of the fullness and depth of being, energies which consciousness brings to light." Tillich wanted to change the socialist mentality which lacks these energies and whose enlightened awareness is "neither symbolically powerful nor historically creative," for he saw it as a major source of socialism's weakness.[86]

Thirdly, Tillich believed his anthropology implies "a new theory of needs."[87] In discussing "the socially producing man" as the "matter" of history, Tillich remarked that how one understands the needs satisfied in common production depends upon one's image of man (see above, p. 122). Tillich's image further challenged a narrow economism, for it prohibits an abstraction of economic needs out of their living connection with other human needs.

"Since all types of human thrusts into reality are really grounded in the central layer of human being, . . . it is not possible to isolate particular needs and derive the remaining ones from them." He recognized "the special urgency of the instinct of self-preservation," but this too he qualified, observing that this urgency takes effect only in life-threatening situations, which, in most cases, do not characterize the actual life process.[88] Rather, he stated life

> . . . is filled by a comples of vital, erotic, aesthetic, and religious impulses which in many instances lead to an ascendancy of the so-called spiritual over the life-preserving tendencies. (Cf. the dedication even unto death of members of the fighting proletariat.) But even this formulation is questionable because in many cases the will for the sustaining of life is not at all concerned with "life at any price," but with a specific quality of life, e.g., life in freedom.[89]

Furthermore, observed Tillich, "even the basic needs of hunger and thirst are in themselves complex," since, apart from the most extreme cases, these needs are "infinitely differentiated and defined by vitalistic, aesthetic, and erotic elements whose composite effect (*Zusammenwirken*) causes a radical change even in the spheres of most primitive need-satisfaction." He supplemented his enlarged and more complex theory of needs with the suggestion that such a theory would help to clarify differentiations within the proletariat as well as to clarify why the middle classes, even when they are at a lower economic level than the proletariat, reject the proletarian consciousness.[90]

Tillich considered his "new interpretation of man" to have "fundamental significance . . . for all aspects of socialist theory and praxis," thought that socialism's dependence on the bourgeois principle had been "most disastrous for its own development," and argued that "the socialist decision" requires "decisive change at this point."[91] In following this theme through *The Socialist Decision*, I have illustrated Tillich's critical analysis of socialism's conflicts.[92] He has demonstrated the importance of the anthropological question for socialism, and he has set forth a view of man that more adequately recognizes the fullness of human life. His architectonic framework, his subtle balancing of the rational and the non-rational, and the precision of his numerous insights are a provocative part of Tillich's socialist theory.

For the Marxist, man produces his own world which in turn produces man. This insight makes it difficult, perhaps impossible, to define an unchanging "essence" of man. Nevertheless, Tillich believed there is a continuity of meaning in the word and reality of man. In this section the focus has been on the simple proposition that man is a unity of being and consciousness. Tillich considered that this proposition describes the structure of human being, restates a central theme of Biblical anthropology, and is in accord with vital elements of Marx's materialism. Three assertions are present in this proposition: 1) Man is to be understood in a wholistic fashion; 2) man is to be understood as living from his vital center; and 3) man is to be understood as uniquely a spiritual being. The interest in the previous pages has been to explore the meaning of the first two statements, especially the more controversial second one, and to show their significance for Tillich's appropriation, analysis, and alteration of historical materialism. As was seen, Tillich's view of the socially producing man went "farther down" than the implicit anthropology of the orthodox Marxism he was combatting. In the next section, where I turn to the third assertion, it will once more be seen that Tillich also went "farther up."

The Spirit, Ideology, and the Protestant Principle
Present within historical materialism is the concept of ideology. As I noted in the opening section of this chapter, Tillich considered Marx's insight into the interconnection between the spirit and the social situation as an enduring contribution for scientific study and for socialism. The concept of ideology is built upon this unity and implies in some manner a false relationship between the two. The concern of this section is with Tillich's interpretation and re-construction of this concept.

In a lecture entitled "The Meaning of the Social Situation for the Life of the Spirit," Tillich sketched his view of man as "a living spirit" in relation to two opposing answers to the question implied in the title.[93] One answer sees "the life of the spirit as a reality for itself, which has its own forms, its own laws." According to this view, whoever participates in the life of the spirit has to leave behind the particularities of his own social situation and devote himself to the task which is the same for all. The spirit is seen "as a higher reality beyond psychic and social realities, as a place in which one can only succeed if one turns away from his existence, from his being there (*Dasein*) as this man in this situation."[94]

The truth that Tillich found in this "idealistic" answer is that one who wants to serve the spirit has to break through the boundaries of his own accidental existence. "Every spiritual creation speaks to us: become different. 'Spirit' is the pain with which life itself cuts into life'" (Nietzsche). If this is the truth in idealism, its error is in believing that the spirit is beyond vital life, in wanting to keep the spirit away from "the blood of life," from natural, psychic, and social life. When this happens, the spirit is conceived as something abstract and transcendent, standing over against life, and therefore violating life. But life does not allow this violation, he continued, and turns from the spirit to itself, to fortuitousness and ease, and becomes empty and formless. The result is that the spirit either is something for one's free hours; that is, it ceases to be spirit and becomes decoration, or it becomes very formal and sacrifices vital life, proud to have fled from the chaos of the soul and of public life. "This," interpreted Tillich, "is the characteristic of our spiritual situation since the breakdown of idealism . . . ."[95]

In contrast to the idealistic answer Tillich posed the opposite claim: "The life of the spirit does not have any independence in itself. It is completely determined by the vital interests of people, by its conscious and unconscious psychic formation, above all by its economic and social situation." For Marx, all spiritual forms are only the super-structure of an economically-determined class situation, that is, they are "ideologies by which a class conceals its own situation and its own will-to-rule." One who accepts this position, commented Tillich, never asks the truth or the spiritual meaning of religious, artistic, legal, and philosophical symbols, but instead asks, "What hides behind them in relation to the class situation, to the will to power? What is their meaning in life?"[96]

Marx's idea has had "a tremendous world-historical effect" because there is a truth in it that is right in relation to all idealism. "Every spiritual form is born by a will to live; every spirit . . . is born and filled by blood, by the blood of immediate, unique life." A further truth that Tillich found in this position is that the call to the spirit and to truth is often nothing but an unconscious or even conscious pretext to assert one's will to power without restraint. He did not, however, accept this as the final word, for to hold consistently to it would make his own position senseless. If one has to explain one's own ideas as an ideology, as a facade, as an expression of a will to power, then one would have to give up any claim to speak the truth. "Spirit is no less spirit," he concluded, "because it is born by blood, because it can be experienced and realized only in the actual process of life. And spirit is therefore no less spirit because it can be misused as a pretext and a facade."[97]

Tillich discovered a truth in both answers, and he considered both inadequate in themselves. "Spirit and life, also spirit and social life, stand together (*ineinander*). They cannot be separated from each other." The spirit-side is directed "toward universality, toward validity," and the life-side "toward the particular, the uniquely-creative." For Tillich "living spirit is both in unity."[98]

He illustrated his thesis of "the living spirit" by examining the concept of property in relation to changing forms of society, from primitive peasant communism through the bourgeois era to the demands of the socialists, seeking to demonstrate the intimate interrelation between the spirit and the social situation. The spirit is always bound to concrete life, and yet, he summed up, "the spirit is more than a product of the social situation, for it creates tensions in every situation and drives beyond each. It creates new societies and with it new formations of the spirit."[99]

From this it can be seen that Tillich's concern is threefold: the unity of life and spirit in man; the locus of the spirit in the blood of life; and the integrity and independence of the spirit. With an understanding of the living spirit as both concrete and creative, he sought to go beyond idealistic and materialistic conceptions of man. His evaluation of the spirit grew out of this understanding of the spirit and its relationship to the social situation.

Interestingly, in contrast to his early endorsement of Marx's socio-economic method, Tillich took up the concept of ideology for serious consideration relatively late. In his writings up to 1926 there are only passing references to it.[100] He discusses it first in his essay "Kairos and Logos" and from then on in various articles.[101] In 1929 he participated in the controversy raised by Karl Mannheim's *Ideology and Utopia*.[102] Only later did he "discover" a connection between Marx's attack on ideology and Luther's protest against self-made gods. On the basis of this theological insight and his increasing involvement with socialist theory, Tillich worked to incorporate a refined concept of ideology into his own religious socialism. In 1934 he spoke of the concept of ideology as "the gold" hidden in what Hirsch had called "'the filth of economic materialism.'" Tillich added that he can scarcely think of a more important concrete theological task than to use the concept of ideology to unveil the practical materialism hiding behind so much theism.[103]

Tillich first discussed the concept in the context of "the question of the dynamic character of truth and reality." He believed that Marx's concept of ideology has raised this question in a "new" way since "reality itself is interpreted as something changeable in its essence. Consequently, the concepts in which the essence of reality is grasped must themselves be changeable, if truth is claimed for them."[104] Ideology, which implies its opposite, non-ideology or truth, poses the question of truth in terms of change and makes the relationship between absolute and relative especially acute.

Tillich described ideology in this fashion: "For Marx . . . productive society is the ultimate reality and ideas are only relections of a special situation of society in the mirror of the spirit. The totality of such ideas is the ideology of a social group." He continued that the word has come to designate ideas "used by a social group in order to justify its political and economic power, especially in situations where this power contradicts the actual historic situation."[105]

In his initial discussions ideology meant for Tillich that ideas are entirely derivative from economic and social realities. Secondly, Tillich recognized that it is often used "for purposes of agitation," as a means to attack "the sanctity" of the spiritual creations of socialism's opponents and "a weapon" to destroy "all the hallowed truths of bourgeois and feudal culture."[106] It is therefore a warning, "a system for the volcano over which our society lives. If an intellectual system is successfully interpreted as a mere ideology," he admonished, "it has lost its formative power."[107] Thirdly, Tillich valued the concept for demonstrating the dependence of the spirit on the social situation. As he wrote in reference to ideology, the social situation "determines one's cognitive functions as much as the system of values in which one lives."[108]

Nevertheless, Tillich had two major objections to the concept in this form, objections which might have accounted for his hesitancy to employ the ideology-concept in his earlier writings. One criticism (also included in the lecture referred to above) was "the formal objection" that "the assertion of the ideological character of thinking must allow at least one exception, namely this assertion itself. If this also is nothing but ideology it is only the expression of a special social situation and cannot even try to claim universal validity."[109] Tillich's second objection was to its reductionism and its failure to appreciate the validity of the spirit. Tillich's rejection of the metaphor "reflection" because it destroyed the unity of being and consciousness applies also to his description of ideology given above.

In his first article on the nature of symbols (1928) Tillich reiterated his criticism of Marx's concept of ideology. He connected the names of Marx and Nietzsche (as he had done before) with two types of "negative theories" of symbols. They have shown "that the psychological and social situation is decisive for the selection of symbols," and Tillich accepted this. The two, however, went further and offered a genetic theory of the symbol itself: "symbols have no other reality than to serve as an expression of the psychological and social situation." He found Marx's thesis--that "symbols are ideologies" and "a political subterfuge" for the sake of dominance in power--untested and unconvincing.[110]

Marx and Nietzsche had helped to explain the selection of symbols, but they had not offered a complete theory of symbols themselves. Tillich's own attempt to do so aimed to demonstrate the integrity of symbols, especially religious ones, by arguing that man's spirit "must be defined precisely by the relation to the unconditioned transcendent." Since "the relation to the unconditioned transcendent is essential or constitutive" for the human spirit, religious symbols have their own validity which has to be respected.[111] Symbols for Tillich did not refer to another world, as both Marx and Nietzsche had assumed, but to the transcendent meaning of life.[112] It should also be remembered in this connection that Tillich took the offensive in socialism's attack on religion by insisting that socialism too is religious.

In spite of his criticisms of the concept of ideology as he knew it from the socialist tradition, Tillich adopted and modified it for his own use in attacking distorted expressions of the spirit. An important factor in this development is the analogy that he found between Feuerbach and Marx and Luther. The assessment of man in these two materialists, he wrote, had "deep roots in the Christian judgment of man."[113] The interpretations of Feuerbach "about the limitlessness of human drives, about the formation of religious ideas by means of the projection and objectivization of the contents of these drives" as well as those of Marx about the historically determined character of man are "unconditionally affirmed" by Tillich.[114]

> Every prophetic religion is inherently suspicious of religion that is based on man's wishes, of the 'self-made God' [Luther], and of the unconscious use of the divine in the service of the will to power. This protest [against false religion] is powerfully expressed the Feuerbach-Marxist theory of ideology.[115]

Tillich believed that religion, which "has in itself the enduring suspicion of ideology," should welcome what Marx and Feuerbach have done, apply it to itself, and consider it not as a hostile act toward religion, but as "a religious act," though expressed in a non-religious way.[116] Tillich saw the concept of ideology as the critical element within historical materialism, and in bringing it into a theological context, he thought he could deepen its meaning.

He interpreted ideology by relating it to the Protestant principle, the protest against a finite reality claiming unconditional status. The Protestant principle presupposes "a radical negativity of the human situation," a situation traditionally implied by the doctrine of original sin. This concept, wrote Tillich, signifies "an original self-contradiction in human existence," a perversion of existence due to the finite elevating itself or refusing to fulfill its finitude.[117] This state points to what Tillich called the "disruption" of man's unity.

According to Tillich, the socialist utilizing the concept of ideology also knows the corruption of human life since in the proletarian situation man's perversion breaks forth "as social fate." Both socialism and Protestantism are one in their ethical-pessimistic assessment of the actual human situation. In uniting the two Tillich aimed to give the plight of the proletariat new significance as representative of the universal distortion of humanity and, at the same time, to add meaning to the Protestant principle of linking it directly to the social realm.[118]

This effort incorporated Tillich's insight that human perversion is both universal and particular; that is, it involves all people, and it is especially pronounced in definite demonic structures. The categories of "the universal" and "the concrete-historical" do not stand in contradiction to each other, he stated, because "the universally-human is never visible except in the concretely-historical . . . . " For historical support he appealed to the example of the early church, which called the Roman state demonic, and to Luther, who attacked the papacy as the Anti-Christ. Today, he claimed, "the proletarian situation compels Protestantism to pursue this insight further. For the proletarian situation is an inescapable consequence of the capitalist demon."[119]

Tillich continued with an historical paradigm in order to establish the meaning of ideology. "In the Reformation Protestantism fought against two ideologies, that is, two ways of concealing the human situation, the Catholic and the humanistic." Ideology means concealment, and the anti-ideological struggle involves, as it had for the Reformers, a radical recognition of the actual situation without the aid of any veils.[120] Ideology is not only "false consciousness" about the universally-human situation, wrote Tillich,

> . . . but the character of ideology is also expressed in that the "self-made God" is the shielding of a concrete sociological tendency . . . . It is not the self will of man in general that makes a God, builds an ideology, but it is a concrete psychically and socially conditioned will to power. The attack on the self-made God (the first and the deepest conception of ideology) was for Luther a concrete attack, not a non-specific declaration about the human situation.[121]

Because the Protestant principle is anti-ideological, Tillich saw that it has a point of contact with the proletarian situation which by its very nature is anti-ideological. He cautioned that this does not mean that the proletariat are exempt from creating ideologies, nor that socialist theory is free from building up its own questionable ideological superstructure; but these too are ship-wrecked on the objective nature of the proletarian situation.[122]

> The final bodily-psychic needs, needs of a sociologically homogeneous mass (not exceptional cases like poverty) rip away the ideological mask; for they have the criterion for distinguishing between reality and concealment: distress (*Hilfe*). Anything that cannot save them from their bodily-psychic distortion is rejected . . .[123]

Tillich's concept of ideology was a critical doctrine which unites "The Protestant Principle and the Proletarian

Situation." In summary, it was constructed on the basis of the following propositions: 1) the radical and universal perversion of human existence; 2) the religious necessity to protest concrete social evils; 3) the understanding of ideology as concealment of distorted reality; 4) the identification of ideologies with idols; and 5) the proletarian situation as the criterion to differentiate reality from concealment. Tillich's anti-ideological struggle ensued from the uniting of the particular and the universal.

A further point should be added. Awareness of the negative came through awareness of the positive. Consciousness of the new for Tillich comes by way of expectation, an attitude that is characteristic of both the Protestant principle and the proletarian situation.[124] Living in the horizon of expectation allows one to see and to be critical of the existing order, in light of the coming truth; ideology, therefore, involves symbols and concepts which contradict the expected future.

In *The Socialist Decision* Tillich wrote of "false consciousness" in this way, calling it "a discrepancy between traditional concepts and symbols and a new historical reality." False consciousness implies true consciousness, "namely a consciousness which is united with the new being. . . . *A false consciousness is nothing other than a defensive self-affirmation of obsolete social structures which are being threatened and destroyed by new ones.*" This of course again raises the question of truth, which for Tillich meant a dynamic concept of truth adequate to changing reality. Thus, he wrote, "true and false in this context, therefore, means agreeing or not agreeing with the underlying structures of a social order." Tillich thought, as will become clearer in the next chapter, that the structure of society is moving toward a post-capitalist society, and truth therefore is linked with this movement. Marxism, he stated, has revealed how much the bourgeoisie has obscured its own structure.[125]

Tillich challenged Protestantism to free itself from its ideological distortion. The proletariat reject the churches and their symbols, he remarked, because they bypass their situation.[126] He appealed to the churches to take up the critical element in their own principle and apply its constant suspicion of idolatry and ideology to itself. He did not ask every

Protestant to become a socialist, but he did think each should know

> . . . that he turns Protestantism, Christianity, and religion into an ideology, that he serves the "self-made God" of his social group, his class or his nation if he does not allow the fact of the proletarian situation to become decisively important for the formation of Protestantism as well as for his own piety.[127]

These words were written in 1931, but in 1932 the situation had worsened. He wrote then: "The basic attitude of Lutheranism has become an ideology." He bitterly attacked the first declaration of the von Papen government as an extreme ideologization of the Protestant principle that, he thought, is likely to have made all attempts to narrow the gap between Christianity and the proletariat impossible for decades. "*Protestantism as ideology* means in the long run the self-destruction of the Protestant church."[128] Again he appealed to Protestantism for the sake of its principle to separate itself from political romanticism, but, he admitted, such an event "would have to appear like a miracle."[129]

Tillich also urged socialists to be self-critical in their use of the concept of ideology. He cautioned against the tendency to label every new idea as ideological, and he welcomed Mannheim's book as a valuable contribution to socialist self-criticism.[130] Because he recognized the possibility of ideas becoming ideological and yet denied all necessarily were ideological, he asked that socialists distinguish between "the genuine significance and the ideological misuse" of concepts and symbols.[131] Moreover, Tillich wanted a theory that unveils its own illusions and concealments. "*Socialism has permanent cause to subject itself to the suspicion of being an ideology.*"[132] With the Protestant principle Tillich placed socialism itself under the judgment of the Unconditional; neither is it exempt from the reality of ideology.

The primary target of ideological criticism was neither Protestantism nor socialism, however, but the dominant ideas of the period, those of the bourgeoisie. In *The Socialist Decision* Tillich characterized the bourgeois principle as "belief in (automatic) harmony," the attitude of "'*laisser-faire, laisser-aller,*'" and traced its significance for the bourgeoisie in economics, politics, and philosophy.[133] This belief is ideological, contended Tillich, because the class struggle shatters its validity: "The proletariat does not experience harmony, but *disharmony*."[134]

> The exposing of the disharmony in bourgeois society, i.e., *the revealing of the class situation, was the most significant and most successful accomplishment of the Marxist theory of ideology* . . . . Therefore the materialistic interpretation of history belongs essentially and inseparably to socialism as long as it is involved in the struggle with bourgeois society.[135]

As is clear from this discussion, the question of ideology was a serious one for Tillich. It was an ethical-political matter--the welfare of the proletariat--and a religious concern-- the worship of false gods. It involved the question of truth and the proper understanding of spirit and social situation. By maintaining its relationship to the proletariat and by transforming its meaning with the help of the Protestant principle, Tillich did, as he wrote, provide "a fresh substantiation for the concept of ideology."[136] Because of its critical theological-political meaning, it is evident why Tillich considered it the "gold" of historical materialism.

The Validity of Marx's Analysis

In the three previous sections of this chapter Tillich's concern with the theoretical aspects of historical materialism has been discussed. Finally, brief mention should be made of the importance of Marx's materialism in providing an empirical basis for Tillich's religious socialism. Tillich was persuaded by the basic correctness of Marx's scientific investigation of bourgeois society.

"Religious socialism," wrote Tillich, "stands fundamentally on the ground of Marx's analysis of capitalistic society." First of all, this meant for him "that the structure of contemporary society is determined by the capitalist economy." The market, he continued, stands at the structural center of the economy and society, and the pervasive influence of the economic structure permeates all of society, which, however, is not the case for previous societies.[137]

In describing the background to "the religious situation" of the present, Tillich pointed to "mathematical natural science, technique and capitalist economy" as the three activities that

formed it, activities whose "carrier" was "capitalist society."[138]
He saw that the present situation is marked by "self-sufficient
finitude," which he equated with "the spirit of capitalist society." In this society, he stated, "it is economic activity
which is dominant and it is its unconditional dominance which
characterizes the capitalist spirit most definitely."[139] Like
Marx, Tillich considered economic activity as central in the
existing order.

Secondly, noted Tillich, religious socialism recognizes
along with Marx that "there is a necessary opposition between
the owners of the means of production and those who are dependent upon this means" which in turn, creates "the differentiation of classes" in which everyone participates, whether he is
aware of it or not. Thirdly, he agreed that Marx has shown that
"the class struggle represents a structural necessity in capitalist society, regardless of the good will of the individual."[140]

Tillich, following Marx, accepted the class struggle as a
conflict inherent in the nature of capitalism, a reality in
which the individual has no choice but to be a participant. Because it is a structural feature of society, he considered moralistic judgments about it to be of no avail, and he thought
that the insight of Heimann, that the class struggle is simultaneously fought from above as well as from below, is important
in appraising its meaning.[141]

In Tillich's theological perspective, the capitalist system is "demonic," which means that it represents "the reign of
a superpersonal, sacred form which supports life, which at the
same time contains the force of destruction in such a way that
the destructive power is essentially connected with the creative
power."[142] The capitalist system is demonic "because of the
union of creative and destructive powers present in it," and
"because of the inevitability of the class struggle independent
of subjective morality and piety." Its effect is that society
and the individual are "'possessed,'" or caught in a structure
of evil (which, however, is not all "bad," but a mixture of
creative and destructive elements). For Tillich, religious socialism's "most decisive religious task" is exposing and combating a demonic capitalism."[143]

In accepting Marx's analysis of capitalism and in giving it
theological meaning, Tillich is not saying that all historical

periods were determined by their economic structure and by class struggle. For Tillich the economic factor can dominate but it does not have to. In other words, he rejected the sweeping economic interpretation of history in *The Communist Manifesto*: "The history of all hitherto existing society is the history of class struggles."[144] Tillich did not think of class struggle as "a universal social phenomenon: but as something limited to the modern period of history.[145]

Tillich could disagree with Marx on this point because of his rejection of the anthropology of economism. But was he then inconsistent in endorsing Marx's description of the contemporary period? No, not necessarily, since he allowed for the possibility of the economic factor dominating in an era. Moreover, he found that Marx and Marxists made their point with convincing probability.[146]

During this period there were two points of contention about Marx's analysis to which Tillich responded. One was the question as to whether the proletariat is still proletariat, or if it had not in fact become bourgeois. This was the position of de Man who argued that therefore Marx's analysis is no longer applicable. In his review of *The Psychology of Socialism* Tillich disagreed with de Man's conclusion. He was in accord with de Man's view that the economic factor is completely embedded in psychic and social realities, but this in itself does not invalidate Marx.[147]

> For Marx the fate of the capitalist era is decided in its economic structure. It is to be interpreted from here and certainly with means that originate from purely economic abstraction. The right of this abstraction is the right of every science to take an element of reality and to think it through consistently. The *homo oeconomicus* is not a reality, but it is a true abstraction.[148]

Tillich recognized that new factors can change the validity of the Marxist analysis.

> Here is the alternative: either it actually happens that the proletariat enter into a real petit bourgeois situation, in which case the structure of society in the sense of the Marxist analysis of capitalism no longer holds. Then a new situation has arisen which must call for a new analysis and synthesis. Or, the proletarian situation remains a broad or narrow reality. And the tendency toward proletarianization which somehow threatens almost all layers of society remains in effect. Then this situation is the

place for meaningful, direct resistance to the capitalist system.[149]
Tillich still thought that the evidence supports the latter alternative and that the Marxist view of things is still valid. The events after 1927, especially the Depression, strengthened this judgment.[150] He considered the question, however, as one to be decided on the basis of empirical analysis, and within his own socialist theory there was room for the changes that a new analysis might require. He believed that it is possible for the proletariat to lose its "calling" and no longer be the decisive group in opposing the demonic structures of modern society.[151]

A second point where Tillich re-examined Marx's analysis is the question of proletarianization. In *The Communist Manifesto* Marx had outlined this process: "The lower strata of the middle class--the small trades-people, shopkeepers, and retired tradesmen generally, the handicraftsmen and peasants--all these sink gradually into the proletariat . . . ."[152] But in the circumstances of 1932 the opposite was occurring. As Tillich observed, "*the fear of proletarianization was turned into a will to struggle against the proletariat.*"[153] Tillich left open the question of a general proletarianization of all non-proletarian groups, writing that it could happen, but that it is not at present. Therefore, he argued, socialism dare not wait for this to occur, but instead strive "*for an alliance of the revolutionary proletariat with the revolutionary groups among the political romantics.*"[154]

Tillich's proposal indicates that his more flexible understanding of historical materialism allowed him to take new factors into account which the dogmatic materialist would never consider. He maintained that the proletariat held the key position in society, but he considered that the lower middle class groups, who also were fighting an anti-bourgeois campaign, might, if they were stripped of their romanticism, become the allies of socialism. He never said that this would happen, but only warned of the dire consequences if it did not. Tillich of course had no way of knowing what would happen in 1933, the situation of 1932 was still undecided, and the options available not promising. Nevertheless, his proposal, especially in retrospect, might be considered far-fetched. It was more appropriate to his ontological anthropology (where the first root was not eliminated, but broken and subordinated to the second) than to the realities of the political situation.

In spite of his efforts to revise the doctrine of proletarianization, Tillich accepted Marx's analysis of capitalism and the class struggle as describing things the way they are and as the scientific basis for his own theological understanding of socialism. Tillich was not a dogmatist in his understanding of the situation but accepted the tentative judgments of economists. He was a socialist because (among other reasons) he found validity in the Marxist's economic interpretation of capitalist society.

Summary

In this chapter Tillich's understanding of one significant aspect of Marxist theory, historical materialism, has been probed. First, the meaning of historical materialism for Tillich was outlined. It was shown that for him its meaning was the human being, "socially producing man." In the second section Tillich's understanding of the socially producing man was discussed in terms of man as a unity of being and consciousness, of the vital and spiritual, and it was seen how this provided a basis for Tillich's dialectical relationship to historical materialism. Tillich's position toward Marx's concept of ideology was then studied, and it was demonstrated how Tillich further developed the concept by relating it to the Protestant principle and how he used it to criticize the concealments and distortions of capitalist society as well as of Protestantism and socialism. Finally, Tillich found in Marx's analysis of bourgeois society a valid interpretation of the existing order which required identification with the proletariat in their struggle against the demonic power of capitalism.

Tillich's attitude toward historical materialism involved both endorsement and criticism. As a socialist and a theologian he dialectically appropriated elements from socialist materialism and Protestant anthropology and theology in order to transform this element of socialist theory. Now, after having followed Tillich's encounter with historical materialism, I will turn in the next chapter to another and very closely related aspect of Marxism, historical dialectic.

CHAPTER 4

NOTES

[1] *SD, GW,* II, p. 320.

[2] Ibid.

[3] For Marx's conception of materialism see Karl Marx and Frederick Engels, *The German Ideology,* ed. with an Introduction by R. Pascal (New York: International Publishers, 1947). Cf. Engels, *Socialism Utopian and Scientific,* in *The Essential Left* (New York: Barnes and Noble, Inc., 1961), pp. 103-46. For one view of Marx's materialism, see Robert C. Tucker, *Philosophy and Myth in Karl Marx* (Cambridge: University Press, 1964), esp. pp. 177-87. For a convenient summary of Marx's view and its subsequent history, see H. B. Acton, "Historical Materialism," *The Encyclopedia of Philosophy,* Vol. 4 (New York: Macmillan Publishing Co., Inc., 1967), pp. 12-20.

[4] "Religioeser Sozialismus I," *GW,* II, p. 154. Originally published in *Neue Blaetter fuer den Sozialismus,* I, p. 9 (September 1930), pp. 396-403.

[5] Tillich did not deny the existence of a practical materialistic attitude among the proletariat, but he saw it as a carry-over from the bourgeoisie. "Kirchenfrage," *GW,* II, p. 17. He had little patience, however, with the bourgeoisie who use "the instinctive-materialistic reaction of the proletariat to discredit the proletarian struggle," and he wrote, "much so-called 'idealism' has its roots in the social and economic security of the upper classes. There is just as little reason to praise this idealism as there is to condemn proletarian materialism." "PPS," p. 14, Cf. "PPPS," *PE,* pp. 167-68.

[6] "Weiterbildung," *GW,* II, pp. 121-22.

[7] "RS (I)," *GW,* II, p. 153. Tillich referred to Haeckel as one "who wanted to derive all things, men and history from the dice game of atoms." Haeckel's views are briefly summarized in John Macquarrie, *Twentieth Century Religious Thought* (New York: Harper and Row, Publishers, 1963), pp. 100-101.

[8] "Kairos," *PE,* pp. 34-35.

[9] "Weiterbildung," *GW,* II, p. 122. Cf. metaphysical materialism was "an interpretation of the bourgeois mechanization of the world." "RS (II)," *Pol. Exp.,* p. 46.

[10] "The Protestant Message," *PE,* p. 193. In his "Theses on Feuerbach" Marx attacked materialism that sees the object only in the form of perception and not as sensuous human activity. Karl Marx, "Theses on Feuerbach," *Writings of the Young Marx on Philosophy and Society,* ed. and trans. by Lloyd D. Easton and Kurt H. Guddat (Garden City, New York: Anchor Books, 1967), pp. 400-402.

[11] "Christentum, Sozialismus und Nationalismus," *GW,* XIII, p. 163.

[12] "Die Theologie des Kairos," p. 315.

[13] "RS (II)," *Pol. Exp.*, p. 46; cf. p. 43. Cf. *OB*, pp. 81-90.

[14] "Zum Problem der evangelischen Sozialethik. Zum gleichnamigen Aufsatz von Wilhelm Loew," *GW*, XII, p. 212. Originally published in *Blaetter fuer religioesen Sozialismus*, VII (1926), pp. 73-79.

[15] "Christentum und Idealismus," *GW*, XII, p. 233. Originally published *Theologische Blaetter*, VI (1927), pp. 29-40.

[16] *SD*, *GW*, II, pp. 321-22.

[17] Ibid.

[18] Ibid.

[19] Ibid.

[20] "Weiterbildung," *GW*, II, p. 124.

[21] For a discussion by Tillich of the relationship of the theoretical and practical as functions of meaning, see "The Philosophy of Religion," *WR?*, pp. 62-63. "The theoretical act is the meaning-fulfillment in that aspect of it which is directly related to form. The practical act is the meaning-fulfillment of reality, insofar as reality is formed into spirit-bearing reality, through breaking loose from immediacy. The practical act is therefore meaning-fulfillment in the primary sense, and the theoretical act is fulfillment in the secondary sense." P. 63. On the social nature of existence, see *Das System des Wissenschaften*, I, pp. 170-77. "Man as a biological and psychological individual essence is an abstraction. Man in the social organism is alone real." P. 183. Against Heidegger, Tillich wrote: "With the abstract use of the concept historicity he covers up the concrete historical connection of his concepts." "Die Theologie des Kairos," p. 315.

[22] *SD*, *GW*, II, p. 322.

[23] "Kirchenfrage," *GW*, II, p. 16. Cf. "Answer," p. 12. This is the only time Tillich spoke of a "causative connection."

[24] "Christentum, Sozialismus und Nationalismus," *GW*, XIII, p. 164.

[25] "Die geistige Welt im Jahre 1926," *GW*, X, p. 95.

[26] "Die Theologie des Kairos," p. 315.

[27] Ibid., p. 319; cf. *OB*, p. 85.

[28] *SD*, *GW*, II, pp. 231-32. Tillich here stated that consciousness is not bound to being in a biographical but in a functional sense. For example, certain thoughts express the proletarian situation no matter who utters them. He saw that distance from a social situation can also be a source of knowledge about it. "The greatest examples for this are Marx and Lenin." Tillich's observation undercuts a narrow view of the relationship of being and consciousness and gives consciousness power to transcend a social situation, but if this statement is carried further it would destroy the unity of the two he insisted upon.

^{29}Perhaps his best statement of the substructure-superstructure image is found in the summary of his philosophy in "Preface to *A Contribution to the Critique of Political Economy*," in *Marx and Engels Basic Writings on Politics and Philosophy*, ed. Lewis S. Feuer (Garden City, New York: Anchor Books, 1959), pp. 43-44. Cf. Tillich's summary, "Weiterbildung," *GW*, II, p. 124.

^{30}*SD, GW*, II, pp. 322-23.

^{31}Ibid. The last phrase is only in the original, p. 154. Cf. Martin Staehli for discussion of Tillich as a materialist. "Materialistische Grundlegung des Christentums," *Internationale Dialog Zeitschrift*, V (1972), pp. 23-37, esp. 23-25, 30-31.

^{32}Ibid., p. 323.

^{33}For a detailed critique of Marx himself that has many parallels to Tillich's criticism of economism see Louis Dupre's *The Philosophical Foundations of Marxism* (New York: Harcourt, Brace and World, Inc., 1966), esp. pp. 219-30. " . . . He [Marx] defines praxis itself so exclusively in terms of a material life process that man's transcendence over nature becomes seriously jeopardized." P. 220. "In the first satisfaction of physical needs he creates and satisfies artificial needs. His production, then, is never entirely determined by material conditions." P. 222.

^{34}For a discussion of the nature of historical "laws" see *Das System des Wissenschaften, GW*, I, pp. 191-202. In a review in 1922, Tillich wrote: "Especially important is the critique of the economic interpretation of history insofar as it derives the law from the economy, instead of seeing that 'economy' is always an ordered composite effect, therefore every particular economy is the working out of a definite order of law." *Rechts philosophie, Zu einem Lehrbuch von Rudolf Stammler, GW*, XII, p. 201. Originally published in *Theologische Literaturzeitung*, XXXXVII (1922), pp. 417-20. Tillich used especially strong language in a brief review condemning the "gross" and "grotesque" misuse of the materialistic understanding of history. See Heinrich Eildermann, *Urkommunismus und Urreligion, Archiv fuer Sozialiwissenschaft und Sozialpolitik*, L (1923), pp. 247-48.

^{35}"Weiterbildung," *GW*, II, pp. 124-25.

^{36}Ibid.

^{37}Ibid., p. 125.

^{38}Ibid.

^{39}"RS (II)," *Pol. Exp.*, p. 46.

^{40}This new interest was influenced by the work of Martin Heidegger and Max Scheler. Tillich's own interest in anthropology, which was not so evident in his writings ten years earlier, will become more intense after 1932.

^{41}*SD, GW*, II, fn. 3, p. 225.

^{42}Ibid.

^{43}Ibid., p. 226.

^{44}*SD, GW*, II, fn. 7, p. 231.

[45]Ibid., cf. "RS (II)," *Pol. Exp.*, pp. 45-46.

[46]Ibid.

[47]"Theses on Feuerbach," Feuer, p. 402.

[48]Cf. Tillich, "The Christian and the Marxist View of Man," prepared for the Research Department of the "Universal Christian Council for Life and Work" (December 1935). This carefully documented paper is in the judgment of this writer Tillich's best statement on anthropology within a Christian-Marxist context. At the beginning of this paper he outlined the reasons for the absence of an articulate anthropology in Marxian socialism and its analogies in Protestant Christianity and pointed then to the implicit anthropologies in both. In *SD* and especially in this paper Tillich has shown both the presence of and the need to ask the question of man. Anthropology does not have to be an attempt "'to endow with a meaning the life of the individual in the world as it now is,'" as Tillich quoted Max Horkheimer as writing.

[49]Cf. Ulrich, esp. pp. 67-81, 175-205. Ulrich at times, however, seemed to imply that one can do without ontological and deductive elements. E.g., pp. 144-45.

[50]"RS (II)," *Pol. Exp.*, p. 47. The question of the nature of the "disruption" and the "threat" to man's being is of course an issue of controversy between Christians and Marxists. Tillich's claim that they are built into the structure of finite freedom that is man remains, in this writer's judgment, more convincing than an historical or sociological explanation.

[51]Tillich wrote that although the Reformation had recovered this insight, it "has become only partially effective for individual ethics and not at all for social ethics." "PPPS," *PE,* p. 167. Cf. German ed., p. 14.

[52]"Philosophy and Fate," *PE,* p. 8. Originally published in *Kant-Studien,* Vol. XXXIV, Heft 3/4 (1929).

[53]Ibid. Cf. "Kirche und Humanistische Gesellschaft," *GW,* IX, p. 50.

[54]"PPPS," *PE,* pp. 166-67. Cf. German ed., p. 13.

[55]"RS (II)," *Pol. Exp.*, p. 47.

[56]Cf. "RS (II)," *Pol. Exp.*, p. 47; "PPPS," *PE,* p. 167; "RS (I)," *GW,* II, pp. 156-57; "Cl. ST.," *GW,* II, p. 190.

[57]*SD, GW,* II, p. 226.

[58]*Rel. Sit.,* p. 59. The concept of "gestalt" played such an important role in Tillich's thinking that Adams suggested "that one might call him a Gestalt philosopher or theologian." Adams (1965), p. 50, footnote. In *Das System des Wissenschaften* Tillich thanked Dr. Alexander Ruestow for the word. *GW, I,* P. 160.

[59]"Nature and Sacrament," *PE,* p. 102. Originally published in *RV.* Here as elsewhere Tillich indicated that vitalistic philosophy sought to reach this level, but it did so by depriving life of the intellect and the spirit.

[60]*Rel. Sit.,* pp. 63-64. The context of this statement is a discussion of Nietzsche, Freud, and the work in other sciences

which pointed to the vital in man. In all of them, he wrote, there is a point at which the reference to the eternal became apparent; he then wrote the quoted statement.

[61] Cf. *RV*, fn. 1; "The Problem of Power," *IH*, pp. 181-84. Here *Maechtigkeit* is poorly translated as "might." Originally published in *Neue Blaetter,* II, p. 4 (April 1931), pp. 157-70. The word applied not only to man but also to nature. An example of its use in relationship to nature is the little essay "Water," where Tillich spoke of water as having its "own intrinsic power of being" that expressed both chaos and fulfillment. Adams has translated this article in his book, pp. 62-64.

[62] "Basic Principles," *Pol. Exp.*, p. 63.

[63] Ibid., p. 68. Tillich insisted that love and power be considered symbolically and not as strict sociological or psychological concepts. To see how Tillich employs these concepts for his concept of the demonic see "The Demonic," *IH*, pp. 89-93. Tillich's ontological grounding of love and power is suggestive, but also obscure; the meaning of love here is not clear. A later definition of the terms is more helpful: "power as the self-realization of the individual as well as of the group; love as devotion to the meaning of the self-realization of another." "RS (II)," *Pol. Exp.*, p. 52. Love here has more of an agape tone than it usually did in Tillich's earlier writings.

[64] Ibid. Cf. "I see that all creations of theonomous forms in society and in law are only possible insofar as they are born by love and power. This dialectic of the creative principle, that can always simultaneously be divine and demonic, is for me the expression of the impossibility to escape God and therefore also the impossibility to base the world on the pure rational form." "Antwort," p. 21.

[65] Cf. "Basic Principles," *Pol. Exp.*, pp. 66-86. One criticism of the emptiness of the autonomous society deserves special note, and that is his perceptions about the "infinite desire for domination," the "infinite activity that is empty" and "the limitless rational will to power in industry." Pp. 74, 5, 6.

[66] In an unpublished manuscript, which apparently was an address to his co-workers around the *Neue Blaetter* given in the early 1930's, Tillich stated there are two fundamental problems facing socialist theory: the problem of life and the problem of transcendence. B. 6 #30 (Harvard Archive).

[67] *SD, GW,* II, pp. 234-36.

[68] Ibid., pp. 244-47.

[69] Ibid., pp. 264-67

[70] Ibid., pp. 285-89.

[71] Ibid., p. 285.

[72] Ibid., pp. 285-56.

[73] Ibid., p. 286.

[74] Ibid., p. 287.

[75] Ibid. For Tillich's interpretation of Lessing as a representative of the bourgeois spirit see "Lessing und die Idee einer Erziehung der Menschengechlechts," *GW*, XII, pp. 97-111.

Originally appeared in *RV*. For his comments on Nietzsche's relationship to political romanticism, see *SD, GW*, II, pp. 258-59. Tillich was attempting to bring certain ideas of Nietzsche into a socialist setting as is clear from his emphasis on the vital. Cf. "Kairos," *Kairos: I*, pp. 18-19.

[76] Ibid., pp. 287-88.

[77] Ibid., p. 307.

[78] Ibid.

[79] Ibid.

[80] Ibid., pp. 338-39. Tillich was consistent that the first root could not be made the exclusive root of political thinking but had to be subordinated to the second. Cf. "Blut gegen Geist," in *Mensch und Staat*, I (1931).

[81] Ibid., p. 338.

[82] Ibid.

[83] Ibid., p. 339.

[84] Ibid. Tillich noted that these matters are still in flux but considered that this new discussion marks the beginning of the struggle for a new understanding of man. Tillich followed this direction, as did the Marxists of the "Frankfurt School." Cf. Tillich's earlier comments on the role of the unconscious, "The Idea and the Ideal of Personality," *PE*, pp. 131-35. Originally appeared in *Logos*, XVI, 22 (November 1927), pp. 68-85.

[85] Ibid., pp. 339-40.

[86] Ibid., pp. 341-42. Cf. p. 288 where Tillich noted the lack of and the mistrust of charismatic personalities in socialism.

[87] Ibid., p. 340.

[88] Ibid.

[89] Ibid., pp. 340-41.

[90] Ibid., p. 341. Cf. fn. 13, p. 334. Tillich here commented that the socialist use of the term "true interest" in relation to the middle classes is an expression of a false materialism.

[91] Ibid.

[92] Besides the conflicts or antagonisms of the socialist belief and the socialist concept of man, Tillich discusses conflicts in its interpretations of society, culture, community, and economy. *SD, GW*, II, pp. 289-304.

[93] "Die Bedeutung der Gesellschaftslage fuer das Geistesleben," *GW*, II, pp. 133-38. Originally given as a lecture at the commencement of the *Verwaltungsakademie* (School of Administration), Dresden, in June, 1927.

[94] Ibid, p. 133.

[95] Ibid., pp. 133-34.

[96] Ibid., p. 134.

[97] Ibid., pp. 134-35.

[98]Ibid., p. 135. For a complete discussion of "spirit" or "*Geist*" see *Das System des Wissenschafte*, *GW*, I, pp. 210-18. Adams gives a careful discussion of this passage in his book, pp. 144-47. He writes, "in the spiritual act, elements of thought and existence achieve form as a cultural creation." P. 144. The emphasis for Tillich was on "creation," as is the case in the next paragraph.

[99]Ibid., p. 138; the discussion of property is found, pp. 135-38.

[100]E.g., "Kairos," *PE*, p. 50.

[101]*IH*, pp. 154-56. Originally appeared in *Kairos: I* (1926).

[102]"Ideologie und Utopie. Zum gleichnamigen Buch von Karl Mannheim," *GW*, XII, pp. 255-61. Originally appeared in *Gesellschaft*, VI, 10 (1929), pp. 346-55.

[103]"Die Theologie des Kairos," p. 315. Cf. *OB*, pp. 85-86, 88; cf. Elizabeth P. Lam, "Tillich's Reconstruction of the Concept of Ideology," *Christianity and Society*, V, 5 (1940), pp. 11-15.

[104]"Kairos and Logos," *IH*, pp. 155, 154. As will be seen in the next chapter, Tillich does not think that Marx has provided a satisfactory answer to the question he raised.

[105]Ibid., p. 154. Cf. "RS (I)," *GW*, II, p. 154; "Loew," *GW*, XII, pp. 216-16.

[106]Ibid., pp. 154-55.

[107]"Realism and Faith," *PE*, pp. 74-75. Originally published in *Theologische Blaetter*, VII, 5 (May 1928), pp. 109-18.

[108]Ibid., p. 75.

[109]"Kairos and Logos," *IH*, p. 155. Cf. "Ideologie und Utopie," *GW*, XII, p. 260.

[110]"The Religious Symbol," pp. 16-17.

[111]Ibid., p. 20.

[112]Cf. *SD*, *GW*, II, fn. 7, p. 319. See above, Ch. 3, "Socialism as a Religious Phenomenon."

[113]"RS (I)," *GW*, II, p. 156.

[114]"RS (II)," *Pol. Exp.*, pp. 45-46.

[115]Ibid., p. 46.

[116]"RS (I)," *GW*, II, p. 156.

[117]"PPPS," p. 11. Cf. *PE*, p. 165. The English version contains a more complete discussion of the Protestant principle, p. 163.

[118]Ibid., pp. 12-13; cf. *PE*, p. 166.

[119]Ibid., p. 15; cf. *PE*, p. 168.

[120]Ibid., p. 17; cf. *PE*, p. 169.

[121]Ibid.; cf. *PE*, p. 170. The English version is somewhat different.

[122]Ibid., p. 17; cf. *PE*, p. 170.

[123] Ibid., pp. 17-18; cf. *PE*, p. 170.
[124] Ibid., pp. 18-19. See above, Ch. 3, p. 130.
[125] *SD, GW*, II, p. 324.
[126] "PPPS," p. 18; cf. *PE*, p. 170.
[127] Ibid., p. 33; cf. *PE*, p. 181.
[128] "Protestantismus und politische Romantik," *GW*, II, p. 216; cf. "Christentum als Ideologie," *GW*, XIII, pp. 179-81. In "Protestantismus," Tillich pointed to Barthian theology as a critical, anti-ideological theology. P. 216.
[129] Ibid., p. 218.
[130] "Ideologie und Utopie," *GW*, XII, p. 260. There he wrote: "Thus Socialism, for example, must again and again ask itself, to what degree its own conceptual constructions still agree with its own and the total situation, and whether perhaps certain power groups in it do not themselves use the party theory ideologically, either by their firm adherence to it or by their modification of it. In this connection socialism has to draw from the general discussion of the concept of ideology something important for self-criticism; indeed it might very well be fatal for it, if it one-sidedly used the reproach of ideology as a weapon against its opponents and not also as a means of self-criticism." Translation by James Luther Adams (unpublished).
[131] *SD, GW*, II, p. 324.
[132] Ibid., p. 325.
[133] Ibid., pp. 266-68.
[134] Ibid., p. 274; see whole section, "The Radicalization and the Shattering of the Bourgeois Principle in the Class Struggle," pp. 273-77.
[135] Ibid., p. 324. For a writing that set out to demonstrate Tillich's religious socialism as an ideology, one would have expected a critical analysis of Tillich's ideology-concept. However, none is present in Amelung's Harvard dissertation. What he has done is to show that Tillich was not a functionalist. See esp. Chs. II and IV.
[136] Ibid., p. 325.
[137] "RS (II)," *Pol. Exp.*, p. 48. The text is in obvious error when it reads: "This is true for all varieties of pre-bourgeois social structure."
[138] *Rel. Sit.*, p. 42.
[139] Ibid., p. 105; "Basic Principles," *Pol. Exp.*, p. 77.
[140] "RS (II," *Pol. Exp.*, p. 48.
[141] Cf. *SD, GW*, II, fn. 6, p. 274; "Cl. St.," *GW*, II, pp. 184-87; "Sozialismus," *GW*, II, p. 148; "Basic Principles," *Pol. Exp.*, p. 78; *Rel. Sit.*, p. 110; "PPPS," *PE*, pp. 168-69.
[142] "The Demonic," *IH*, p. 91. Tillich wrote here that capitalism is demonic because it combines a creative-destructive tension in its production of goods and creates havoc in lives. P. 119-20. It should be remembered that along with capitalism Tillich considered nationalism a demonic power.

143"RS (II)," *Pol. Exp.*, p. 50. Cf. "Basic Principles," *Pol. Exp.*, p. 78.

144Marx and Engels, in Feuer, p. 7.

145"Basic Principles," *Pol. Exp.*, p. 78.

146Cf. *Das System des Wissenschaften*, *GW*, I, p. 146, where Tillich spoke of "*Uberzeugung*" and "*Wahrscheinlichkeit*" as the basis for the empirical sciences.

147*GW*, XII, p. 239.

148Ibid., p. 241.

149Ibid., p. 242.

150"Sozialismus," *GW*, II, pp. 145-46.

151"RS (II)," *Pol. Exp.*, p. 50; "PPPS," *PE*, p. 174. The notion of "calling" and its possible loss is in this context an important way of relativizing socialism's agent of change. This is one point where an orthodox Marxist could not follow Tillich, but this idea or its equivalent is essential for the Christian's evaluation of a group chosen to play a key role in historical change.

152Feuer, p. 15.

153*SD*, *GW*, II, p. 263. Cf. Adolf Hitler's statement: "Those among whom I passed my younger days belonged to the petit bourgeois class and the ditch which separates that class, which is by no means well off, from the manual laboring class is often deeper than you think. The reason for this attitude, which we may almost call enmity, lies in the fear that dominates a social group which has only just risen above the manual laborer--a fear lest it may fall back into its old condition or at least be classed with the laborers" (from *Mein Kampf*; quoted by Holborn, p. 713).

154Ibid., pp. 333-34.

CHAPTER 5

TRANSFORMING HISTORICAL DIALECT

Tillich considered "the real greatness" of socialist philosophy to be its philosophy of history. "Here we find its most significant creation, the Marxist dialectic of history." He identified three issues posed by dialectic: the substratum, the movement, and the goal of history.[1] In the preceding chapter the substratum, historical materialism, was the area of inquiry; in the present chapter the topics are the movement and the goal of history, that is, historical dialectic in a narrower sense. Historical dialectic and historical materialism belong together as two aspects of one socialist theory, but for the sake of this study they are being analyzed in separate chapters.

Tillich himself, it will be recalled, made the same division in calling the two "the central problems of Marxism."[2] Historical dialectic, an attempt to account for the nature of socio-political change, is at the center of Marxist theory. Tillich wrote that the relationship between Marxism and the proletarian movement is especially dependent on it, "for historical dialectic gives the theory of the movement."[3]

A proper understanding of historical dialectic is therefore crucial for socialism. In addressing his co-workers around the *Neue Blaetter,* Tillich said it is their task "to discover anew for socialism the meaning of dialectic on which socialism stands theoretically."[4] Above all this task meant bringing it into explicit relationship to the prophetic attitude. In order to understand Tillich's interpretation and transformation of historical dialectic, this chapter first looks at his view of historical change. In the second section the relationship between necessity and freedom--the issue Tillich thought was the key one--will be studied, followed by a discussion of "expectation" and its meaning for historical dialectic. Finally, Tillich's approach to the future, to the goal of history, will be examined.

Dialectical Change

Historical dialectic is a theory of socio-political change that asserts the unity of necessity or fate and freedom, and perceives the coming of a new social order from the tensions of the present. This in skeleton form is the meaning it had for Tillich. Contained within this brief definition are a number of issues that need to be clarified. Much of this discussion will concern the meaning of fate or necessity and its relation to freedom, especially in their connection with Tillich's prophetic principle. First, however, the focus is on his understanding of change as present within historical dialectic.

Marx, in seeking to explain the dynamics of capitalist society and to furnish the proletariat with a theory of struggle, gave historical dialectic classical expression.[5] Tillich considered that Marx's "real dialectical conception of history, his insight into the struggle character of history and simultaneously into the inner reason of historical development, is the last great historically effective conception of historical becoming."[6] In Tillich's view, however, socialism has squandered the true meaning of dialectic, and, therefore, in light of Marx--and Hegel and the prophetic tradition--he aimed to formulate afresh the theory that guides the socialist movement.

Tillich, in one of his first discussions of Marx's historical dialectic, suggested that his static substructure-superstructure image had only a "preliminary right" because of Marx's conception of the dialectical nature of historical change (see above, Chapter 4, p. 126). In this view, he explained, "the gestalts [of history] change without ceasing, one being born from another in a living, creative process. And dialectic seeks to grasp the essence of this change."[7] Tillich saw the purpose of dialectic as that of understanding historical change, and for this purpose he found the image of birth more appropriate than the architectural image. One also notes that he introduced the important concept "gestalt": an historical time is to be seen as a living, structural whole.

Furthermore, a gestalt is a wholistic structure of meaning. "Dialectical relationship is a relationship of meaning, and only meaning-bearing groups can enter into such a relationship." He rejected a causal-mechanistic schema as being inappropriate for a relationship among meaningful gestalts, and he added, in principle Marx had affirmed the notion of historical gestalts. "When Marx summarized and characterized an age, then he had cut through the undifferentiated flow of an unbroken series of causes and introduced an epochal gestalt view."[8]

Historical dialectic involved the periodization of history. Such a view of history was naturally congenial to Tillich's own epochal consciousness. Like Marx, he understood the present to mark the end of the bourgeois period of history, but, unlike Marx, he believed the present means not the end of religion but a new religious era. An important characteristic of dialectical thinking, whether in a theological (Joachim of Flora), logical (Hegel), or sociological (Marx) form, is that it is epochal thinking.[9] Tillich believed it is necessary to understand a period in time as a structural whole in order to comprehend the dynamics of change that lead beyond it.

The dynamics of change in dialectical thinking are tension, conflict, and discontinuity. "Dialectic is the historical category absolutely," remarked Tillich, "for all historical movement goes through affirmation and negation (*Setzung und Gegensetzung*), claim and contradiction." The task of the philosophy of history is therefore to discover "the elements that meet in tension and effect the movement." Tillich thought that Hegel's idea that these elements are "logical categories" is "impossible" because it "contradicts the inexhaustible ground of life of all events." Marx, who believed they are "economically-grounded class oppositions" (which, Tillich commented, held for the capitalist age but not necessarily for others), has shown "that every particular gestalt of society is realized by real power groups."[10]

In accepting this view (which he later attributed to Hegel, as will be seen), Tillich insisted that the bearers of the new gestalt idea are therefore simultaneously the bearers of power which develop in the "womb" of the old structure. He considered them always to be "revolutionary," regardless of whether they overcome the old through legal or illegal means. Thus, he argued, "every gestalt appears as a temporary compromise between the polarities of tension from which new powers and tensions break forth."[11] Tillich did not think one can give "a schematic presentation of this living dialectic," so he offered a summary very much in line with his ontological categories:

> In all the oppositions, somehow the opposition
> of the ground and abyss of meaning, of form and life,
> of morality and mysticism, of rational formation and
> irrational, creative will will return. It is that
> which the St. Simon school has characterized in a
> schematic way as the change from an organic to a
> critical age.[12]

With this model of change one analyzes a period as a whole in order to discover the decisive tension or contradiction, convinced that at this point the new will issue forth. This approach is essentially critical in its view of the existing order, since it recognizes a structural limitation in the present gestalt. Tillich's dialectical thinking embodies a critical, revolutionary "principle of negation," but it is balanced by another side: "Dialectical thinking subjects every moment of time to its 'Yes and No.' It does not negate the past unconditionally, and it does not affirm the future unconditionally."[13] This understanding is reflected in his concept of demonic whereby he evaluated capitalism as a creative as well as destructive force. In contrast to Hirsch, who saw the Weimar period in a totally positive light, Tillich never made "an absolute value judgment," "never called an age sinful." He added, however, that "we have called powers demonic."[14]

Tillich's dialectical approach is well illustrated in his brief remarks at Heppenheim where he and others were debating the meaning of a renewed socialism. "We can say nothing at all outside a gestalt of reality," said Tillich in cautioning against the hope of trying to find a place outside the present situation. But he did not think that the only alternative is then to describe the given reality.[15]

> Every living gestalt contains in its depths the
> conflict between a present and a becoming gestalt. We
> go out from this intuition (*Anschauung*) of the becoming gestalt and the conflict which it set in motion
> in the existing gestalt: this is dialectical thinking.[16]

He continued that the in-breaking of the becoming gestalt is "the concrete presupposition of every critique."[17] Then he posed a question:

> We stand before the decision: do we see in the
> proletariat the coming of the becoming gestalt or
> don't we? The socialist is one who thinks that the
> tension expressed in the proletarian situation of our
> present moment announces the new, coming gestalt.
> This is dialectical thinking.[18]

Tillich inquired if "the consciousness of standing in this tension of gestalts" might be a common foundation for the group's work.[19]

Frequently in his talk Tillich used the words *Schauen* and *Anschauen* to characterize his approach. In order to discover the tensions of history, one looks to reality. He contrasted his dialectical posture with both a spectator stance and "an abstract knowledge of values" by insisting that looking is itself action, "responsible intuiting." He was quick to point out that the dialectical method is therefore one of risk: "Our intuition is a *venture*. Socialism is a venture that can fail . . . . Socialism is a venture from the present into the future."[20] Historical dialectic is, as he wrote elsewhere, "an intuition of the coming [gestalt] out of the tensions of the present."[21]

Tillich's method includes rational knowledge as well as intuitive knowledge and risk. He accepted Marx's analysis that the class struggle is "a structural necessity in capitalist society" (see above, Chapter 4, p. 149), and that there "arises the marked tendency to overcome the form of society on which that structure depends," a tendency that can be represented dialectically, as Marx had done.[22] Tillich, like Marx, recognized the class struggle as the critical point of tension, and he thought the proletarian situation represents the coming of the new gestalt. For him the next period of history is to be realized through this social tension.

Tillich contrasted dialectical analysis with that of positivistic forms of science, rejecting the latter as the only form. Dialectic "knows no objects whose 'essence' is fixed, but functional relationships in which the particular 'is' something different according to the moment of development. Its being posits itself in social tensions."[23] One looks to the whole and understands the parts on the basis of the encounter between the old and the new.

Throughout this discussion the word "tension" or *Spannung* has often reappeared. The reason for this is that tension characterizes the nature of life which dialectic seeks to grasp. "To be alive is to go beyond one's self . . . . Where there is life there is a tension between 'being one with one's self' and 'separating from one's self.'"[24] History for Tillich, as previously indicated, "drives forward from every present into the future," "is tension towards that which is to come," and "points beyond itself."[25] Tillich understood historical reality as dialectical, that is, as tension-filled change, moving beyond itself in a continuous process of identity and separation.

Tillich's understanding of historical change was indebted in part to Hegel, particularly the young Hegel. His 1932 essay, "The Young Hegel and the Fate of Germany," reveals this influence and demonstrates some of the background to his idea of fate.[26] According to Tillich, the highpoint of Hegel's early development came when he "found the idea of fate as the solution of his questioning"; from then on his philosophy became "an interpretation of fate." Tillich believed that the early experience of Hegel as well as the principle of his later philosophy is expressed in the sentence: "'What is contradiction in the realm of the dead is not contradiction in the realm of the living.'" He interpreted this to mean that "the beginning point of Hegelian questioning is the world of the dead, of standing over against (*Gegenueberstehenden*), or unreconciled contradiction. His goal is life as union, as reconciled contradiction."[27]

In the course of his discussion Tillich advanced the thesis that Hegel came to see that reconciliation is only possible when that which stands over against us is understood as fate, as "that which is our own (*das Eigene*) that has become foreign to us, as life that has turned against life." Fate is seen by Hegel as life separated from itself, yet it is life. For Hegel, "the unity of life is stronger than the violation and the contradiction," and therefore one has to allow fate to take effect and one has to bear the pain of separation. "Then, however, reconciliation is possible . . . . The synthesis is more original than the antithesis."[28]

Hegel, in applying this idea to politics and history, contended, that "it is impossible to master fate with force. The impulsive revolutionary, the utopianist, are broken on reality." Hegel did not mean by this that one should accept what is, for one must place reality under the judgment of something better, interpreted Tillich. But demands do not help "unless fate itself breaks into itself, unless it goes beyond the old gestalt with the power of a new gestalt whose [fate's] truth flows from it [the new gestalt]. Fate reconciles itself with itself through the progress of historical gestalts."[29] This idea finds frequent expression in Tillich's writings.

Tillich stated further that fate for Hegel thus came to mean "the movement of life itself that constantly creates gestalts; it [fate] drives by violation of itself into cleavage (*Zwiespalt*) and to reconciliation in new gestalts." This "abstract thought" of Hegel is made "concrete" in that "the new gestalt is an expression of this reconciliation." Because history is seen as the "separation (*Entzweiung*) and reconciliation of life with itself," the role of the moral demand is viewed as being able to do nothing but recognize and co-actualize (*mitvollziehen*) through action the way life itself is going. With this idea of fate, asserted Tillich, the young Hegel "discovered the real dialectical interpretation of history and of human, historically conscious activity. Through Marx it became for Germany a fate-determining idea of the first order."[30]

The fate of history for Hegel is, according to Tillich, actualized by the attack of a new power against an old. The attacker is both "the energies that bear new life" and "the carrier of truth, a truth which was intended in the old gestalt of life but was not realized," Tillich found in Hegel's notion of the new power a normative element present from the onset. Both Marx and Bismarck adopted this side of the doctrine of historical fate, the former finding the coming truth and power in the proletariat and the latter in the power-state (as did the later Hegel). Tillich believed Marx grasped the dialectic better and measured the reality more adequately, and therefore he became "the executor of the early against the later Hegel."[31] Marx, in discovering the self-separation of the life of Western humanity in the opposition of classes, dissolved the synthesis of the later Hegel and pointed to a deeper, more lasting reconciliation than Hegel had considered.[32]

Hegel's insight that life is a movement of separation and reconciliation is incorporated into the basis of Tillich's theory of change, as is the idea of fate as "the correlate of human action" and as "a universal historical category."[33] His differences with Hegel, especially the later Hegel (for example, with his idealism, his notion of synthesis, and his belief that the Prussian state represented reconciled reality), are important. These differences, however, should not obscure points of similarity between the two.[34] The task of philosophy and theology as the interpretation of fate, the centrality of a doctrine of historical fate, the ontological priority of unity to separation, the view of one's own age as marked by division and separation and the coming of a new gestalt characterized by synthesis and reconciliation, and the coordination of moral action with the movement of history are ideas that Tillich found in Hegel and that one finds in Tillich. As this essay demonstrates, Tillich read Hegel through Marx, and, as it also makes clear, he read Marx through Hegel. Central to all three is a conviction that history involves conflict between the old and the new, a movement which is best characterized by historical dialectic, whose originator was Hegel.

One significant difference between Tillich and some of his later interpreters pertains to this question of dialectical change. Some, especially in the post-World War II, "end of ideology" period, rejected his historical dialectic in favor of a non-dialectical, gradualist, "piece-meal engineering" approach to change.[35] This view was stamped by its historical fate at least as much as Tillich's had been, an interpretation that receives support by noting that Tillich's own position at this time was not dissimilar from those of the critics of his earlier ideas (see below, Chapter 6, Section 6). There is little doubt that Tillich's sweeping epochal attitude is largely irrelevant to a pragmatic, so-called non-ideological attitude. Today, however, the truth of the latter approach has been questioned, and there is new concern about structural limitations and new interest in exploring alternatives to the present. In this setting Tillich's dialectical thinking, which did not envision change happening all at once but did seek to conceive fundamental structural change, is not irrelevant.

The Unity of Freedom and Necessity

Tillich understood historical dialectic to be a theory of change that maintains the unity of freedom and necessity. Inherent in the conflict of gestalts is a "necessary" direction; in history's struggles there is, as he had said of Marx's ideas, "the inner reason of historical development." Tillich called this inner reason "necessity" or "fate" (words he used interchangeably), and he linked it with the free, creative power of historical groups. With his socialist analysis of the capitalist structure, Tillich noted at the decisive point of tension, class opposition, the "marked tendency" to go beyond capitalism, a tendency borne by the proletariat. Tillich's efforts to formulate anew the theory of historical dialectic were done in relationship to this movement of history and its reciprocal relation to human action. He was concerned with the meaning of necessity and freedom and their unity in this process of change.[36]

Fate and freedom are preeminently for Tillich "the historical categories." When the two are connected, freedom, the going beyondness of life, is brought into relation "with the whole of existence," which also includes standing before the Unconditional. "Both are one in every event which constitutes history."[37] One cannot speak of one without the other, for, as Tillich defined it, "fate is the transcendent necessity in which freedom is entangled." This statement includes three claims. First, fate implies freedom; without freedom there is no fate but only blind necessity. Secondly, "freedom is subjected to necessity. It puts freedom into an embracing frame of reference." Thirdly, it means that the two can never be separated "but that, in every fateful event, freedom and necessity interpenetrate each other." A person feels both a sense of responsibility for what he does, and yet, at the same time, observed Tillich, he feels that he is conditioned by events that go back for generations, events embedded in much earlier expressions "of the continuing and living fabric of humanity. He feels that the necessity implied in the concept of fate is a universal necessity, a necessity that transcends every special chain of events." It is in this sense that "freedom and necessity are conditioned by each other and are inextricably interwoven."[38]

Schicksal (like *Notwendigkeit*) combines the meaning of "fate" and "destiny" for Tillich, although it lacks the connotations of blindness connected with the former.[39] It refers to the unbroken web of relationships in which a person lives, and it suggests a positive, meaningful, and inevitable direction to history (although the word "inevitable" is too strong or at least should be understood in a non-natural scientific manner, as Tillich would insist). Fate is "the correlate of human action" (from Tillich's essay on Hegel) as well as "the impulse of events themselves" (a description of expectation given by Tillich, see above, Chapter 3, p. 103). It is a word that speaks both of the past and the future, offering to freedom a universal framework. The "God wills it" of the prophetic tradition and the "*es muss*" of Hegel and Marx express Tillich's notion of transcendent necessity.[40] In all three, "one finds the peculiar notion that history moves forward toward its goal, as it were, *behind the backs of the participants in historical action.*" In Marx, for example, Tillich saw this uttered in his idea that "the movement of a capitalist economy, quite contrary to the knowledge and intention of its participants, leads to its transmutation into the classless society." In him and the others, interpreted Tillich, "being moves toward what should be, without the demand being championed by conscious human action, indeed often in opposition to all human knowing and willing."[41]

Tillich considered necessity (or fate) and freedom the key components of historical dialectic, but he also thought that their meaning has been seriously misconceived by socialists. "Since Engels the profundity of the dialectical idea has been less and less understood. Western socialism has never adopted it, but rather has put the ethical, utopian element in the center."[42] The first sentence refers to the mainstream of the German socialist tradition and the second to an ethical socialism whose major spokesperson was de Man, who had originally come from Belgium. In developing his own constructive proposal, Tillich "battled" on these two fronts.

According to Tillich, the orthodox socialist view of the dialectic has been determined by a mechanistic way of thinking derived from metaphysical materialism. In addition, having been influenced by Neo-Kantianism, these socialists have made the dialectic into a purely methodological matter.[43] In *The Socialist Decision* Tillich spoke of this position as belonging to an older generation of socialists who still hold the leadership of the SPD. Rooted in the period of militant and progressive socialism and determined by the positivism of the late nineteenth century, they maintain "the scientifically-grounded belief in

a necessary development leading to the socialist society." For
them, therefore, "the socialist struggle is itself a calculable
consequence of this calculable process." They believe that
this process creates the struggle, not vice versa, and that
step by step the economic development leads inevitably to victory.[44]

For such a view, which emerges in a "'thingified' world,
necessity can only imply the law of cause and effect and of
calculability." More than anything else, wrote Tillich, this
variety of Marxism "has broken the power of socialist action,"
for if necessity is a calculable process, one can only act in
a calculating manner. He acknowledged that as a result Marxist
intellectuals have achieved a high degree of success in predicting the technical organization and the development of capitalism, "but what for socialism is the decisive factor, the human response to these developments, was judged wholly incorrectly." With their primitive understanding of man, explained Tillich, they are unable to account for the reaction of the proletariat, the bourgeoisie, and the political romantics.[45]

Tillich thought the fault of this theory is that it
"viewed man and history in terms of a thing with attributes,
and thus fell into insoluble contradictions." In such a view
"freedom is excluded, for a thing is totally conditioned"; nevertheless, one has to affirm freedom for the sake of the political struggle. For Tillich, this contradiction can only be
resolved "*when the model of a thing is abandoned*." This requirement, he wrote, is the prerequisite for understanding the
dialectic and recognizing the unconditionality of freedom and
the possibility of the new."[46]

Tillich accounted for the rise of "a voluntaristic, ethical socialism" as a reaction to this vulgar Marxism. This attitude is especially prevalent in a young generation which had
experienced the Russian Revolution and had witnessed the tremendous powers of the will that prevailed in it, against all
calculations. For them human action became the decisive factor
and "freedom took the place of necessity. The motives of ethical socialism . . . covered up the Marxist foundation. The
spirit of youth rebelled against the spectator attitude." As
a result, he continued, demands were raised that had no basis

in reality, and along came the dangers of utopianism--"the arbitrariness and caprice of the demand, the inclination toward romanticism, the overestimation of the thinking and willing of individuals, and estrangement from the movement of the masses." Tillich also pronounced a negative judgment on this position. Ethical socialism, too, has "grievously misunderstood" the dialectical method and is "equally far removed from reality" as is orthodox socialism, for its action is not related to necessity, to "the inner meaning and aim of every particular historical process," to "the impulse of history in each of its moments."[47]

Tillich's critical estimate of de Man's attempt to go "beyond Marx" arose from this vantage point. In reviewing *The Psychology of Socialism* he wrote that socialism "in its creative beginning has a principle of self-criticism that must not simply be pushed aside. Neither Marx nor Marxism is historically exhausted." He repeated his belief that in a changed and contemporary form this principle has continuing significance for German socialism and for Western culture in general.[48]

> In the determinism of Marx is something entirely different from mechanism and mathematics. In it is "dialectic" and to that de Man obviously has no access. The consciousness of destiny which is the depth of dialectical thinking and the power of its effectiveness is missing from his voluntarism. The willing of the proletariat is nothing if it is not in its basis bound with the basis of present events in general; and the certainty of the proletariat that its willing leads to the goal is either born by the authority of a genuine feeling of destiny or it is impotent. . . . Only the will that is formed through the intuition of the time of fate is penetrating and revolutionary.[49]

De Man, in rightly rejecting determinism, has in Tillich's eyes also lost the depth of Marxism, having undercut its sense of destiny or fate. In de Man it is "the accidental will" of the proletariat that fights for socialism, while "for the genuine Marx it is the essential will (*Wesenwille*) in which the meaning of a new age penetrates." Marx, Tillich noted, has seen "a turning of the times" in all areas of life whereas de Man sees only an improvement in the situation of the workers. "We must be on guard," he wrote, "that the going beyond Marx is not reversed into a falling behind Marx." He urged that the "historically-conscious thinking," "the ontological layer of depth," "the universality of the Marxist interpretation," "the consciousness of destiny," and "the spirit of prophecy" characteristic of Marx not be lost to socialism.[50]

These phrases and this review indicate that Tillich considered "fate" and its proper apprehension essential for the socialist dialectic. Marx's dialectic pointed to a dimension of reality beyond the empirical (or below the surface, as Tillich was more likely to say) which one grasps (or which grasps one) by intuition and faith. This reality is not available to the "flat" approach of de Man, and so his voluntarism remains unconvincing, for Tillich's dialectical viewpoint.

One notes that Tillich also used a pragmatic, political argument to dispute de Man's socialism. Tillich found immense value in the Marxist dialectic in bestowing on the struggling proletariat the consciousness and the certainty of being a fateful people at a fateful time. With de Man this is lost, and the proletariat is in danger of being absorbed by the capitalist system. De Man seemed willing to accept this, but Tillich was not and therefore dismissed the reformist option for the revolutionary, for the belief that the proletariat offer a possibility for a new societal gestalt. He recognized that this demand can only be sustained when there is certainty that reality itself is on the side of the demand.

> Vulgar Marxism wasted this power because it turned the dialectic into a method of calculation which is forever changing and constantly a source of disappointment. Ethical socialism can never evoke this power because it presents a demand which is unrelated to being and is not one with the impulse of history.[51]

The consequences of socialism's perception of its dialectic is an important factor in Tillich's consideration of its meaning.

Tillich's two-sided battle was waged against "a belief either in meaningless necessity or in meaningless willfulness as the heart of things. In place of the meaningful framework of fate and in place of spiritual reality, whose highest form is creative freedom, there appears the demonic pair, necessity and change."[52] He rejected orthodox Marxism because of its meaningless necessity and ethical socialism because of its meaningless willfulness in favor of a concept that offers freedom a meaningful structure. He sought to be a "bridge" between the two generations representing these poles by going "back to the real Marx and to a concept of dialectic which maintains the connection of freedom and necessity."[53]

The unity of historical dialectic is established, according to Tillich, only on the basis of its religious character (see above, Chapter 3, Section 1, p. 73; Section 2). Tillich's view of freedom has already been discussed (see above, Chapter 3, esp. pp. 76-77, 102). To be meaningful freedom requires a framework, which finally is accessible only by faith. For Tillich freedom is undergirded by faith in necessity. "Genuine dialectic is faith in historical predestination and has in itself the entire authority of activity which the consciousness of being bearers of destiny brings."[54] The necessity of faith does not destroy freedom but rather gives it meaning and power. In describing predestination, Tillich wrote of its "paradox" in that "it unites in itself human freedom and transcendent necessity." This paradox, he stated, is not "an intellectual construction but an accurate image of the real behaviour." He cited Calvinism as an example in which "the Yes to transcendent necessity is simultaneously a Yes to immanent freedom." In the proletarian movement he discussed the same paradox: "it combines the certainty that the expected future is coming with the feeling of responsibility for its coming."[55] The unity of universal necessity and historical responsibility, expressed so perspicuously in the last sentence, is for Tillich the proper meaning of historical dialectic.

Tillich's interpretation of the socialist dialectic is theological. The key to his reconstruction is the recognition of its religious character and its transformation from a prophetic-eschatological perspective. He summarized his position when he wrote that religious socialism "regards the unity of the socialist dialectic, a unity of expectation and demand of that which is to come, as a conceptual unity and at the same time as a concrete and contemporary transformation of the Christian eschatological tension."[56] In an unpublished talk from the early 1930's he stated its theological character in this fashion: "Dialectic is faith in destiny . . . Dialectic is the unity of freedom and necessity. This faith, which in other times has been proclaimed under the religious symbol of the kingdom of God that is dawning, is my conception for the solution of the socialist antimony."[57]

At this point it is clear that Tillich's kairos concept was developed in relation to his understanding of historical dialectic (the reverse is of course also true). Kairotic thinking is dialectical thinking. The kairos points to "the concrete tensions [from which] the new creation proceeds"; it is a unity of necessity and freedom, for in it "the holy that is given and the holy that is demanded meet."[58] The kairos marks the dialectical turning of the times. As he wrote in relation to the Kairos, "the meaning of dialectical thinking from here is nothing else than the certainty of standing in this grace. For historical fate is grace."[59]

Here and elsewhere Tillich equated fate and grace; he also used the ambiguous phrases "faith (or belief) in the kairos" or "faith in fate." These phrases should not be misinterpreted to mean that Tillich thought history itself is God or the Unconditional. Rather (as in a phrase such as "faith in the church"), they should be seen as an affirmation of the concrete locus of the Unconditional's revelation, the place of "religious realization."[60] To believe in fate in Tillich's language is to acknowledge the coming of God's grace in history.

Furthermore, Tillich's understanding of fate as grace is dependent upon his interpretation of Christian doctrines that concern history--creation, providence, and eschatology. For Tillich the goodness of creation and the triumph of time over space mean that "a 'gracious' destiny that brings salvation in time and history subdues a demonic fate which denies the new in history."[61] He considered "the certainty that fate is divine and not demonic, that it is meaning-fulfilling and meaning-destroying" to be "the inmost kernel of Christianity."[62]

These affirmations stand behind Tillich's speaking of fate as grace. Expressed differently, Tillich with his doctrines of kairos and fate is making these beliefs concrete. This concreteness, done with awareness of the daring involved and carried out in a subtle and dialectical fashion, is one of the most remarkable characteristics of his theological interpretation of socio-political realities. It is also one of its most problematic features. The most obvious reason for saying this is that history did not cooperate with his proclamation, a contingency that his theology allowed for, however, his uniting of fate and grace also gives his religious socialism an optimistic coloring at points which appears foreign to many in the last quarter of the twentieth century. But perhaps the major reason for its problematic nature is the unfathomable difficulty of the question itself. If one accepts with Tillich the belief that historical fate for the Christian is meaning-fulfilling and the conviction that grace becomes concrete in history, in spite of all the contradictions, then one is left struggling with his question: Where is this grace? When is historical fate grace-ful?[63]

In this section Tillich's understanding of historical dialectic as the unity of freedom and necessity has been outlined in relationship to the demonic pair, necessity and chance, that he intended to avoid. His most complete discussion of the meaning of this view of dialectic came in his elaboration of expectation, the subject for the next part of this study.

Historical Dialectic as Expectation

Previously the anthropological, theological, and socialist meaning of expectation, the central concept of *The Socialist Decision,* was discussed (see above, Chapter 3, Section 4). Now it is necessary to make explicit the relationship of historical dialectic to it. Expectation, the human posture directed to the new, which is both openness to the future and the impulse of history, is a unity of freedom and necessity. Expectation expresses the tension both of prophetic eschatology and historical dialectic. Tillich's continuing exploration of this term spelled out various aspects of this unity and tension.

Expectation for Tillich is a unity of promise and demand. "The expected is that which will come, and, to the extent it *will* come, it is not dependent on human activity. And the expected is that which *ought* to come, that which is demanded, and to the extent that it is demanded, it is achieved only through human activity." In this tension, he remarked, is "the depth of the socialist principle." In describing the prophets he made the point that their message was always directed to discerning the promise and demand of a unique situation.[64] Characteristically, he emphasized the concreteness of these two theological (Gospel-law) concepts, and argued that they come together in reality.

Because of the demand, expectation is not "passive waiting," "inactive observation," or "irrelevant theory" but involved action. In contrast to political romanticism which also knows the demand but aims at preserving the origin, Tillich saw the prophetic and socialistic imperative transcending the origin and pointing to the new. The demand "places every power, 'high and low,' under its criticism." This for him is the deeper meaning of "*the demand for equality,*" since "the unavoidability of the imperative, which addresses everyone, makes everyone equal."[65]

Because the demand places every power under its judgment, Tillich argued that it embraces possibilities for both self-sacrifice and self-fulfillment. In the presence of the unconditionality of the demand, the fullness of one's being becomes insignificant so that there "arises the extraordinary possibility that human existence may be fulfilled through the severest diminution of being." He considered the positive evaluation of humility in the prophetic and Christian traditions based on this possibility. The unconditional character of the demand also includes the imperative "that each person shall be treated in accordance with his destiny, that each person shall be allowed to enjoy the fullness of being without which, normally, his humanity will be destroyed." He understood the meaning of the demand to incorporate both "the ideal of universal fulfillment of each person's being and the extreme case of radical diminution of being." But the latter meaning, he maintained against a possible perversion, cannot rightly be made into an ideology that glorifies the situation of the poor and defends an unjust rule.[66]

Tillich did not elevate equality as an abstract principle to the pinnacle of his moral hierarchy nor propose egalitarianism as the universally valid moral system of socialism. He feared such proposals because of their neglect of the concreteness of the demand and its unity with promise.[67] Rather, in speaking of the "deeper" meaning of the demand for equality, he was emphasizing that everyone is subject to the unconditional seriousness of the demand while maintaining the particular character of each demand.[68] It is in this light that he interpreted the demand of the prophets, who, he wrote, "fought against

the repression of the poor by the powerful, and threatened the
whole people with destruction on account of such injustice,"
and of Marx who "*fought against the 'thingification' of man and
for a real humanism.*" Today, he declared, "the proletarian
situation as the crisis in bourgeois society and as the refuta-
tion of political romanticism" proclaims the demand to action
of expectation.[69]

Clearly, socialism for Tillich is a moral concern. Socialism's attack on bourgeois morality or "necessity's" inevitability does not in his view eliminate the moral imperative. In as-
serting that socialism is what ought to be, Tillich believed
he was making explicit something that is usually hidden but is
present in Marx and in the proletarian movement. He appealed
to the unconditional demand because it is intrinsic to the
freedom that characterizes the human as human. In spite of
Tillich's fear of legalism, utopianism, and abstraction, he
supported socialism as a movement for justice. What he did object to is the separation of the demand from the promise.

Tillich also understood expectation as a unity of goal and
origin. One way the concept of expectation unites the two is
by showing that "the goal is the fulfillment of what is intended by the origin," which is the source for "the content of
the socialist expectation."[70] Theologically, one can rephrase
Tillich's statement by saying that the eschaton is the fulfillment and not the destruction of creation. Tillich saw this connection between goal and origin as meaning three things: first,
the demand and promise have to engage those to whom they are
directed; secondly, the presence of the demand and promise presuppose unfulfillment; and thirdly, fulfillment is in accord
with the true origin. The correspondence between the beginning
and the end in myth and reason (e.g., Marx's primitive communism) means, observed Tillich, that the expected must have the
features of the origin, even if changed by history. "The origin cannot be effaced in the fulfillment."[71]

Tillich's immediate interest in pursuing this relationship
is to offer a basis for understanding the continuing existence
of the powers of origin in the socialist society. He foresaw
that the society expected by socialism will not be one in which
being is abrogated and constituted by consciousness, as it is

for the bourgeois principle, but rather one that will fulfill being "in its real power, its particularities, its tensions, and its forces of *eros*." The demand, however, means that "being comes to its fulfillment only through the negating of its immediate power." The powers of origin will be present but as something new, changed by the imperative of justice.[72]

Therefore, "the classless society" is not for Tillich a complete contradiction of the present, not a future molded by an abstract norm of justice unrelated to the origin, but one in which the powers of origin are alive. "The factors of soil, blood, and social group," of "traditions and symbols," and of "faith and devotion" will be present. Tillich recognized that differentiations among the proletariat, geographical distinctions, and possible alliances with farmers, for example, are important in preparing "*the structures of the classless society*."[73] He insisted that the coming socialist order will not be one of automatic harmony nor of submission to the powers of origin.

> The opposition (*Gegeneinander*) of the powers of origin can never cease; and in this opposition there is the danger of violence and violation. Space and its juxtapositions (*Nebeneinander*) will not and should not be abolished. But socialism can challenge these powers with the demand of justice and check their unbroken influence for an unforeseeable period of history.[74]

In stating that the origin provides the content for the socialist expectation, Tillich is giving a vital and legitimate value to the shared experiences of the various groups in society.[75] He is altering the meaning of the classless society so as to embrace diversity and to include the specific features of the people who will comprise it.[76] He knew that in the future man will remain in his wholeness and not be a disembodied mind. In accordance with the entire argument of *The Socialist Decision*, these values and realities are, however, subordinated to the second root and the norm of justice, for these powers, if unchecked and unbroken, are demonic and portend barbarism. Here as throughout the book, time triumphs over space.

Tillich conceived expectation as uniting goal and origin in a second way by showing that "the origin engenders the power through which the goal is realized," providing "the way to its [expectation's] fulfillment."[77] This is another way of expressing the crux of his understanding of historical dialectic: the unity of being and obligation, of promise and demand, of necessity and freedom. His thesis is that "*the demand cannot move life if life itself is not moving in the direction of that which is demanded.* . . . Only when being moves itself toward its fulfillment can one speak of promise and thus of expectation." Here too Tillich discussed the symbol of providence and its rationalized forms in Hegel (who, however, finally lost the ought in the is) and Marx. The decisive model for Tillich is the notion of providence which expresses "the confidence that that which is is not utterly removed from that which ought to be; that in spite of all the nonfulfillment of being, being moves in the direction of its own fulfillment." Providence is the unity of *Sein* and *Sollen*.[78]

Tillich quite expectedly found a structural similarity in Marx's dialectic where "*the socialist demand is confirmed by being itself*."[79] In the dialectic there is "a direction, an impetus," in which history goes from the origin to final fulfillment, "but it moves this way through human *action*." He considered it impossible to speak of fulfillment if human action is bypassed, for "the fulfillment of being is fulfilled human action that corresponds to the demand." On the other hand, this action is not arbitrary since it is in tune with "the impulse of history," which, Tillich again made clear, is not "an objective process" or "a succession of external events," but "the inner meaning and the aim of every particular historical process."[80]

> Socialist action has an inherent certainty that it corresponds to the meaning and impulse of history. For it concerns the fulfillment of the origin in the goal, understood in terms of the contemporary situation. It is the prophetic movement in our times; it is the movement which puts itself under the demand of justice.[81]

Historical dialectic, symbolized by expectation, is a unifying conception. Obligation is grounded in being, freedom is united with the meaningful structure of necessity, and action receives its power from the promise. The dual demons of chance and necessity are avoided by affirming freedom and embracing the vision of a meaningful destiny. Tillich also understood historical dialectic as both a rational and a religious construct. Expectation unites the prophetic and the rational.

Because socialism is a prophetic movement on autonomous soil, it expresses its substance in rational terms. Tillich's descriptions of socialism's antagonisms suggest the dangers he saw in this connection (see above, Chapter 3, pp. 99-100; Chapter 4, pp. 133-138). Yet he could also speak of "its uniqueness, its profundity," "its contemporaneity and its veracity--in contrast to the frivolous self-abnegation of autonomy and rationality in political romanticism." Prophetic and rational expectation are in tension but not in contradiction, for living expectation is, he claimed, always both.[82]

Tillich described how the double character of expectation is effective in relationship to the goal of socialism:

> Insofar as expectation has prophetic character, it transcends the known, the calculable, the manipulable aspects of being. It points to a new creation, something wholly other. Insofar as expectation has a rational character, it remains within the dimension of the knowable. It too looks for something "other," but not "wholly other." That which is coming stands in unbroken connection with what is present now. *Prophetic expectation is transcendent; rational expectation is immanent.*[83]

The prophets, wrote Tillich in illustrating his description, saw the coming reality in continuity with the present, but they depicted it with concepts that presuppose a total transformation of the present. Or, they saw the coming order breaking in through a world catastrophe, yet they described it with pictures taken from everyday life. Tillich believed that the socialist expectation shows the same transcendent-immanent oscillation. Socialism's immanent demands for equality and freedom actually presuppose "a radical transformation of human nature" and therefore of nature and its laws. He found "the classless society" to be "just as much a transcendent symbol as an immanent object." Therefore, stated Tillich, "*both prophetic and socialist expectation are a witness of life to its fundamental openness. They are a protest of life against false concepts of transcendence which inevitably call forth, in opposition, false concepts of this-worldliness.*"[84]

Tillich also discerned the prophetic and rational nature of expectation operative in questions related to the way of socialism.

> Insofar as expectation is prophetic, it reckons with the incalculable, which cannot be known from the

> context of being. Insofar as the expectation is rational, it seeks to eliminate the incalculable and to reveal the powers of destiny as demonstrable and controllable causal sequences. *Prophetic expectation acknowledges factors that are in principle incomprehensible; rational expectation only factors that have not as yet been comprehended.*[85]

He recognized this relationship as present in both the prophets and socialism. The prophets, who reckoned with the miraculous, nevertheless pointed to all the available historical, political, and social factors; and socialism maintains a firm commitment to its expectation in spite of the changing character (favorable and unfavorable) of the evidence. "The reality of a living expectation always and everywhere precedes an abstract analysis of its components."[86]

Tillich applied the same insight to the historical dialectic itself. It also is both rational and prophetic, a symbol as well as a concept. "A sense of transcendent destiny is just as apparent in its background as are the investigation of historical factors and a policy for the shaping of history in the foreground." The two are interdependent and do not limit each other. Rational analysis has an element within itself that is inaccessible to it, and the prophetic belief in providence always looks to the historical situation. "A living historical consciousness, as it exists in socialism, represents this unity. The person in action assumes it at every moment." The tension of the prophetic and rational in socialism is for Tillich "a genuine expression of a living expectation."[87]

Once more Tillich unites phenomena; the reality requires it. Distinctions are drawn between the prophetic and the rational, both are affirmed, and both become one in the person and movement that live and act in expectation.[88] The person living with this attitude knows that neither rational prediction nor religious anticipation is sufficient in facing the future. His attitude toward the future is one of confidence in spite of the "in spite of's." He combines careful study of continuities and yet awaits the new and the uncalculable, for what is coming is both rational and transrational.

Tillich's discussion of expectation is suggestive. In it he captured the future thrust of the Biblical tradition and articulated it in contemporary form. Missing, however, is consideration of the concept of promise in relation to its giver.[89]

Tillich also offered a significant description of the phenomenon of expectation, all the more so, since it is described as a social phenomenon. Finally, his account of expectation was his most complete and convincing portrayal of the *dynamis* of socialism.

Expectation has a social locus. The proletarian situation was called by Tillich "a favored place" for learning "*the interrelation of human being, historical reality, and the socialist demand.*" Because it stands "on the negative side of society" and experiences the injustice of the social structure in its own existence, the proletariat's natural reaction is one of "tension toward a new order of things, toward justice." Marx, wrote Tillich, was right in linking socialist knowledge and action with the proletariat, for here socialism grows out of existence itself with dialectical necessity, offering initial proof for the historical dialectic.[90]

> Being and obligation are thus linked together once again in a concrete human situation. The socialist challenge and historical existence are as one in the knowledge and action of the proletariat. At the same time, a structure of human existence itself is disclosed in such thought and action, thus demonstrating that socialism is the decisive concern of Western humanity as a whole.[91]

Tillich's socialism is dependent on the proletariat. Once more he confirmed and elaborated the original point discussed in Chapter 3: socialism is an expression of the proletarian situation. Its universality is present in its particularity, revealing expectation as a structure of human existence, and making socialism crucial for Europe and beyond. The significance of socialism extends beyond the proletariat, and yet for Tillich it is completely dependent upon this fragile, historical agent of change.

The proletarian situation represents the unity of *Sein* and *Sollen* in concrete reality; it is the place where necessity and freedom are united, where the demand for justice comes directly from historical existence. It is the locus where the Unconditional breaks into reality and yet remains transcendent. It is for Tillich the place of truth, for a dynamic concept of truth which unites "Kairos and Logos."[92] The proletarian situation, which by its nature is eminently anti-ideological, provides the criterion for distinguishing between ideology and truth.[93]

Therefore, in his review of *Ideology and Utopia* he disputed Mannheim's contention that the intelligentsia is the place where the best possibility of knowledge exists. Although they might be to a degree sociologically less bound than other groups, they are not so psychologically.[94]

> In accordance with the dynamic theory of knowledge it would, however, be consistent if that group which stands in the dynamic process at a decisive position, that is, where the real situation is evident, should become the bearers of the essential possibility of knowledge--at the moment, for example, the proletariat.[95]

Tillich believed that socialism has rightly discovered in the proletariat "a vantage point from which alone the real state of existence can become visible for the mind of our day."[96] The test of true knowledge is the proletarian situation.

For Tillich, true knowledge, which is born of the kairos and which shares the ambiguity of all free decisions made in history, is not absolute knowledge.[97] The only absolute knowledge is "the fundamental judgment about the relationship of the Unconditional and the conditioned." In this relationship the Unconditional is "the guardian" which averts "the encroachment of a conditioned point of view on the sphere of the Unconditional."[98] Socialism is under the Protestant principle as is the proletariat (who can lose its favored place). The truth of socialism is not absolute truth since it is subjected to the Unconditional.

A brief summary of the salient points of Tillich's concept of historical dialectic discussed thus far may be helpful, even if it risks oversimplification.

1) Historical dialectic is a revolutionary theory of change, that is, it understands the tensions of the present--class struggle--as leading to a fundamentally new social gestalt.

2) In this process of change historical dialectic asserts and demonstrates the unity of freedom and necessity.

3) Vulgar Marxism and ethical socialism destroy this unity, in effect basing their positions on a belief that either freedom or necessity is meaningless. Objecting to both, Tillich affirmed the creativity of freedom within a meaningful structure.

4) Necessity, fate, or destiny (which are to be comprehended both rationally and religiously) refer to the "direction"

or "impulse" of history which paradoxically is not dependent on human action but which is not realized without it.

5) Expectation, a symbol for historical dialectic and for the kingdom of God, unites being and obligation, promise and demand, origin and goal, necessity and freedom, the rational and the prophetic. Tillich sought to express the wholeness of living expectation as found in the proletariat and in the prophets.

6) Historical dialectic is grounded in the proletariat whose predicament represents the favored place for dialectical change. The dialectic gives to this class the certainty that its struggle is worthwhile and that a meaningful future is coming while creating a passionate sense of responsibility for its coming.

7) Socialism is the prophetic movement of the present because it acts in accord with the necessity of history and stands under the demand of justice. Because it struggles to overcome the demonic power of a class-structured society in which all are involved, its significance is universal.

History's Future

Historical dialectic posits the end of history, the necessary outcome of historical development. Tillich considered that questions about the goal (*Ziel*) of history raise "the most difficult problems, which are the least resolved, in which, however, philosophical-historical thinking culminates."[99] Much of what has been discussed thus far, particularly in relation to the concept of expectation, indicates Tillich's basic position, a position that strives for an alternative to both this-worldly and other-worldly utopias. Because of its importance, however, Tillich's transformation of historical dialectic's view of the future will be probed further and in a more direct way. First his dialectical attitude toward the utopian element he found in socialism will be examined, followed by a discussion of his concepts kairos and theonomy as they relate to history's future. Finally, there will be a brief discursus on the content of Tillich's own vision of the coming society and his notion of synthesis.

Tillich identified a utopian element in the language about the future of the socialist dialectic and in the dynamic hopefulness of the proletarian movement. Marx's prospect of a classless society, his belief that after the revolution prehistory would end and history begin, and his description of the communist order in which the free development of each would be the condition for the free development of all are features of Marxism that Tillich considered utopian. In the proletariat, he wrote, "all the hidden yearning, all the inner and external distress, the burden of guilt and the meaninglessness of fate, the corruption of the world and the injustice of the social order, all this pours itself into the passionate hope for the future absolute."[100] The utopian drive in socialism is religious in an eschatological fashion.[101] Tillich disputed Mannheim's distinction between relative and absolute utopias, arguing instead that one should ask to what extent the absolute is hidden within every relative utopia. Tillich believed that the absolute is the hidden power of all utopias, especially the socialist.[102]

Tillich wrote that since Thomas More "utopia" or "no place" has referred to sketches of a future social order "which contradict the conditions of worldly and human existence, which can find no space and time, that is, no realization." Utopia has thus become a "nickname" for designs that are considered impossible to realize. The person of "average sensibility, middle-class security, and uncreative doubt" constantly casts suspicion on "every extraordinary design, every revolutionary expectation, every creative idea" by labelling it "utopian." Such a person is in effect saying that he does not want to be made uncomfortable or disturbed. This reaction, however, misses the true meaning of utopia.[103]

Tillich discovered the roots of utopia in the "dissatisfaction" (*Unzufriedenheit*) which makes the human being human and which leads to "the expectation of the wholly other and the wholly new." He considered utopia "the political expression for this expectation."[104] Then, in his first direct reference to the Marxist philosopher Ernst Bloch, he elaborated:

> The spirit of utopia (a coinage of Ernst Bloch) is the power which changes reality. It is the spring (*Triebfeder*) of all great historical movements; it is the tension which thrusts humanity beyond every calm and security into new insecurity and unrest. Utopia is the power of the new.[105]

Utopia (like freedom and expectation) means "going beyond" the present.[106]

At this point, Tillich criticized the treatment of utopia by Mannheim who had brought utopia and ideology into an analogical relationship by saying they both transcend reality. Tillich objected, "The 'going beyond' in the two cases is so different that only the sound of the word and not the meaning creates a similarity." Ideology, thinking which conceals the real existence of a group, has nothing to do with a "real forward-pushing tension." The going beyond of utopia, however, is a tension that belongs to human existence, an idea that is not yet realized but is going to be. Because it lacked this push to the new, the notion of a conservative utopia advanced by Mannheim was for Tillich confused.[107]

In affirming the spirit of utopia as the power of the new, Tillich stood opposed to reactionary and progressive philosophies of history.[108] He found in Marx the "prophetic spirit" that created the new, but he believed that socialism to a great extent had lost this spirit and had taken on a bourgeois, progressive form.[109] He stated:

> It was a great victory of the capitalist spirit, perhaps the greatest victory that it has won, when it took captive the strongest of the movements directed against it. The ultimately transcendent goal of socialism was made finite and temporal in its actual definition of ends.[110]

Much of Tillich's religious socialism is given to recapturing socialism's utopian spirit so that it might be a genuinely transforming force.[111]

Tillich, however, is also cognizant of the dangers of utopianism, that is, the falsification of the going beyond of historical existence. He found this distortion of the utopian spirit in the history of socialism, and he opposed it with a variety of arguments, many of which have already been mentioned. These arguments may be summarized in the following way:

1) Utopianism elevates a conditioned reality to the status of the Unconditional. "Utopia wants to realize the eternal in time and forgets the eternal is the shattering of time and all its contents."[112] To identify a finite reality as ultimate is to create an "'idol.'"[113] Tillich recognized in utopianism an element of "unbelief" that remains in bondage to the finite.[114]

The most fundamental criticism he leveled against a literal belief in utopia is that it violates the Protestant principle.

2) Tillich often coupled this stricture with the warning that unfulfilled utopian hopes lead to profound disappointment. "Where a finite reality is exalted into a transcendent status, metaphysical disillusion always inevitably follows." He added that this "may lead to despair, but it ordinarily ends in apathy, in compromise, and in a feeble belief in progress."[115] Tillich saw that such vacillation typified much of the German socialist movement.

3) Utopianism failed to understand the symbolic meaning of words which anticipate the future, and therefore it takes them literally. Tillich insisted that the transcendent element in utopian visions has to be referred to in non-objectivied, symbolic language (see above, Chapter 3, pp. 101-103.

4) Utopia in the negative sense is based on a mistaken concept of human nature. Religious socialism, wrote Tillich, "rejects every utopia, that is, every expectation of perfection within history" because of the inescapable and essential threat to human existence.[116] Secondly, a belief in a future harmony fails to reckon with man as a unity of being and consciousness and with the continued existence of the powers of origin in human life.[117] For Tillich any belief that finds its final goal in this world overlooks the irrational, the creative-destructive ground and abyss of all.[118] Moreover, it "leaves nature untouched and wishes to erect a national and spiritual structure on an irrational natural foundation."[119]

5) Utopian thinking is undialectical. Two distinct targets are objects of this criticism. First, Tillich labeled ethical socialism as utopian because it loses contact with the real possibilities of history (see above, Chapter 5, pp. 173-175). On a second front, dialectical thinking becomes undialectical when it believes the new social order will be the final one of history. But, Tillich asked, why should the classless society be the end of historical dialectics? "Why should the proletariat, after its victory, not succumb to cleavages similar to those experienced by the victorious *bourgeoisie*? An absolute state as the end of the dialectical process is a contradiction of the dialectical principle." The "limits" of the dialectical view of history become manifest in the fact that it neither has

to stop the process arbitrarily, or it has to fall back to a doctrine of infinite repetition.[120]

Tillich's affirmations and negations led him to search for a way that transcends utopianism and yet preserves the spirit of utopia, that eliminates its idoltry and maintains its power for action. "The most important source of religious socialism," he wrote, "lies in the effort to overcome the unbelieving element in Utopian socialism, the bondage to the finite and temporal, without abolishing the eschatological enthusiasm."[121] In his "*Auseinandersetzung* with utopia" his idea of the kairos emerged.[122] The kairos concept has been seen as an expression of Tillich's epochal consciousness (see above, Chapter 2, p. 23), as a theological principle modeled after justification (see above, Chapter 3, Section 3), and as an historical dialectical principle. Tillich's idea of the kairos is also an attempt to resolve the dilemma posed by the utopian element in the socialist dialectic.

Tillich explained this connection in his open letter to Hirsch. In contrasting his dialectical attitude toward socialism with Hirsch's enthusiastic endorsement of National Socialism, he commented that there is "one decisive point" where the religious socialists had to become "unyielding critics and transformers."[123]

> The danger of utopianism adheres to every prophetic-eschatological movement. Utopianism is the absolutizing of a finite possibility, even if this possibility lies in expectation. We had to oppose this, but we did not and should not have wanted to break the force of the demand and the passion of expectation. The kairos idea was discovered in this distress--I remember the day exactly. It was discovered (which perhaps many do not know) in struggling with the problem of utopia. With it a position was found from which we had the possibility to appreciate the significance of the historical moment for the formation of the future without becoming utopians. For at the end of every utopian enthusiasm stands disillusionment and despair.[124]

With the concept of kairos Tillich expressed his Yes and No attitude toward utopia and its spirit.

In his kairotic thinking Tillich answered the questions of utopianism by transcending the limits of historical dialectic and relating change directly to the Unconditional. In other words he combined dialectical thinking with paradoxical thinking.

The kairos is "not perfect completion in time," but "fulfilled time, the moment of time which is invaded by eternity."[125] What happens in the kairos is absolute, yet not absolute, but under the judgment of the absolute.[126] The Unconditional does not arrive in history but is always the coming, that which is at hand, the new which is breaking through the old.[127] "Socialism must recognize that the fulfillment of the meaning of human life is not possible in the sphere of the human. The fulfillment of meaning is only given as a momentary breaking in of what is beyond being and freedom into the interplay of being and freedom."[128]

The notion of kairos thus combines the "forward" thrust of the historical dialectic with the "upward" relationship of the divine-human paradox. In the overcoming of the demonic structure of capitalism and the appearance of a new gestalt, Tillich discerned "'the fullness of time'" in which the kingdom of God (as it were) touches reality and reveals a new fulfillment of meaning; yet the kingdom remains transcendent.[129] The difficulty of a utopian vision is for Tillich only resolved by setting the present tensions and future development of history within the context of the paradox of transcendence.

Insofar as expectation is a parallel concept to kairos, it holds the same relationship to socialism's utopian elements as does the idea of kairos. In the more non-theological language of *The Socialist Decision* Tillich stated this relationship by suggesting that "socialism, at least in principle, must look beyond itself and its possible success in a future social order. Socialism is not its own end." The reason for doing so lies in the nature of expectation.[130]

> Expectation as such, expectation as a human attitude, comes into existence in a definite content of expectation pertinent to a particular time. *Expectation is always bound to the concrete, and at the same time, transcends every instance of the concrete.* It possesses a content which is dependent on the spiritual of social group that manifests it, and yet it transcends this content.[131]

Tillich added that this posture, which is embodied in socialism, is "the most perilous."[132]

The present kairos for Tillich marks the coming of a new theonomous society, a society open to the Unconditional without claiming to be unconditioned itself.[133] In contrast to autonomy, which represents a society turned away from the eternal and resting content in time and finiteness, theonomy is a society that is turned toward the eternal and in which this orientation is recognizable in its life and organization.[134] In Tillich's thinking the dialectic of autonomy and theonomy coincides with the dialectic of capitalism and socialism. The theonomous society is the socialist society, and the socialist order is a theonomy. Stripped of what he considered their debilitating utopianism, Tillich embraced and--so he would have said--deepened socialism's goals in his vision of the future.

What is this vision? What did Tillich incorporate in his view of the coming social order? Tillich never spelled out in detail the shape of his goal; in fact, he rejected such an attempt as undesirable for the utopian or prophetic spirit.[135] Furthermore, theonomy is a symbolic and not an empirical way of speaking of the future.[136] But if the image of theonomy does not provide a picture of specifics, it does indicate what Tillich considered important for a new society. Theonomy is his concrete religious and ethical norm for societal reconstruction; it is the affirmation implied in the negation of bourgeois society, the becoming gestalt that is the concrete presupposition of every critique.[137] Therefore it is necessary to pinpoint some prominent aspects of theonomy to understand the content of his vision.[138]

Theonomy is above all for Tillich an autonomous society permeated by the meaning-giving quality of the Unconditional. Theonomy gives an answer to the question implied in autonomy, "the question concerning a religious substance and an ultimate meaning of life and culture."[139] In his later writings (1930 and after) Tillich frequently replaced "theonomy," which he feared had been abused by reactionaries,[140] with the "meaningful society." He raised "*the demand for a society in which it is possible for every person and every group to fulfill the meaning of their lives, the demand for a meaningful society.*" He considered this concept as an alternative to the usual concepts of justice, freedom, or community (as in the time after the Revolution, he added), but one that includes all three concepts.[141] The meaningful society, explained Tillich, gives a positive turn to Marx's classless society. It is a society in which the intrinsic power of life (*Lebensmaechtigkeit*) of every individual and group can be realized and which as a whole fulfills its own power and meaning by pointing to the unconditional meaning of life which bears all but which is never directly statable.[142]

The image of a meaningful society, although admittedly a vague notion, appears to this writer at least to be a novel, intriguing beginning point for speaking of the gestalt of the good society, one particularly congenial to Tillich's anthropology and theology. The question of meaning for Tillich is the deepest and most encompassing, and therefore its answer is the most crucial. In making the meaningful society the goal Tillich placed this question within a social context and set the task of social transformation within the horizon of the question of meaning. He was not saying that a social order can guarantee meaning, since there is never an automatic bestowal of meaning. Nor did he indicate that the elimination of adversity is the key to meaning. He also recognized the possibility of meaning in a society that as a whole he considered meaningless. It should be remembered as well that the threat to meaning is intrinsic to human freedom. Nevertheless, the point seems valid that one social order may be more conducive to meaningful life than another. For Tillich, of course, this depends more on a new breakthrough of import than on social manipulation. The goal of a meaningful society, however, can be considered a worthy end, perhaps the most worthy end, of social transformation.

To be sure, this would depend on the content of such a goal. For Tillich not all societies are meaningful; neither did he consider meaning an entirely subjective concern. As he developed it, the meaningful society is not all-inclusive but contains definite criteria. The following quotation, which implies much of his understanding of historical materialism and dialectic, indicates some of the normative meaning of the meaningful society. The answer to the question of meaning, he wrote,

> . . . contains the answer to all the individual questions; it encompasses just as much the material, economic foundations as the psychic life and the spiritual forms of expression. It exceeds all these and more. It embraces the individual and the group, while with the individual freedom is predominant, with the group, community. It cannot be utopian for it speaks

only of the possibility of the meaning of life. It
cannot be ideological for the meaning of life can only
be asked from the concrete tensions of the present.
It cannot be reactionary for the meaning of life is
never fulfilled, only always being fulfilled. And it
is not a pallid ideal, but either the living reality
making life possible or it is nothing at all.[143]

The quest for a meaningful society has to arise out of the dialectical tension of the existing order. Its anchoring in reality is essential for Tillich in distinguishing it from other alternatives. One also notes that the concern with meaning means valuing the well-being of the whole person.

In this selection from "Socialism," Tillich made freedom and community the paramount values. Freedom for Tillich means that distinctively human capacity to go beyond one's self and the possibility to fulfill one's own destiny. In *The Socialist Decision* Tillich described the unconditional demand to allow a person to enjoy the fullness of one's existence (see above, Chapter 5, p. 179). This, of course, is the meaning of justice.

Community is equally significant. In 1919 he identified the "*idea of socialism*" as "a new order in which the consciousness of *Gemeinschaft* is the basis of social construction."[144] His attack on the class struggle assumed this ideal: "The formation of classes means that a radical rupture has taken place in the human community and that its solidarity before the eternal has been radically destroyed."[145] He believed that it is not possible to build a meaningful society unless the class split of capitalism is overcome.[146] With his concern for community (which he tended not to use because of its romantic connotations) Tillich was searching for a way of articulating the common good. A society in which there is "recognition of legitimacy and concern for the meaning of the other," in other words, where power and love interact creatively and not destructively, presuppose "a comprehensive principle of meaning." A group with such a principle he called "community," and he saw as "the socio-ethical ideal of religious socialism" "the development of a meaningful society, in which the possibility exists to recognize the meaningful power of being of another, or, what amounts to the same thing, the formation of a community as the unity of power and love."[147] What stood in the way of creating this trustful relationship among people has to be opposed by Tillich as demonic. Also, a comprehensive principle of meaning is dependent upon the relationship to the Unconditional.

It should also be recalled in this connection that the meaningful society includes autonomy. Theonomy, a unity of autonomous forms and religious substance, is a society in which import bears and breaks through but does not shatter or destroy human autonomy.[148] Tillich marked a theonomous situation off from religious or political heteronomy by its affirmation of the requirement to be obedient to the rule of reason, to acknowledge the validity of the unconditioned form, which in a sociopolitical context means endorsement of the concepts of justice, equality, and human rights, the recognition of personality, and the emancipation from bondage to nature.[149] He considered democracy as a corrective to the conflict of social powers.[150] Finally, it should be added, Tillich's goal included not only a new relationship between God and humankind and among people but also a new relationship to nature and to technology.[151]

The meaningful society of theonomy represents in some way the "synthesis" of history's dialectical process. Tillich wrote that he "stands without reservation" on Troeltsch's "idea of the contemporary cultural synthesis as a criterion of the interpretation of the meaning of history." In opposition to Troeltsch, however, he appealed to the doctrine of justification to find the ultimate within the relative syntheses of history. "The intended 'cultural synthesis' is an ethical goal and a criterion for understanding history only insofar as in it the meaning of every possible cultural synthesis, the ultimate meaning of action and creation, is manifest." In this symbolic view of history the synthesis of autonomous creativity with religious traditions into a theonomous unity "is the social-ethical goal in an absolute sense. Its realization in the endless tensions between autonomy and theonomy is the great theme of history in all periods."[152]

Tillich, like Troeltsch and Hegel, believed synthesis and unity to be ontologically and axiologically more significant than antithesis and disunity, but he differed from both by seeing this unity only in the paradox of justification. He wrote that in opposition to the Hegelian notion of synthesis he placed himself "on the soil of polarity, of dynamic tension, of individual creativity, of justification, and of paradox." For him "the perfect synthesis" is "a regulative principle" and "a corrective" for the tension of history (which arose from the conflict of form and import).[153]

> Not integration, but polarity is our fate, and integration is the ideal, which certainly corresponds to a root in being itself. . . . We stand in the tension and only in paradox, in breakthrough, in faith is the integration, the synthesis of fullness, the unity in God realized.[154]

Theonomy, continued Tillich, refers to certain historical moments in which the integration of the elements of tension are approximated. In each synthesis, however, there are so many new tensions that the integration is only a moment, "a razor's edge," on which basis the synthesis can be represented only symbolically.[155]

> Each such historical-symbolic theonomy is the image of the absolute synthesis, the eternal integration. It is the creative goal toward which all history in every moment moves. Its growth is the eternal kairos, which to be sure becomes conscious as a kairos only in times of great crisis.[156]

Tillich also differed with Marx insofar as his classless society implied the Hegelian notion of synthesis. He turned away from the idea of a total integration for a partial or fragmentary one created by the paradoxical breakthrough of the Unconditional and apprehended through faith. Tillich's differences with Marx at this point are evident; his own proposal is, however, ambiguous, oscillating between a graspable, conceivable future and one that often appears to be of a different quality only through the eyes of faith. It is not always clear as to what is actually to change in the new society to make it a symbol of the absolute synthesis. The ambivalence, it appears, is a result of the uniting of historical dialectic and paradoxical thinking, or, said differently, of the uniting of the autonomy-theonomy dialectic with that of the capitalism-socialism dialectic. Both are always present, although the historical dialectical thinking is more pronounced in his later writings, and the paradoxical more readily evident in his earlier ones. By relating the two Tillich is able to correct and transform utopian concepts of syntheses present in socialism; but he does not adequately describe the changed reality that will emerge from the breakthrough of the Unconditional.

To summarize, then, Tillich's vision of the future is socialist; he anticipated the coming of a new social order in which the class conflict of capitalism is overcome and in which there is a new degree of economic justice and a new sense of belonging. He wanted therefore to cultivate the utopian spirit, the drive toward the new, within historical dialectic and to weed out the untrue and distorted utopianism that threatens its realization. This is the intent of his concepts of kairos, expectation, and theonomy. Tillich, in a way that combined his socialist and religious ends, articulated the goal of socialism as the meaningful society. The meaningful society is not for him the final synthesis of history's dialectical process, but it is a symbol of the final unity of God and man and therefore a worthy goal for history's future.

Summary

Tillich considered historical dialectic to be a theory of socio-political change that asserts the unity of necessity and freedom and perceives the coming of a new social order from the tensions of the present. Tillich's conception has been interpreted in this chapter in three parts: as a critical and revolutionary theory of change that views historical movement as one of tension and conflict and of separation and reconciliation; as one that unites transcendental destiny and historical responsibility, a unity that converges in the proletariat; and as a theory that envisions the new society, but not the ultimate social order. Special attention was given to Tillich's elaboration of expectation, which is his most extensive discussion of his interpretation of historical dialectic. Tillich went behind Marx and Hegel to the prophetic attitude of the Biblical tradition and placed the socialist dialectic within the context of transcendence, transcendence paradoxically present in history. Tillich, it was seen, adopted many elements of Marx's conception, criticized others from his theological perspective, and sought from there to give a new formulation to the dialectic, the theory of the proletarian movement.

This completes the presentation of Tillich's encounter with socialist theory. In the preceding two chapters the meaning of his critical appropriation and transformation of historical materialism and historical dialectic has been demonstrated.

Tillich responded seriously to the theoretical issues of socialism from the inside and from a theological perspective. Not only was he profoundly critical toward what he considered socialism's errors, but more significantly, he aimed to offer a new Yes, a new theoretical basis for socialism. In the next chapter Tillich's distinctive approach to socialism will be viewed further from a theological standpoint.

CHAPTER 5

NOTES

[1] "Weiterbildung," GW, II, p. 124.

[2] SD, GW, II, p. 320.

[3] Ibid., p. 325.

[4] Unpublished manuscript, B. #2. 17 (Harvard Archive), p. 19.

[5] See Ch. 4, fn. 3. Marx's dialectic is evident in The Communist Manifesto, Feuer, pp. 1-41. Also note his remarks on dialectic in the Prefaces to Capital, Feuer, pp. 133-46, esp. 145-46. Engels' views can be found in Socialism: Utopian and Scientific.

[6] "Christentum, Sozialismus und Nationalismus," GW, XIII, p. 163.

[7] "Weiterbildung," GW, II, p. 125.

[8] Ibid.

[9] "Kairos," PE, pp. 40-41.

[10] "Weiterbildung," GW, II, p. 125.

[11] Ibid., p. 126.

[12] Ibid. Tillich in a sense here absorbed Marx's dialectic into his own understanding of form and Gehalt as the basic principles of historical interpretation. Another way of stating this is that the bourgeois-socialist dialectic is also for Tillich a dialectic of autonomy and theonomy. See below, the final section of this chapter. In his early writings there are occasional references to St. Simon and French socialist romanticism. Cf. "Kairos," PE, p. 41. The influence does not appear to have been significant.

[13] "Kairos," PE, p. 41. "The principle of negation," which is present in Tillich's thought, came in a reference to Hegel.

[14] "Die Theologie des Kairos," p. 313.

[15] Sozialismus aus dem Glauben, p. 102.

[16] Ibid.

[17] Ibid.

[18] Ibid., p. 103.

[19] Ibid.

[20] Ibid.

[21] RV, fn. 1, p. 304. Cf. "Sozialismus," GW, II, p. 148; "The State as Expectation and Demand," Pol. Exp., pp. 97-98. For Tillich's interpretation of Marx as an example of this method see "Glaeubiger Realismus I," GW, IV, p. 82.

[22] "RS (II)," Pol. Exp., p. 48.

[23] "Das Problem der Macht," *GW,* II, p. 195; cf. *IH,* p. 182. In one text, Tillich defined dialectic as "the art of determining the relation of ideas to one another and to existence." He thought the "subjective" use of the word was surpassed when it was seen "that dialectic grasps truth only when the ideas themselves are dialectical. Thus, from an art of discovering relationships, dialectic becomes an expression for a certain kind of actual relationship." "Kairos and Logos," *IH,* pp. 164-65. It is not readily apparent that this abstract definition is crucial for his discussion of historical dialectic.

[24] "Sozialismus," *GW,* II, p. 139. See above, Ch. 3, Sec. 5, "Socialism as Living." Df. "The Problem of Power." *IH,* p. 182; *RV,* fn. 3, p. 287.

[25] *SD, GW,* II, p. 310. See above, Ch. 3, Sec. 4, "Expectation: The Symbol of Socialism."

[26] *GW,* XII, pp. 125-50. Originally published as *Der junge Hegel und das Schicksal Deutschlands,* in *Hegel und Goethe. Zwei Gedenkreden* (Tuebingen: Mohr, 1932).

[27] Ibid., p. 126.

[28] Ibid., pp. 142-43.

[29] Ibid., p. 144.

[30] Ibid., pp. 144-45.

[31] Ibid., pp. 144-46.

[32] Ibid., p. 148. In the last pages of the essay, Tillich forcefully defended "the Jewish principle" of "opposition" (*Entgegensetzung*) as part of Germany's fate and attacked the nationalist movements of the right: "Those spiritual and political movements which today by jumping over the real oppositions, above all, those of the capitalist system, want to force a national unity, a reconciliation, an 'integration,' do not fulfill German fate; they confuse and violate it and induce reactions of an injured fate, which could mean complete ruin. They must, even if they win in the first assault, fail on the appearance (*Scheinhaftigkeit*) of reconciliation." P. 150.

[33] Ibid., p. 144.

[34] Tillich noted in his lecture that Hegel rejected the idea of justification or the paradox. P. 142. This is the crucial difference between Tillich and Hegel, at least as seen by Tillich, in their notion of synthesis. See below, Sec. 4. For a discussion of Tillich's understanding of dialectic, particularly in relation to Hegel and Marx, see Adams, "Tillich's Interpretation of History," Kegley and Bretall, pp. 294-309, esp. pp. 296-302. One should note that Adams did not draw upon this friendly interpretation of the young Hegel.

[35] Perhaps the most sustained argument along this line was given by Adams, "Paul Tillich's Dialectical Social Analysis," (paper read at the American Theological Society, Midwest Division, April 22, 1955). He concluded, "But for the time it would appear that in our society dialectical sociology is inadequate." PP. 22-23. Another is William Wright Paul, "Paul Tillich's Interpretation of History" (unpublished Doctor's dissertation, Columbia University, 1959). He explicitly argued for Karl

Popper's "piecemeal social engineering" approach. P. 190. For discussion of the "end of ideology" see the essays in *The End of Ideology Debate,* ed. by Chaim L. Waxman (New York: A Clarion Book, 1968).

[36] *SD, GW,* II, p. 325.

[37] "Kairos and Logos," *IH,* p. 157.

[38] "Philosophy and Fate," *PE,* pp. 3-5.

[39] Cf. Ibid., translator's footnote, p. 3. In his *Systematic Theology* Tillich used the word "destiny."

[40] *Masse und Geist, GW,* II, p. 84.

[41] *SD, GW,* II, p. 326.

[42] *RV,* fn. 24, p. 302.

[43] "Weiterbildung," *GW,* II, p. 125.

[44] *SD, GW,* II, p. 220.

[45] Ibid., pp. 326-27.

[46] Ibid., p. 327.

[47] Ibid., p. 221, 327.

[48] *GW,* XII, p. 240.

[49] Ibid.

[50] Ibid., pp. 241-42.

[51] *SD, GW,* II, p. 329.

[52] "Basic Principles," *Pol. Exp.,* p. 71.

[53] *SD, GW,* II, p. 222.

[54] "Weiterbildung," *GW,* II, p. 126.

[55] "PPPS," p. 21; cf. *PE,* pp. 172-73.

[56] "RS (II)," *Pol. Exp.,* p. 50.

[57] B. 2 #17, p. 20.

[58] "Basic Principles," *Pol. Exp.,* p. 61. Cf. Ch. 3, p. 111.

[59] "Weiterbildung," *GW,* II, p. 128.

[60] The reference, of course, is to his book by the name, *Religioese Verwirklichung.* See "Zur Einfuerung," p. 9-24. Also, his writings on revelation, "Die Idee der Offenbarung," *GW,* VIII, pp. 31-39. Originally published in *Zeitschrift fuer Theologie und Kirche,* VIII, 6 (December 1927), pp. 403-12; "Revelation and the Philosophy of Religion," *Twentieth Century Theology in the Making,* ed. by Jaroslav Pelikan, Vol. II (London: The Fontana Library, 1970), pp. 46-55. Originally appeared in *Die Religion in Geschichte und Gegenwart,* Hersg. v. Hermann Gunkel und Leopold Zsharnack, 2 Auft., Bd. 4 (Tuebingen: Hohr, 1930), pp. 1227-33.

[61] "Philosophy and Fate," *PE,* p. 8.

[62] Ibid., p. 14.

[63] One is reminded of Dietrich Bonhoeffer's question, "How does fate become providence?" *Letters and Papers from Prison,* ed. by Eberhard Bethge, trans. by Reginald H. Fuller (New York: The Macmillan Company, 1962), p. 138.

[64] *SD, GW,* II, pp. 312-13.

[65] Ibid., p. 313.

[66] Ibid., pp. 131-14.

[67] Cf. "The ethic of religious socialism, like its entire outlook, is dynamic. It does not recognize an abstract system of values that is universally valid but, rather, it discerns as an attribute of being itself a demand that changes according to the nature of the encounter between man and another entity." "RS (II)," *Pol. Exp.,* p. 51. In 1919 Tillich wrote, ". . . a form of society constructed on the basis of community and love has nothing to do with the egalitarian ideal, but must recognize a rank ordering of ability and must also affirm national particularity." "Kirchenfrage," *GW,* II, p. 15. This was not Tillich's position later--equality did have something to do with community, especially as a corrective against injustice--but equality as an ideal is not the basis of his socialist ideal. Note in the text he spoke of its "deeper meaning." A major reason for this attitude is the importance he gave to *Maechtigkeit* or intrinsic power. See "RS (II)," *Pol. Exp.,* pp. 52-53; "The Problem of Power," *IH,* esp. pp. 179-87.

[68] Cf. "The 'formal' grounding of the *demand* for justice is unavoidable, if its unconditionality is not to be touched. Therefore the Kantian formalism remains valid, even if the *ideal* of justice receives its fulfillment from a concrete situation, e.g., the proletarian situation." *SD, GW,* II, fn. 6, p. 229. (See above, Ch. 3, p. 96.) Note how Tillich followed this interpretation in understanding the prophets and Marx. This formal grounding does not do away with the dynamic character of Tillich's ethic.

[69] *SD, GW,* II, p. 314.

[70] Ibid. The section is entitled "Expectation and Origin," pp. 314-17.

[71] Ibid., pp. 314-15.

[72] Ibid., p. 318.

[73] Ibid., pp. 335-36.

[74] Ibid., pp. 336-37.

[75] Tillich would recognize "the ethnic factor" as a valid concern, but one subordinated to the concerns of justice.

[76] Tillich often expressed reservations about the notion of a "classless society," but here he accepted and filled it with new meaning by recognizing the validity of pre-bourgeois realities continuing to exist. Cf. "Sozialismus," *GW,* II, pp. 146-48; "The Problem of Power," *IH,* p. 188.

[77] *SD, GW,* II, p. 314.

[78] Ibid., pp. 315-16.

[79] Ibid., p. 317.

[80] Ibid., p. 328.

[81] Ibid.

[82] Ibid., pp. 317-18.

[83] Ibid., p. 318.

[84] Ibid., pp. 318-19.

[85] Ibid., p. 318.

[86] Ibid., pp. 318-19.

[87] Ibid., pp. 319-20.

[88] Juergen Moltmann has made a similar distinction with the terms *futurum* and *adventus*: "The *futurum* is *extrapolated* from the factors and processes of past and present. This is the method of prediction and 'futurology.' Future as *adventus Dei*, however, cannot be extrapolated from history but is historically *anticipated*, insofar as it announces itself." In a footnote Moltmann arrived at the same conclusion as Tillich: "In the practice of history both ways of becoming certain of the future must constantly be combined." "Theology as Eschatology," *The Future of Hope*, ed. by Frederick Herzog (New York, 1970), p. 14. What Moltmann placed in a footnote Tillich made a central argument. Tillich found this unity not only true of "the practice of history" but also true for the prophets.

[89] The concept of "promise" is not explicitly developed in *SD* or other religious socialist writings. The statement (p. 24), for example, that "only when being moves itself toward its fulfillment can one speak of promise . . ." seems to get the movement itself ahead of the promise. Promise is not however first of all dependent on the movement but the reason for one's being able to trust in fulfillment. One does not discover here why one should trust the promise or from where it originates.

[90] *SD*, *GW*, II, pp. 329-30.

[91] Ibid., p. 330.

[92] For a complete discussion of how Tillich related these two concepts to overcome the alternatives of relativism and absolutism, ses *IH*, pp. 123-75.

[93] *SD*, *GW*, II, p. 329. See above, Ch. 4, p. 000.

[94] "Ideologie und Utopie," *GW*, XII, p. 261.

[95] Ibid. Trans. by Adams. Tillich added: "It might be added that the intelligentsia who have inwardly penetrated the proletarian situation have the special function to give theoretical expression to their awareness of it."

[96] Ibid. He commented further that "the concrete accomplishment of such an idea is *ultimately* more important than the abstract stating of the problem of ideology."

[97] "Kairos and Logos," *IH*, pp. 171, 174. Cf. p. 138.

[98] Ibid., pp. 170-71.

[99] "Weiterbildung," *GW*, II, p. 126.

[100] *Masse und Geist*, *GW*, II, p. 80.

[101] Ibid., pp. 83, 127. Cf. Ch. 3, Sec. 3.

[102] "Ideologie und Utopie," *GW*, XII, pp. 257-58; *RV*, fn. 27, p. 303.

[103] "Utopie," *GW*, XIII, p. 172. Originally published in *Mensch und Staat*, 1931.

[104] Ibid.

[105] Ibid. In 1926 Tillich had spoken of the "spirit of utopia" but without reference to Bloch. For Bloch's comments on Tillich see *Werk und Wirken Paul Tillichs*, pp. 40-45. Cf. "Kairos," *Kairos I*, pp. 9-10.

[106] Ibid.

[107] "Ideologie und Utopie," *GW*, XII, pp. 256-57. Trans. by Adams.

[108] "Kairos," *Kairos I*, pp. 8-9. Cf. "Kairos," *PE*, p. 40; *SD, GW*, II, p. 268.

[109] Ibid.; "Weiterbildung," *GW*, II, p. 126.

[110] *Rel. Sit.*, p. 112.

[111] "Kairos," *Kairos I*, pp. 9-10; "Cl. St.," *GW*, II, pp. 189-191.

[112] "Kairos," *Kairos I*, p. 10.

[113] "Kairos," *PE*, pp. 35-36.

[114] *Rel. Sit.*, p. 175; "PPPS," p. 20; *PE*, p. 172; "Eschatology and History," *IH*, pp. 274-75; "Cl. St.," *GW*, II, pp. 188-89.

[115] "Cl. St.," *GW*, II, p. 189.

[116] "RS (II)," *Pol. Exp.*, p. 47.

[117] *SD, GW*, II, p. 287, 335, 6.

[118] "Weiterbildung," *GW*, II, p. 126.

[119] "Basic Principles," *Pol. Exp.*, p. 63.

[120] "Kairos," *PE*, p. 42. Cf. "Weiterbildung," *GW*, II, p. 129.

[121] *Rel. Sit.*, pp. 175-76.

[122] "Kairos," *Kairos: I*, p. 10.

[123] "Die Theologie des Kairos," p. 314.

[124] Ibid. Cf. *OB*, pp. 78-79. The first time Tillich used "kairos" in print was in 1922.

[125] *Rel. Sit.*, p. 176. Cf. Ch. 3, Sec. 3.

[126] "Kairos," *PE*, p. 42.

[127] "Weiterbildung," *GW*, II, p. 127.

[128] "Cl. St.," *GW*, II, p. 190.

[129] Ibid., p. 191. Cf. "Kairos," *PE*, p. 48.

[130] *SD, GW*, II, p. 337.

[131] Ibid.

[132] Ibid.

[133] "Kairos," *PE*, p. 47 Cf. Ch. 3, pp. 000-00.

[134] *Rel. Sit.*, p. 176.

[135] "Cl. St.," *GW*, II, p. 188.

[136] "E. Troeltsch: Historismus und seine Probleme," *Journal for the Scientific Study of Religion*, I, 1 (October 1961), p. 114.

[137]"Loew," *GW*, XII, p. 218; "Kairos," *PE*, p. 38; "Protestantism as a Critical and Creative Principle," *Pol. Exp.*, p. 18. See p. 202 of this chapter.

[138]For Tillich's most detailed description of the coming society see the last part of *SD*, *GW*, II, pp. 332-63.

[139]"Kairos," *PE*, p. 46.

[140]"Theonomie," *RGG*, V, pp. 1128-29. Significantly, the article is very brief. For a translation see Adams (1965), pp. 60-61.

[141]"Sozialismus," *GW*, II, p. 143.

[142]Ibid., pp. 147-48.

[143]Ibid., p. 143.

[144]"Kirchenfrage," *GW*, II, p. 14; cf. "Answer," p. 11.

[145]*Rel. Sit.*, p. 110.

[146]"Sozialismus," *GW*, II, p. 148.

[147]"RS (II)," *Pol. Exp.*, p. 53.

[148]"Theonomie," *RGG*, V, pp. 1128-29; "Kairos," *PE*, pp. 44-45; "The Philosophy of Religion," *WR?*, pp. 72-76.

[149]"Basic Principles," *Pol. Exp.*, p. 73; cf. p. 69. Cf. also *OB*, pp. 36-45.

[150]*SD*, *GW*, p. 346.

[151]See, for example, "Basic Principles," *Pol. Exp.*, pp. 74-76; "The Idea and Ideal of Personality," *PE*, pp. 120-24; "Logos und Mythos der Technik," *GW*, IX, pp. 297-306. Originally published in *Logos*, XVI, 3 (November 1927), pp. 356-65.

[152]"Historismus," pp. 113-14. Other things that Tillich wrote that he accepted without reservation and which have been apparent in this study are: " . . . the idea of the individually-creative, the conception of the interpretive principle as a risk, the fundamental transformation of the neo-Kantian theory of values by the idea of their creative, unique realization. . . ." P. 113. Tillich here also wrote that Troeltsch's periodization of history had "symbolic and not empirical validity," that this attempt "contains no scientific judgment concerning the present," and that to assert that the present was developing toward a new communal period "was very questionable to say the least, if it is to be understood in an empirical sense." It was not historiography or even philosophy of history but rather "an ethical-prophetic attitude." Such statements create questions about the material reality of theonomy.

[153]"Antwort," p. 20.

[154]Ibid. Ulrich, who in his study claimed that Tillich failed to mediate the polar elements of his ontology, himself failed to deal with Tillich's idea of paradox by which he had attempted this mediation. Ulrich, who also found "Antwort" an important source, did not however quote this statement. Ulrich, pp. 23-24; 67-68.

[155]Ibid. With this statement, too, theonomy lacked more historical being than it appeared to in other contexts.

[156]Ibid.

CHAPTER 6

THE THEOLOGICAL PERSPECTIVE

The central occasion of Tillich's religious socialism was the transformation of Protestant Christianity and Marxist socialism in expectation of a new social order. Tillich placed himself within both antagonistic traditions, affirmed both, criticized both, and constructed anew the theoretical bases of both in an effort to contribute to the creation of a meaningful, socialist society.

> *Thus Christianity and socialism must continue to develop and become one in a new world and social order whose foundation is an economic order which is structured by justice, whose ethos is an affirmation of every person because he is a person, and whose religious import is an experience of the divine in all humanity, of the eternal in all temporal nature.*[1]

In Chapter 2 the "difficult, unknown, and important way" that Tillich followed in pursuit of this vision was sketched, and what Tillich meant by socialism was explored in Chapter 3. In Chapters 4 and 5 his interpretation and transformation of socialist theory were discussed. In the present chapter Tillich's theological perspective will be examined more closely, and an initial attempt will be made to appraise his religious socialism from a standpoint within Christian theology and ethics.

In addition to attempting to reshape socialism from a theological perspective, Tillich was simultaneously seeking to relate theology to the social situation and to give it new form. These efforts were two sides of the same religious socialist project. In the opening section of this chapter the concern will be Tillich's theological principles for understanding the relationship between religion and politics. In the following two sections Tillich's understanding will be compared to two alternatives, the attitude of his own Lutheran tradition and that of Karl Barth. Section 4 will consider a crucial doctrine in this theology of politics, the doctrine of eschatology. Here the question will be discussed as to the significance and limits of Tillich's understanding of the kingdom of God. In the following part the focus will return to socialism and Tillich's understanding of it. What might be learned, positively and negatively, from his placing socialism within a theological perspective? The chapter and study will conclude with a brief overview of Tillich's relationship to socialism and politics after 1933 in order that the period from 1918 to 1933 can be viewed in the context of his whole life.

A Theology of Politics

Tillich, in the beginning of his essay on the early Hegel, made the claim that "the two roots," "the living powers," of Hegel's thinking were "the religious and the political." "Hegel's philosophy arose out of the question of religious and political realization, not 'in general,' not in an empty air space, but in his time, in his space."[2] What Tillich wrote of Hegel is true also for him: the vital sources of his early life and thought were religious and political. He too was driven by a practical, concrete concern: political and religious realization in his time and space. Even the label "religious socialism" demonstrates Tillich's "two-in-one" existential interest.

Tillich stated this interest most clearly in his "Introduction" to *Religioese Verwirklichung*. Because his remarks exhibit the two sources of his thinking as well as bring together some of the essential features of his religious socialism, they deserve to be quoted at length.

> In the present kairos religious realization in the profane must be first and above all social realization. *And social realization which is more than the organization of social welfare is socialist realization.* For the opposition of socialism is directed not against the individual evils of the capitalist economic order but against capitalism itself. Capitalism is a creative-destructive, that is, demonic, order. Religious realization which wants to bypass it is ideology, does not encounter the decisive reality of the present, builds on demonized ground, and justifies it by covering it up. This recognition drives me to *socialism* and effects a resolute "yes" to the anti-demonic struggle of the proletariat. The simultaneous recognition that various forms of proletarian being and socialist consciousness are those of the opposed liberal-capitalist attitude drives me to *religious* socialism and effects a resolute "no" to the expressions of the emptiness of meaning in socialist theory and praxis. The wrestling with this problem for many years in the Berlin Circle of the *Blaetter fuer Religioesen Sozialismus* has become spiritually and humanly determinative for all the participants. It is the background not only

for the arguments of the third part, but of all parts
of the book and for my entire interpretation of the
present—*since the kairos-idea was also born here.*
The working community of this circle, which continues
in spite of external separation, breaks every inclination to seek spiritual or religious realization by
overlooking the social situation.[3]

Tillich in this summary tied together religious and political—religious and socialist—considerations in a practical concern, a concern shaped by his friends from his early days in
Berlin and one that permeated his whole life and thought. Again,
he pointed to the demonic nature of capitalism and selected the
proletarian situation as the criterion for evaluating the au-
thenticity of religious realization in the present. One notes
also his dialectical understanding of the relationship between
religion and politics: religious realization means socialist
realization, and socialism requires religious criticism.

As is clearly evident here and throughout this study, the
religious and political spheres of life are in Tillich's view
to be united. His own major concepts—kairos, theonomy, demonic,
expectation, and prophetic (to name some)—possess this double
quality. Whether one begins with their religious or their political meaning, one is necessarily led to the other. This relationship is intrinsic to his philosophy of religion and his
theology of culture, since, he insisted, religion (especially in
its broad but also in its narrow meaning) has political significance, and politics has an inherent religious dimension. There
is for him no way neatly to separate religious and political
elements into totally distinct hunks of life without doing violence to both. The theologian could and should not view religion apolitically nor view politics as a purely secular phenomenon. Fundamental to Tillich's whole project is the proposition
that the posing of the theological question (the relation between God and man) is a political concern, and reversely, the
posing of the political question (the meaning and structuring of
the good society) is a theological concern. Therefore he viewed
the task of theology in light of the proletarian situation and
placed socialism in theological perspective. This interrela-
tionship is one of the most characteristic and noteworthy features of Tillich's religious socialism.

Tillich, in his dispute with Hirsch, wrote that "the

relationship between theology and politics can never be characterized by an 'and.'" This is especially so, he added in reference to socialism, when a political movement is shaped by a comprehensive "*Weltanschauung*." He distinguished between judging political action from the viewpoint of the struggle for power and expediency and that of taking seriously the worldview of a political group and placing it under the judgment of theological categories. The latter, he explained, "is not politics but it is 'theology of politics.'" He saw it as an essential part of a theology of culture which theology cannot bypass "if" --and this is the significant condition--"it wants to maintain the unconditional claim of the Christian proclamation." Therefore, argued Tillich, the issues he raised in his religious socialism and in his criticism of Hirsch "must be recognized as legitimate theological questions." Any theology that would surrender its right to criticize political worldviews would "have mutilated itself. In the moment when politics substantiates itself according to a worldview, its argument must be subjected to responsible theological criticism."[4]

Once more, in a very direct way, Tillich asserted the possibility, desirability, and necessity of a theological interpretation of political realities. The conviction crucial for such an undertaking is that God's reality has meaning for all life-- "the unconditional claim of the Christian proclamation." Tillich interpreted both National Socialism and socialism theologically because of his belief that no political movement stands outside of or apart from the ultimate reality of which the Christian message speaks. From the beginning he thought "that a rejection in principle of socialism in the name of Christianity contradicts the universality of Christianity."[5] He believed that the proletarian situation challenges the belief that Protestantism heralds news that is intended for all people and is not simply a religious possibility for some. ". . . Insofar as socialism is the expression of the proletarian situation, it poses for Protestantism the question concerning the meaning and validity of its own unconditional and universal claim."[6] Tillich's "theology of politics" was based on the faith that the Christian message does have universal significance, and therefore he sought to discern and understand God's (as well as the demonic's) presence "in, with, and under" the public and social activity by which human beings structure their lives.

Tillich's theology of politics incorporated a normative view of the relationship between the divine and the human, a topic which has been discussed as the prophetic attitude and which will again be picked up in Section 4. At one point in his polemic against Hirsch, Tillich, using slightly different categories than he previously had, presented his criteria in a way that is helpful in framing the present discussion on the principles of a theology of politics. He suggested that the basic question for all Christian theology today (just as in previous ages it had been the relationship between the two natures of Christ, or between nature and grace, or between justification and good works) is "the relationship between divine and human action." He averred that the kairos doctrine was an attempt to resolve this question and to avoid the dangers that lay on both the right and the left. Hirsch's demonic sacramentalism (by which he meant the identification of the divine with the finite) demonstrated the error that exists on one side. "My question was: Is this mistaken way, the 'Chalcedonian' mixture of the divine and the human, necessary if we want to avoid the Barthian error, the 'Chalcedonian' separation of both? Is there no 'Chalcedonian' solution to the question of 'the kingdom of God' and 'the kingdom of man'?"[7] Tillich's theological norm, which he developed with his paradoxical understanding of transcendence, is that the human and divine realities are united without being confused.

Tillich's understanding of God's relationship to history was augmented by a parallel interpretation of the proper response of human beings to God's reality in social and political affairs. This side of the relationship, which he usually discussed under the rubric of religion and politics, is the main concern of the succeeding pages. A profitable place to see how he elucidated this connection is in the opening paragraphs of his answer to the consistory where he outlined in a lucid manner "The Relation of Christianity to the Social Order in General and to the Socialist Order in Particular."[8]

Christianity as well as religion in general is first of all, he wrote, "an experience of God in and beyond all things, an *Erlebnis* that is possible in every time and in every situation and which is independent of every social and economic form."

On this basis he rejected all attempts to equate Christianity with a particular social order and thus to rob it of its inward, personal character.[9] Also, however, he rejected all forms of Christianity that only cling to "pure inwardness," for "Christianity carries within it the power and the will to shape the life of humanity in its own terms."[10]

When Christianity moves "from within outwardly," it encounters independently developed forms that it seeks to shape and by which it is itself shaped.[11] He observed that in this "mutual penetration" Christianity has been connected with differing philosophical consciousnesses, aesthetic experiences, ethical ideals, and social and economic orders.[12] Sociologically, it has been closely associated with a variety of orders, including "the Lutheran church with agronomy and the absolutist-patriarchal state authority, the modern church with high capitalism, nationalism and the military state."[13] Christianity cannot exist apart from interaction with definite sociological structures, as the history of the church demonstrates, but this for Tillich did not mean it is equally suited to every social order. Rather it has "a greater *affinity* for certain forms of social order than for others. The ethics of love carries a ferment of criticism into every social and economic form which is the more inciting the more those are based on coercion, oppression, and self-interest." Thus, Christianity could enter into a closer-relationship with medieval society than with the late Roman society. Now, appealed Tillich, this love ethic demands that Christianity "must in the present moment enter into opposition with the capitalist and militarist social order in which we stand and whole ultimate consequences have become evident in the World War."[14]

The four brief paragraphs summarized here are Tillich's first account of the relationship between religion and politics, and, although the language will not be common later, the direction of the argument remained a part of his religious socialism. Tillich began with a normative description of religion, supplemented it with a Troeltschian historical, sociological observation on the plurality of Christian realities, implied the necessity of religion having social form, asserted the priority of love and its "affinity" for certain social orders, and in light of the present situation called for support for socialism. Religion is not socially determined and it does have moral implications. The argument is a theological-ethical one which moves from a general statement on religion to a concrete demand. It includes both the ultimate perspective of religion and the particular historical context.

What is especially to be noted is the two-fold normative character of religion. Religion has both an "inwardness" and a "power and will" to shape all facets of life, or (as in the words of the revised edition) the religious principle has an "*unconditionality,*" and it is simultaneously "*concrete.*" These two poles establish the broad parameters for the proper disposition of the religious person and community toward the political-social order. To reduce religion to a sanction of a social system or movement or to exhaust the religious experience in political action is to deny its inward character; to "privatize" religion as an affair between God and the soul or to flee from the task of constructing the world is to reject the exo-centric drive of religion. Tillich considered that "true" religion contains an underived and inexhaustible unconditionality as well as an active concreteness. The two belong together and in their dialectical unity they comprise Tillich's theological guidelines for determining the proper relationship of religion to politics.

Tillich later expressed this relationship with the concepts *reservatum religiosum* and *obligatum religiosum*. These concepts were first mentioned in a discussion of theonomy. In the ideal theonomy "all culture is actualized religion, and all religion is actualized as culture." Because of the demonic, however, there can never be a simple identification of religion and culture. Tillich maintained that religion "contains within itself a No, a *reservatum religiosum*, and a Yes, an *obligatum religiosum.*" The culturally negative attitude of early Christianity, of mysticism, and of Lutheranism was interpreted by Tillich as illustrative of the religious withdrawal, of the religious spirit falling back upon itself before the predominance of the demonic. The *reservatum religiosum,* which, he said, has always to assert itself, "is the ground for the delimiting of a sacred alongside a secular sphere." Yet, argued Tillich, religion becomes open to demonic distortion if it forgets the other side, the *obligatum religiosum*. Religion is never able to do without culture; to renounce the "world," one has to use the world's forms. "The *reservatum* without the *obligatum* is impossible and untrue." On the other hand, the *obligatum* without the *reservatum* is just as untrue because it forgets the Unconditional, and as a result its creation, a culture religion, "not only dissipates religious substance but also robs culture of its import." Tillich believed that "the only proper attitude toward culture and also toward socialism is that characterized by the double demand of *reservatum* and *obligatum religiosum*."[15]

From this point Tillich accounted for the significance of the churches and the confessions as "the representatives of the *reservatum religiosum*." One might call them a reminder of the *sui generis* nature of religion, or, as Tillich put it, "they are the focal points of the religious spirit." He cautioned that this does not mean they are any less cultural than other aspects of culture, and he warned against both trying to make symbols and insisting that one is absolute. He appealed to the churches to negate themselves before the Unconditional and simultaneously urged believers to maintain the validity of "an emphatic yes" to their own confessions.[16] Although he did not fully develop a doctrine of the church in his early writings, he did give the church an important and independent role in his systematic outline.[17]

The dialectic of religious responsibility and reservation set in the horizon of the paradoxical breaking in of the kingdom of God gives Tillich the principles of his theology of politics. The Uncondiitonal is concretely present without being identical to any socio-political reality. Tillich's eschatology, which articulated a Chalcedonian solution to the question of divine and human activity, provides an all-encompassing perspective for prophetic criticism and new creation. The response of faith is to shape the world in light of the coming kingdom while recognizing that what is coming in history can never be equated with the kingdom. There is something more both to God's reality and the meaning of religion. While neither is exhausted in political action, neither is separated from it. Tillich united religious and political (socialist) realities not into an identity but into a dynamic relationship.

Tillich's own typology provides an overview of the relationship of his position to other possibilities within the theological tradition. "Considered in terms of church history," he wrote, "religious socialism is an attempt to unite the radical nature and the transcendence of the religious perspective with the concreteness of an immanent will to shape the world." He thought it an alternative to 1) an exclusive Protestantism that sacrifices the concrete to the transcendent, 2) a humanistic piety that does the opposite, 3) a pietism that ignores its *obligatum religiosum,* and 4) "a hierarchical Catholicism that betrays the concrete situation with the aid of a sacrosanct ethic possessing metaphysical and sacramental sanctions."[18]

In the typology of H. R. Niebuhr, Tillich can be viewed as a theologian of paradox who saw "Christ as the Transformer of Culture."[19] On the basis of the dialectic of *reservatum* and *obligatum* he could not accept either the opposition of "Christ Against Culture" nor the accommodation of "Christ of Culture." Although he spoke of synthesis, he opposed the layered view of reality of "Christ Above Culture" and saw synthesis only in paradox. Tillich was a paradoxical thinker, but he challenged the dualism and the conservatism of "Christ and Culture in Paradox." The thrust of his theology of politics was the conversion of the present reality in light of the breaking in of God's reality. Like Augustine, whom both Niebuhr and Tillich considered a prime example of the transformist motif, Tillich looked toward a new society permeated by the presence of God.[20]

In light of this discussion of his criteria for relating religion to politics, I will, in the next two sections, explore in some detail Tillich's attitude toward two different understandings of this relationship. First, his interpretation of the traditional social teachings of Lutheranism (Christ and Culture in paradox) will be studied, followed by a look at aspects of his encounter with Karl Barth.

A Critique of the Lutheran Ethic

Tillich's early absorption of and later reaction to the conservative socio-political beliefs of his own Lutheran tradition have already been recounted. His debt to his religious background was immense, as for example in his understanding of paradox, of the corruption of human existence, and of the irrational.[21] But when it came directly to social ethics, Tillich believed that the evangelical churches were totally unprepared to respond creatively to the social question and that their present positions were disastrous for society's future. Tillich's religious socialism included a withering attack on their theological-ethical attitude on the basis of his very different perspective.

The social teachings of the evangelical churches represented the most deep-seated and wide-spread posture in Tillich's Protestant context. Tillich's critique of these ideas is significant not only because of its incisive content but also because it came before Hitler's rise to power and antedated the criticism and defense of Lutheran social thought during and after the time of National Socialism.[22] The failure of the churches to attend to the issues of religious socialism (Tillich's and others') was not without importance for their unpreparedness in facing Nazism.[23]

Tillich's root indictment of what he understood to be the Lutheran position is its lack of a theological ethic geared to social transformation.[24] Protestantism, he wrote, "lacks a prophetically grounded, socially critical principle. It lacks on Lutheran soil the will to shape reality according to the image of the kingdom of God."[25] In the language of the linear metaphor he used on occasion, Lutheranism had neglected the horizontal in favor of the vertical.[26] As a result it had been unable to penetrate the proletarian situation; it had bypassed the class opposition of capitalism and become an ideology. Lutheranism's weakness was that it had not developed an understanding of the kingdom of God that embraced socio-political life and was thus not capable of incorporating the critical and revolutionary expectation of oppressed groups.

Historically, Tillich traced this deficiency back to Luther's decision concerning the Peasants' War which, he stated, made permanent the fixation of Protestantism on secular authorities and which led it to accept absolutism and reject democratic-revolutionary tendencies.[27] A system of local princedoms in which the prince was the highest-ranking bishop became the bearer of Lutheranism, and "the Protestant churches became a department of public administration."[28] He wrote that as long as the church had the freedom of word and sacrament, it could subordinate itself to any social and political order without resistance. Only indirectly, through office holders who were Christians, would it attempt to infuse the public realm with a Christian spirit.[29] The churches cultivated the duty of obedience, insisting with Paul and Luther that obedience to authorities was obedience to God.[30]

Tillich observed that the Protestant churches disavowed the capitalist revolution in its initial stages and later tried to divert the proletarian movement into the patriarchal-princely system, a reference that could include the intentions of Wichern, Stoecker, and Bismarck. When this failed, they turned against the socialist movement while in some measure coming to terms with capitalism. After the Revolution of 1918, he wrote (in 1928), the churches linked themselves to the conservative elements that ruled before the war, forming an "intimate connection" with the German National Party. The result is that their influence on socio-political developments "is extremely slight."[31] Tillich also argued that the major theological movements in German Protestantism--orthodoxy, pietism, and liberalism--had all contributed to its non-transformist and anti-proletarian tendency.[32]

In the last years of the republic when he detected the churches' close alliance with the surge of political romanticism, Tillich intensified his criticism of them. He warned in the prophetic "Ten Theses" on "The Church and the Third Reich" in 1932 that an open or veiled alliance of the churches with National Socialism "must lead to the future dissolution of German Protestantism."[33] He declared that to the extent that it "justifies nationalism and an ideology of blood and race by a doctrine of divine orders of creation, it surrenders its prophetic basis in favor of a new manifest or veiled paganism and betrays its commission to be a witness for the *one* God and *one* humanity."[34]

Theologically, two issues need to be singled out. The first is the question of irrationalism and the second the dualism of the two kingdoms. "Apparent obedience to the word that the kingdom of God is not of this world turns out to be, as so frequently it does in history, obedience to the victorious forces and their demons."[35] Tillich's remark is not only a criticism of an individualistic understanding of the kingdom but also an attack on the willingness to subject oneself to whatever powers might be in control out of obedience to God's rule. He found such an attitude characteristic of Lutheranism because of its belief "in an irrational divine *providence*" expressed, for example, in Luther's idea of "'the masks of God.'" The masks of God, the historical powers in which and through which God works, are, he wrote, an expression of the miraculous rule of God in the world, a rule that is simply to be tolerated and neither calculated nor criticized. From here emerges that feature of Lutheran teachings which its opponents see as Machiavellian: "the lack of every ethical norm in the consideration of the political process." For this reason today, claimed Tillich, "the *'Fuehrer'* can be interpreted as a mask of God."[36]

According to Tillich, there was no theory of natural law for nature or society in the old Lutheran theology because such a theory would have limited the direct action of God. In this situation, there were no functionaries who performed according to a normative law but office holders (*Amstraeger*) who were responsible not to a thing but to a person, in the final analysis, to the divine person. This background accounted for the fact that in his Lutheran context it is not world-formation on the basis of a divine-human natural law that is demanded but acts of love flowing out a religious fullness. Tillich believed that the irrational "from above" and "from below" meet and squeeze out the middle sphere of law. Just as Luther struggled against the law, so those influenced by Lutheranism oppose "'formal democracy'" and reject the democratic state as a "'system.'" The democratic form of life is understood as an unbearable mechanization of the irrational powers. . . . The democratic state has become for the Lutheran consciousness a thing, a law." What is wanted, he noted, is to have the state embodied in a person. "This living, stirring *personalism* and *irrationalism* has stamped in its very depths the consciousness of peoples educated as Lutheran."[37]

In signaling the importance of these beliefs for Lutheranism in the context of 1932, Tillich was demonstrating the affinity that it had with political romanticism in both its conservative and revolutionary forms. Because he recognized that these attitudes were so deeply ingrained in one of the key religious traditions of the German people, he feared for the future. He augured that either Lutheranism would acknowledge the laws of social life in spite of the irrationalities of providence, or it would refuse to do so and thus help to destroy the system, the destruction of which would mean the coming of chaos to Europe.[38] Tillich's objection to political romanticism applied also to Lutheranism: it eliminated the norm of justice and undercut the priority of the second root of human existence. Tillich himself was hardly untouched by this strain of his tradition, but he knew the grave potential for evil within it, "broke" it, and subordinated it to rational and prophetic obligations.[39]

A second, related criticism of Lutheran social theory by Tillich concerned its dualism of the religious and political realms. He rarely mentioned the two-kingdom theory by name, but insofar as it sharply divided the two realms, he attacked it. His understanding of the coming kingdom is inclusive of both realms; there is no ultimate dualism. His view of religion as directness to the Unconditional prevents a separation of religion and politics. Tillich's own idea of *reservatum religiosum* and *obligatum religiosum* recognizes crucial distinctions between the religious and the political, but they are not identical with the divisions of the older two-kingdom idea. His understanding and criticism of aspects of the two-kingdom theory can be seen in his reaction to issues surrounding the relationship of the churches and the Third Reich. Two of his "Ten Theses" read as follows"

> 7. Protestantism according to its essence does not have the possibility to be represented in one definite political alternative. It must verify in itself its own freedom that Protestants can belong to any political party, even those which fight Protestantism in its ecclesiastical realization. It must however place every party as well as every human (even ecclesiastical) action in general under the judgment and hope of the prophetic, early Christian kingdom-of-God proclamation.
>
> 8. In this way it can show to the political will of the groups combined in National Socialism a true and just goal adequate to its social distress and free the movement from the national and humanly destructive demons to which today it is subjected.[40]

Tillich, on the one hand, refused to equate Protestantism with one political program, and, on the other hand, he believed that its message offers a direction for all political action.

He preserved the freedom to decide freely among various political options and yet insisted that all judgments are to be seen in the light of the criteria of the kingdom. Concretely, this means that the churches do not have to disregard the political interests of the lower middle income groups supporting National Socialism, but it does mean they cannot remain neutral or indifferent toward Nazism. Instead Tillich believed they should reveal its demonic character and seek to reorient the goals of its supporters, which was in part Tillich's purpose in *The Socialist Decision*. For Tillich, then, the proclamation of the kingdom is addressed to corporate life (which he found lacking in the Lutheran ethic), but he also was cognizant that this proclamation does not offer a detailed political platform.[41]

Another sample of Tillich's understanding of and relation to the two-kingdom doctrine is his earliest response in the spring of 1934 to the church conflict in Germany.[42] He wrote that the action of the resisting group of evangelical ministers does not have "any consciously political character." He traced the background for this to Luther who had "created a deep gulf" between the religious and the political realms, encouraging obedience to governments who were to oppress the evil in human nature. This gulf accounts for the fact that the Lutheran churches remained silent in face of the treatment of Jews, communists, and trade unions, "but the moment questions of doctrine were involved, the church, as represented by the emergency association of ministers, began to organize its resistance." This resistance, observed Tillich, "could not be surprising to anybody who had lived since his childhood within the sphere of the Lutheran attitude." Although it is not directly political, it is so indirectly, for it challenges the absolute claim of the totalitarian state; therefore, he predicted, its consequences will go far beyond the aim of its instigators. The struggle "must result in religious resistance to the fundamental political idea behind the present form of government. In this way there is implied in the religious resistance a political resistance against the latent religious claim made by the absolute state."[43]

Tillich's analysis demonstrates what he considered the strength and weakness of the Lutheran view. As a Lutheran he totally agreed that political authorities had no right to determine or to interfere in the internal life of the church, but the whole of his religious socialism was directed against the corollary of this position that prompted the churches to remain silent in the presence of injustice. Tillich thought the church conflict was an event "of extraordinary importance both in regard to questions of principle and to the actual future of Protestantism, and indeed of Christianity as a whole."[44] He thought so on the basis of his statement quoted at the end of the last paragraph which subtly restates his own concept of the interconnection between the religious and political dimensions of life. The church conflict in spite of itself is political because it challenges the religious basis of National Socialism.

Tillich saw what would be called the "Confessing Church" as a timely and courageous actualization of the *reservatum religiosum*. Interestingly, this is exactly what he perceived as missing in Hirsch's theological justification of Hitler's victory. In his criticism of Hirsch he commented that the *reservatum* corresponded to the position of the New Testament insofar as it had not felt a direct obligation for nation, state, culture, and society. "Your attitude," he charged, "is the *obligatum* without the *reservatum*." He interpreted Hirsch as giving the *reservatum* to the individual in his relationship to God but not to the church, which Hirsch had considered as defenseless against historical powers. But if this were so, said Tillich, then the church would not only be defenseless, it would not be.[45]

> Religious socialism knew when it took up the doctrine of the *reservatum religiosum* that it must never dissolve the religious into the socialist, that the church is also something apart from the kairos. . . . You have taken over the *obligatum* but have abandoned the *reservatum*—the reproach which is basically the theme of my whole letter.[46]

This criticism should, however, be supplemented by another. *Obligatum* in this passage does not have a normative content. But for Tillich it did, and so he also objected to Hirsch's understanding of the *obligatum*. Social responsibility is to be seen in an eschatological horizon. In discussing a Chalcedonian solution to the relationship of divine and human action, he described Hirsch's position as being the direct and unbroken consecration of a human kingdom and therefore a mixture of the divine and human. Tillich found in this mixture the presence of

a faulty two-kingdom doctrine. He elaborated that in Hirsch's
thought one kingdom is related exclusively to the inwardness of
the individual and the other exclusively to the ordering of social and political life, a separation which "has the consequence
that these orders evade the criticism coming from the expectation of the kingdom of God." Tillich remarked that in Barth
they also evade the criticism, but Barth has secularized (*pro-
fanisiert*) these orders and has placed them under pertinent
norms "which consciously or unconsciously contain an element of
prophetic criticism." But because Hirsch gives them religious
sanctification, then, noted Tillich, he destroys every possibility to attack the demons working in them. This question
about the relationship of the kingdom of God and the kingdom of
man is the issue at stake in all present theological work.
Therefore, he added, he had endeavored sharply to mark his kairos concept off from the similar categories of the two kingdoms
with which they had often been confused.[47]

The decisive reason that Tillich rejected the Lutheran social ethic as he experienced it in Germany is its separation of
divine and human action into two realms which in effect exempts
one realm--the public one--from the judgment and the hope of
the kingdom that is "at hand." Tillich discovered this separation in the Lutheran church, in the emergency association of
ministers, in Hirsch, and in Barth. Hirsch, in Tillich's eyes,
had most vividly demonstrated the error of a two-realms theory
since he both defined one realm in terms of the individual and
in the other, seen from a different angle, demonically confused
the divine and human.

Tillich's understanding of the unity of the religious and
the political aspects of life set him off from the dualism of
the traditional Lutheran teaching. His conception of prophetic
eschatology and of the religious reservation was, however, his
defense against equating the divine and the human, the religious
and the political dimensions. He never drew a one-to-one relationship between the Gospel and a political view, but he did
believe that the Christian proclamation pointed the way for socio-political action. He affirmed the value of responsible
autonomy in the political realm, but he denied that this realm
is devoid of religious meaning. With the notion of *reservatum
religiosum* Tillich kept what is true about the two realms

teaching--the inexhaustibility and the integrity of faith, for example--and with an expanded and concrete interpretation of prophetic eschatology he offered a critical and enticing framework in which the *obligatum* can express itself in transforming the world. This dialectical concept is a genuine achievement of his theology of politics.

Troeltsch at the end of *Social Teachings* concluded that the old answers have lost their power and that therefore "thoughts will be necessary which have not yet been thought." Tillich's religious socialism is one such thought that had not been thought before, even though it too stumbled on Troeltsch's "brutal facts" of history.[48] His theology of politics is a significant alternative to the Lutheran ethic which he found so deficient. Tillich's effort to think new thoughts was also challenged by the new thoughts of another theologian, Karl Barth, a subject to be taken up in the succeeding pages.

Barth's Challenge

In 1911 Karl Barth wrote, "Jesus *is* the social movement and the social movement *is* Jesus."[49] Although Tillich never made such an equation, he did want to demonstrate the affinity between Christian faith and socialism, and, it can be conjectured, the Tillich-Barth controversy would have been very different had Barth continued in this vein. But the Barth he encountered in 1919 and later had other interests. An account of the historical origins of their differences has been given (see above, Chapter 2, pp. 29-30). Barth wanted to pull apart those things that Tillich sought to bring together: God and man, theology and politics, religion (or revelation) and socialism. Barth's rejection of religious socialism meant in Tillich's eyes the denial of the possibility, desirability, and necessity of viewing socialism from a theological perspective. Barth's challenge necessitated that Tillich legitimate his whole enterprise and incorporate in his thought the validity of Barth's protest. In responding to Barth he created an alternative to dialectical theology, at the peak of its influence, an alternative directly concerned with political realities.

The Tillich-Barth controversy during these years as well as Barth's attitude toward socialism have been discussed elsewhere.[50] The concern here is narrower, namely, Tillich's view of Barth in relation to political affairs and his insistence vis-à-vis Barth of the theological appropriateness of religious socialism. If the Lutheran social ethic represented the most prevalent attitude among the churches, Barth was the most prominent voice of progressive theology. Tillich considered the option connected with Barth "by far the most important theological movement of present German Protestant theology."[51] In the early 1920's he welcomed the prophetic protest of Barth's Romans commentary and spoke of his "religious socialism as influenced by Barth."[52] In 1922 he wrote of his "spiritual affinity" with Barth and Gogarten who "without mutual influence" had also arrived at the "unqualified affirmation of the Unconditional."[53] Barth at this time referred to his "subterranean community of work" with Tillich.[54] In the late 1920's, however, Tillich stated that he could no longer take part in this fellowship because Barth's theology had lost its dynamic character and had consummated in supernaturalism.[55] Later in the Confessing Church struggle he gave his qualified support to Barth while deploring the "Grand Inquisitor" present in his dogmatic orthodoxy.[56] He thought that only Barth's one-sided emphasis on the separation of the divine from the human was able to save German Protestantism, but he warned that "an instrument that is a mighty weapon in warfare may be an inconvenient tool for use in the building trade."[57]

Barth like Tillich was a Social Democrat, but unlike Tillich he was a socialist for secular, political, and moral reasons. Tillich believed that Barth's separation of theology from politics had detrimental effects on German Protestants, for it strengthened the traditional dualism of the two realms and further undercut its social responsibility.[58] This Lutheran-Barthian mixture is evident, for example, in Rudolf Bultmann. In 1922 in an article entitled "Religion and Socialism," Bultmann wrote that "no cultural ideal, not even that of socialism, can be directly grounded on religion," for this would destroy both the transcendent character of religion and the autonomous character of human responsibility. The one (indirect) contribution that religion can make to socialism is, he concluded, to create the willingness to devotion and sacrifice. "And sacrifice is the greatest power for world formation."[59] Such a dichotomy and its subsequent individualism suggest the negative impact that Tillich saw in Barth's influence.

Tillich's response to an article by the dialectical theologian Wilhelm Loew, "On the Problem of the Evangelical Social Ethic," also is illustrative of his perception of the weaknesses of Barthian theologians.[60] As Tillich described it, Loew's position was a variety of what Christian ethicists in the 1960's would call "situational" or "contextual ethics": "Take the concrete situation entirely seriously and then make the daring decision in the consciousness that God has spoken his word over the world--that is the evangelical social ethic." In reply, Tillich, stating that Loew had not given an adequate description of the concrete situation, insisted that the universal is an element of every decision. He thought Loew had ignored the community where the universal is expressed in language and noted that in institutions, where the issue is one of law and right, the universal prevails. In place of Loew's ethic Tillich reasserted the idea of theonomy as a norm for concrete judgment.[61] He was critical of this spin-off from Barth for its failure realistically to provide a framework for social responsibility.

Later Barth himself seemed to acknowledge the unfortunate consequences of his theology which Tillich encountered. In a letter to Eberhard Bethge he wrote that when he went to Germany in 1921 his earlier political concern in the form of religious socialism "moved out of the centre somewhat" as he attempted "to give a new interpretation of the Reformation."[62] He explained:

> Germany, burdened with the problem of her Lutheran tradition, was very much in need of a 'refresher course' in just the outlook which I presupposed without so many words and emphasized merely in passing, namely ethics, co-humanity, a servant church, discipleship, socialism, movements for peace--and throughout all these in politics.[63]

Barth commented that Bonhoeffer sensed this void and acted to fill it.[64] He might have added that Tillich too had recognized the void and had offered his own refresher course.

But Barth's reaction to Tillich was not that he was offering needed instruction to the Lutheran Church but that he was erecting "a systematic principle over against the Chruch." Barth feared that the religious socialists' "will to social action could be a substitute for careful concentration upon her own business, hitherto neglected by her" and "an invitation to a distracted assumption of alien responsibilities." Barth's priority lay with the correct understanding of the Gospel and the right administration of the sacraments. Tillich for him was too much "an historian of the spirit," too much an heir of liberal theology in his attitude toward the church, and too much influenced by the "pseudo-eschatological 'situation' of the years immediately following the war" to arouse his interest.[65]

Barth's most extended criticism of Tillich's religious socialism (and perhaps one of the most pointed of any) came in a private letter in early 1933. The issue was continued membership in the SPD at a time when Hitler was consolidating his dictatorship. In a letter to Barth, dated March 29, Tillich explained why he had withdrawn from the party and apparently suggested that Barth consider doing the same. Barth's letter of April 2 told why he would not leave the SPD. This little-known exchange of private letters provides interesting material to study their different approaches to politics in spite of, or perhaps because of, the unexpected rationale for their decisions.[66]

In his letter Tillich presented his case in practical, political terms, writing that "the party does not wish its office holders to sacrifice their official quality for membership in the party." He cited two reasons for this, one being that the party considered the actual influence of its officials in their positions as essentially more important than "formal confession to the party," and the other being the impression he held that the party in its manifest form had been liquidated following the final prohibition of its press.[67]

> Under these circumstances there exists among my Frankfurt (also Hamburg, Berlin, etc.) friends, especially among those who have belonged to the SPD from the beginning, the understanding that membership in the party must not be made into a *punctum confessionis*. This also is not a matter of an ideology of mine but of the immediate tactical reaction of the politicians among us. The situation becomes different in the moment where a declaration is placed before us which demands a meaningful commitment (*inhaltliche Bindung*). In this moment the duty of confession would self-evidently enter, exactly as in Italy.[68]

Barth in his reply juxtaposed his own understanding of socialism and his commitment to the SPD to that of Tillich's.

> Membership in the SPD does not mean for me confession to the idea and worldview of socialism. According to my interpretation of the exclusiveness of the Christian confessions of faith, I can "confess"

to no idea nor worldview in a serious sense. So I
have also to "Marxism" as such no inward, necessary
relationship. . . . As an idea or worldview I can
carry toward it neither fear nor love nor trust.[69]

One wonders if Barth had not read more into the word "confess" than Tillich implied in his letter where it appeared to mean loyalty to the party and its principles. Perhaps Barth did not think such fidelity is a legitimate concern for the Christian; Tillich, however, did not believe he was violating his Christian commitment by being loyal to political principles.[70] On a more important level, however, the passage demonstrates that Barth's position was directly counter to Tillich's. He rejected all interest in those elements of socialism that Tillich found especially crucial. He dismissed as theologically insignificant what Tillich called the religious quality of socialism, which is not its ideas or worldview in themselves, but their meaning-giving power. For this Tillich did have respect and trust, if not exactly fear and love, and therefore he could acknowledge faith in what is finally-meant in socialism. Whereas Barth discovered no or perhaps only a negative religious meaning in socialism, Tillich probed and wanted to strengthen its religious background.

Barth's reference to the exclusiveness of the Christian faith did point to a fundamental theological difference between Tillich and himself. For Barth God has revealed Himself once and for all in Jesus Christ; for Tillich God is not without traces in all of life. Therefore the former built a thick wall between Christian faith and socialism, and the latter sought points of affinity. Therefore Barth considered Tillich an historian of the spirit, and Tillich thought of Barth as a ghetto theologian. From his exclusive position Barth poked at a tender spot in Tillich's theology, since Tillich's theological views were not so clearly grounded in the distinctive claims of the Christian faith. In spite of a Christological weakness, it was narrow of Barth to place Tillich's presupposition outside the bounds of sound theology.[71] Tillich's conviction that God discloses Himself concretely in all reality, that God's reality is not totally absent from the strivings of the proletariat, that socialism might flicker signals of the Ultimate, is not out of line with the universal tendency of the Christian faith. Tillich confessed belief in what is finally-meant in socialism because he was grasped by what is finally-meant in Christianity; in both cases he considered it the same unconditional reality.

Barth continued his letter by explaining why he had joined the SPD, stating that it had been for him "utterly a practical-political decision." He had wanted to select "the party 1. of the working class, 2. of democracy, 3. of non-militarism, 4. of a conscious, but reasonable affirmation of the German people. I saw these requirements of a sound polity fulfilled in the SPD and only in it. Therefore I chose this party."[72] Tillich's reasons for supporting the SPD did not contradict these of Barth --his first socialist writing, for example, included close parallels to these four points--although he was never so confident that the SPD fulfilled these requirements. He too saw the question of party membership as a practical-political matter belonging to responsible autonomy, as his own joining of the SPD demonstrates. But he would have denied that such a decision is "completely unideological," as Ernst Wolf called Barth's political attitude in this letter.[73] There is for Tillich an ideology, that is, a set of ideas, behind such a decision explaining why one supports the working class or democracy, an ideology not unrelated to one's fundamental religious attitude. In this regard Tillich's religious socialism is a gestalt or "plausibility structure" for making political decisions.[74] Such a structure is, he rightly insisted, indispensable for conscious decision making.

In 1933 party membership came to mean something for Barth other than a practical choice. In the hostile environment of the Nazi Reich, Barth made the question of theological concern, a question of freedom in the Gospel. If membership were forbidden, then, wrote Barth, everything depended on "the freedom of the pure political decision, on taking a position and evangelical practice of it."[75] The freedom and the use he made of it--to be in the SPD and to allow himself to be addressed as "an SPD man"--this, he asserted,

> . . . (in distinction to the idea of socialism) belongs to my existence, and whoever no longer wants me as such, he cannot have me at all. I could no longer be believable to myself and also to others if I allowed myself to be forced in this civil context to another decision than this one which corresponds to my conviction politically. You understand me: just because in distinction from you I have no retreat

line to an esoteric socialism. Mine is only exoteric, and exactly for this reason I cannot resign from the party book. . . . Contrary to mere advice and above all to a demand of the present state I will have to stick by my decision. . . . It can do much, this state; it can, for example, retire or remove one at its discretion; but it cannot do everything, it cannot, for example, force a free man to become another for its sake. I say this without the defiance of the hero and the desire of the martyr. That's not it.[76]

This remarkable statement testifies to the spirit of resistance that is to be so important in the Confessing Church. Two days later Barth wrote the Nazi Minister of Education that he could not withdraw from the SPD as a condition for continuing his teaching activity.[77]

Whereas Tillich considered party membership to be a tactical question to be decided in consultation with other party members, Barth now viewed it as a "Here I Stand" issue. Tillich too recognized that a time might soon come when personal witness and symbolic resistance might be the act that was demanded, but at this point he believed that the immediate political consequences of the action were the decisive factor. While Barth made the question one of personal integrity and freedom in the Gospel, Tillich saw it as a practical matter of determining the most effective way of resisting the Nazis.[78]

Although I am inclined to think with Tillich that the issue at hand was one to be met primarily on the basis of political wisdom, I recognize that support can be found for Barth's conclusion. It was, however, unfortunate that in his comments Barth implied that Tillich's "idea of socialism" (Tillich would have said "socialist principle") was not part of his being. Barth was also unfair when, in appraising Tillich's decision as a retreat into "esoteric socialism," he suggested that Tillich's theoretical constructions were an excuse for refusing to take a stand.[79]

Nevertheless, one might ask, has not Barth selected a particularly happy tag in labeling Tillich's socialism as "esoteric"? Tillich's religious socialism was certainly esoteric, if by this is meant frequently obscure, difficult, and complex, in much the same way that Barth's writings often were. It was esoteric, if by this is meant that it remained the intellectual property of a relatively small group and did not penetrate either the socialist movement of the Protestant churches. And if it means the loss of the particular in an ontological category, then his theory had an esoteric tendency.[80] But if it means a shelter from reality in a make-believe world, then the answer is no; it was not esoteric.[81] If by esoteric is meant unimportant or irrelevant, again the answer would have to be no. Barth was right that his socialism was exoteric in comparison to Tillich's, but it might be that a simple socialism is in the long run more illusory than a thought-out, elaborate one.

There are some ironies in this exchange. For one it was Tillich, not Barth, who two weeks later was dismissed from his University post for his resistance to Nazi violations.[82] Secondly, it was Barth, not Tillich, who, equipped with a strong theological and deontological stance, proved in the Confessing Church (not in the party) to be the more effective opponent of Hitler. Finally, it was the religious socialist who insisted that a political decision be treated as an autonomous, secular question while it was the more "secular" theologian who made it into a theological issue (albeit a personal question of freedom in the Gospel). Tillich, however, did not perceive Barth's attitude as ironical. Three years later after a very friendly visit in Basel, Tillich wrote in his diary that he had told Barth that "his letter contradicted his theology. To which he can only add that he could not have done otherwise three years ago."[83]

In a lengthy article on Barth in 1935 Tillich summarized his objections to Barth's failure to deal theologically with political realities.[84] In its concluding pages he criticized Barth for his separation of the divine from the human, of the religious from the political, for his supernatural view of the kingdom, and for his lack of a doctrine of demons. Barth, he continued,

> . . . believes in a godless objectivity of human action ravaged by sin and without any relation whatever either to the divine or the demonic. This seems to me to be one of the weakest points in Barthian teaching; and on this ground his refusal to recognize a theological ethics is also based. Now belief in an objective existence, indifferent with respect to both divine and human dominion, is an illusion.[85]

The belief that all life is constantly lived "on the divine mountain-top and in the demonic abyss"[86] necessitated for Tillich a theology of politics, even if some might consider it esoteric.

Tillich added a finishing touch to his dispute with Barth in a review of a book by him in 1940.[87] Tillich noted in this book "a turning point" in the theology of the one who had so vehemently opposed his religious socialism. For the first time, he wrote, National Socialism has become for Barth a theological problem. Barth now saw Nazism both "'as a political institution and as a religious salvation institution'" which had to be dealt with not only politically but also "'directly as a question of faith.'"[88]

For Tillich these statements had wide-reaching consequences. If there are political movements and ideas which unavoidably have religious significance, then "where is the borderline between political systems with quasi-religious character and those without it? On what side, for example, does American democracy belong?" If one asks for a religious interpretation of National Socialism, does it not follow "that the church in *every* case must ask about the religious elements of a political system? And does not the further demand ensue from here for a theological interpretation and critical examination of politics in general--a demand which religious socialism has always raised?" Tillich thought that when the moral question is coupled with the religious, as Barth had done, then the demand is strengthened. If one applies the criterion of the just state to capitalist democracies and finds them lacking because of the destruction of justice in the class struggle, then how is this theologically distinct from Barth's call to resist National Socialism on religious grounds? "I see to be sure a political but no theological distinction. If, however, there is no theological distinction, can Barth then maintain his earlier rejection of religious socialism and its theological interpretation of history?"[89] Tillich's rhetorical questions can be supplemented by another: Has not Barth vindicated Tillich's fundamental theological intent?

Barth complained that Tillich had remained too much influenced by the "pseudo-eschatological" mood of the post-war years, a surprising charge coming in the apocalyptic situation of 1932, which Tillich recognized so clearly.[90] Certainly Tillich was deeply affected by the war and its aftermath, but Barth was too, a fact not at all to his discredit.[91] The difference was the meaning they gave to the period. In 1934 Tillich described their divergent interpretations. For him, he wrote, the time is "'the socialist hour.'"[92]

For Barth, who paid tribute to the kairos without wanting to, it is the hour of freedom for the church from the secular elements that had penetrated into it during the bourgeois centuries, a view, to be sure, which is only possible because secularization as an historical phenomenon has become fragile in itself.[93] Tillich added that both interpretations are risks.[94] That the two construed the historical situation in contrasting ways helps to account for their pointed disagreements. That both should be considered as genuine risks of faithful theologians is due to the perennial tension that exists for faith between the poles of identity and concrete political decision.

Barth's opposition to Tillich is a reminder of the limitations of Tillich's theology, especially in the realm of Christology. He did not, however, undermine Tillich's contention that the Christian has the responsibility of setting political alternatives within a theological purview. On the contrary, Barth himself demonstrated the necessity and validity of a theology of politics. Tillich's religious socialism was a fitting theological enterprise, however full of risk it might have been.

The Coming of the Kingdom

Tillich's religious socialism represents a recovery of the doctrine of eschatology and its significance for historical change. Repeatedly, Tillich related his theological perspective to prophetic, early Christian eschatology. Throughout this study its critical and contructive meaning has been continually encountered. The paradox of justification takes on socio-political meaning in the frame of reference of the kingdom of God. His concepts of kairos, expectation, the demonic, and the Protestant principle are shaped by his prophetic posture. He was eager to strengthen the future orientation of the eschatological hope and to avoid its perversions. His disputes with socialists, with the churches, with Barth, Hirsch, and others frequently revolved around the relationship between eschatology and history. Tillich rightly recognized that eschatological symbols, especially the kingdom of God, are crucial for all theological reflection on society.[95] Because of its importance for Tillich and for social theology and ethics in general, it is necessary to take special note of the value and limits of his eschatology.

Perhaps one of Tillich's best statements of his eschatology comes in the following quotation in his response to Hirsch where he contrasted his own view with that of Hirsch and Barth.

> Perhaps you remember our distinction between a sacramental and a prophetic attitude. It is the distinction between the claim of holiness for a given in time and space and the holiness that "is at hand" in the sense of Jesus's proclamation of God's kingdom, therefore, that is simultaneously promised and demanded. This eschatological moment belongs inseparably to the kairos doctrine, in early Christianity and in religious socialism. It unites us with Barth insofar as we contest with him the graspable presence of the divine in a finite being or event; it separates us from Barth because the eschatological has with him a supernatural character whereas with us it has a paradoxical character. We do not place the Transcendent in an undialectical opposition to history, but believe that it can only be understood as genuine transcendence when it is understood as that which anywhere breaks into history, shattering and changing it. In this conception you and we are together. The theology of kairos stands exactly in the middle between the theology of the recent National Lutherans and dialectical theology. It considers the second as a deviation into the demonic sacramental. Against both of these it represents the prophetic, early Christian paradox that the kingdom of God comes *in* history and yet remains *above* history.[96]

If a choice needed to be made between the two, Tillich declared himself for Barth's eschatological attitude. "Even if a high price must be paid for this in a supernatural narrowness and an orthodox rigidity, it is better than the abandonment of the eschaton to an absolutely-set finite reality." Tillich's final verdict on Hirsch was that he had perverted "*the prophetic, eschatologically-conceived kairos doctrine into a priestly, sacramental consecration of a present historical event.*"[97]

Here as elsewhere Tillich spoke of transcendence precisely in its relation to history, to its breaking in, shattering, and changing of human life; it is "Beyond" in the midst of life.[98] Tillich believed that in this Hirsch was trying to state something similar, but he did so in a way that collapsed God into a possessable entity, and therefore he stood with Barth and the Protestant principle in opposing such an equation.

The most striking mark of Tillich's paradoxical eschatology is its orientation to concrete historical reality. Far from wanting to flee into another world, Tillich was persistently concerned with God's reign being "at hand" in the here and now. While always aware that the kingdom is more than its manifestations, he was driven by the question, "'How is the kingdom of God working in time and space?'"[99] He considered eschatological statements unrelated to history as "meaningless";[100] the eschaton divorced from our reality cannot be ultimate reality for us. The theological intent of Tillich's religious socialism was to discern, understand, and act upon the concrete socio-political meaning of the prayer, "Thy kingdom come."

The concreteness of the kingdom is coupled with other eschatological assertions, among which the following are especially noteworthy:

1) The coming of God's rule is primarily a gift. The kingdom is not only an "ideal" for "unending approximation" (as it so often has been in Christian social thought), but more so "a reality . . . a real breaking in 'among us' . . . . It is the presence of God, it is grace."[101] Human action in this light, even in the public realm, is response to grace, response to the actual, contemporary transforming presence of God's reign that is "at hand."

2) God's in-breaking is universal. Eschatology, as Tillich defined it, "is the theoretical expression of the Christian belief that in every historical event in past and future there is a relationship to an ultimate fulfillment which lends meaning to relative and conditioned fulfillment."[102] He did not restrict the eschatological reality to the Word, to the proclamation about Jesus Christ, although this proclamation gave to him the ultimate criterion for all revelation, the criterion of the cross. For Tillich God's reality is operative in all reality.

3) The coming of the kingdom has corporate as well as individual meaning; the eschaton is also the criticism and transformation of historical gestalts. Tillich's willingness to contemplate divine action in relation to social structures and social groups is reminiscent of the Old Testament experience of God who acted in relation to a people and peoples.[103]

4) As in the Biblical tradition, the "signs of the kingdom" appear among the poor and oppressed. Tillich looked to the proletariat, to the group most hurt by the present order, as the basis of hope for the new (eschatological reversal), and

considered their welfare as the criterion for justice. The concrete expectation of the kingdom is an expectation of an enlarged human community in which the previously excluded live in meaningful relationship with the former excluders.

Tillich, in understanding the paradoxical coming of the kingdom in terms of concreteness, grace, universality, corporate entities, the oppressed and community, gave fresh meaning to vital though often neglected Christian themes. Tillich's interpretation broke through an individualistic and other-worldly view of the eschaton and brought it into relation to history and its transformation in a highly dialectical fashion. This side of Tillich's eschatology is a valuable way of envisioning the kingdom of historical life, making connections without identifications, offering the possibility for saying both no and yes, and giving hope without illusion.

In moving from the concrete to what might be called the ultimate meaning of Tillich's eschatology, I need to raise some questions. While Tillich boldly illumined the *coming* of the kingdom, his lights grew dim when he spoke about the coming *kingdom*. A non-historical and non-eschatological conception overshadows the meaning of God's reign as the goal of history. Tillich's view of the eschaton does not do justice to the intentions of the Biblical message, even as he saw it, nor does it offer the rationale for a universal perspective needed for social responsibility.

Tillich recognized that the Jewish prophets (and early Christianity) looked forward to "an epoch beyond which no new epoch can be imagined," that is, to an ultimate future. In adopting elements from what he called the "absolute form" of the philosophy of history, he maintained the "tension" of this orientation, but the hope of the ultimate future disappeared.[104] In its place came the assumption of "the relative form" of the philosophy of history in which "'every epoch is immediately under God'" (Ranke).[105] Thus in the essay "Eschatology and History," he wrote, "the end of historical time is its relation to the ultimate. Thus the ultimate stands equally close to and equally distant from each moment of history."[106] For Tillich the Unconditional "is independent of the modes of time," and "the meaning of history is untouched by the modes of past and future" since transcendence is that to "which all modes of time are equally related."[107] In other words, the eschaton is de-futurized, and history's relation to the ultimate is vertical-ized. The Unconditional is the eternal beneath and above all time; "the present is eternity."[108] Thus, in interpreting the eschatological symbols, Tillich placed them in a foreign onto-logical framework that robs them of their intended meaning and posits the question of the temporal and eternity for the ques-tion of the eschaton and history.[109] The future beyond which no future can be imagined is no longer considered a divine pos-sibility and promise, but evaporates into the eternal present.

In *The Socialist Decision* Tillich described the conflict that exists between ontology and eschatology. "Ontology stands on the soil of the myth of origin and is bound to space. It must make time into something spatial. It is the final and most abstract version of the myth of origin." In a footnote he added that ontology has validity only when it is "broken" by the philosophy of history.[110] Eschatology for Tillich, it will be recalled, had its origin with the prophets who raised "*time over space*" and envisioned a "'new heaven and a new earth,'" that is, a new structure of being "that cannot be grasped ontological-ly."[111] Tillich decided for the priority of time over space and did to a degree "break" his ontological thinking through con-sideration of the forward direction of history. In the final analysis, however, it is not sufficiently opened up for Tillich consistently to carry through an historical-eschatological ap-proach to reality.[112] Eschatology is subordinated to ontology, and time is made into something spatial. A concept of the new in accord with his ontological assumption of the eternal present replaces the universal hope of a "new heaven and a new earth," of a future non-ontological new being.

Tillich understood that for Jewish and Christian monotheism "the world has a unitary meaning, a unitary origin and goal."[113] Yet his presuppositions do not seem to permit him to lend sup-port to the Christian conviction that history does have a single goal. For Tillich history's *telos* is not the kingdom of God but theonomy. "For even theonomy is not the kingdom of God, but only an indication of it, even if, as such, it is the meaning and goal of history."[114] This puzzling statement illustrates well the problematic nature of Tillich's combination of ontology and eschatology. Having in effect eliminated the promise of the kingdom of God, he is forced to find the goal of history within history itself in the paradoxical reality of theonomy. Yet he did not explain how a reality "in" history can be the goal "of" history.

Furthermore, there are for Tillich several or perhaps many theonomies, which is to say, there are several or many goals of history. But if this is so, how can theonomy be called "the meaning and goal of history?" Since he never made one theonomy the goal and meaning of history, there are two possible ways to account for what Tillich was saying, both of which reveal a non-historical element in his thinking. Either he has fallen into "a doctrine of infinite repetitions"[115] of autonomy (and heteronomy) and theonomy, in which case there is no one goal; or he reduces all particular theonomies to a basic ontological possibility which as an ontological attitude is the goal of history. If the latter is so, then the uniqueness of historical realizations is lost.[116] Whatever the better explanation, Tillich, in making theonomy the goal of history, undercut the concept of a unitary goal for the world and jeopardized the meaning of historical-eschatological thinking (including his own). Jesus, after all, did not anticipate the coming of theonomy (nor of the church), but of the kingdom of God.

Tillich's confusion over the goal of history has substantial ethical implications, for in undercutting the unitary goal of history he is also endangering the hope and goal of the unity of all humankind. In drawing upon the prophetic, eschatological strain of his thinking, Tillich spoke profoundly of "the unity of humanity." "The myth of the nation (*Volk*) or the unity of humanity, that is the present point of struggle between paganism and Christianity."[117] The import of such a statement goes far beyond the situation of 1931 when it was written. Yet Tillich's understanding of the kingdom does not fully support this claim, for from the perspective of the eternally-present Unconditional the future unity of humankind is ultimately not that important.[118] A strength of Tillich's religious socialism is that he realized that the vision and hope of a united human race are essential for responsible moral action; a weakness in it is that it does not provide a theoretical basis for sustaining this vision and making it intelligible.

A number of other questions can be raised about the adequacy of Tillich's theology from this conflict in his thinking between ontology and eschatology. A few will be suggested, although an elaboration of them exceeds the limits of this study.

1) Is not Tillich's basic Christological category of "center" essentially dictated by his ontology?[119] The symbol of the center not only lacks New Testament support but also fails to express the forward direction of eschatology.[120] This is especially true in that it depends upon an anthropology that assumes "that the center of human consciousness always lies in the past. It cannot be sought in the future, for the meaning of the future is determined by it."[121] This assumption is difficult to reconcile with Tillich's description of expectation.

2) Why does the concept of promise play a relatively minor role in Tillich's religious socialism? Why is there no word about who or what is the source of the promise? Is this insufficient attention to promise in part responsible for Tillich's total disregard for the crucial prophetic concept of covenant, the faithful response to the promise?

3) One might also ask if transcendence is not more adequately conceived (with both Biblical and contemporary criteria) as the future that is coming (as Tillich did in *The Socialist Decision*) than as the eternal emerging from the depths of the present.[122] The non-eschatological metaphor of "depth" is most fitting for one who locates ultimate reality below the temporal order, but it is not easily compatible with looking "ahead" in expectation to God's reign which is "at hand."

4) Finally, what is the relationship of one kairos to another? Are the different kairoi without any historical connection, or are they somehow linked in a united direction?[123] The notion of the kairos would have been strengthened if it had been set within an eschatological framework that would have perceived the in-breakings of the kingdom in relation to each other and to the ultimate destiny of history, the "future absolute."[124]

Like other theologians before and after him who focused on the issues of historical change and responsibility, Tillich turned to the symbol of the kingdom of God for theological guidance. His understanding of the "at handness" of God's reign is an original and provocative paradigm for relating the eschaton and socio-political realities. Because of the antagonism in his thought between ontology and eschatology, however, what he wrote about the ultimate future is not adequate to hope, "the final human possibility,"[125] nor to the intention of the New Testament. A question that Tillich's eschatology leaves open is whether or not one can unite concern for concreteness and for the epoch beyond which none can be imagined without falling into the escapism, the literalism, and the trancendentalism that he rightly opposed.

A Proleptic Model

Tillich placed socialism in theological perspective. In the preceding three chapters Tillich's interpretation of socialism from this viewpoint was discussed, and in this chapter his theological perspective has been appraised. Now it is time to attempt to pinpoint what might be learned from Tillich, both positively and negatively, for the continuing encounter of Christians and socialists.

In the Introduction reference was made to Dom Helder Camara's appeal "to try, today, to do with Karl Marx, what St. Thomas, in his day, did with Aristotle." Although he considered Augustine more than Thomas his model, Tillich did seek to incorporate the values and insights of Marx into Christian perspective. If his efforts did not result in a new synthesis comparable to Thomas' Summa, they do give us a not-to-be-forgotten precedent for such an attempt.[126] His struggles with Marx and socialism a half-century ago helped make Marx and socialism legitimate concerns for Christians today.

"Neither Marx nor Marxism is historically exhausted."[127] If these words of Tillich from 1927 can be properly reiterated today, and if the same can be said of Christ and Christianity, then the encounter of these two traditions will be a lively, difficult, persistent, and crucial issue for years to come. And if Camara's call is a timely one, and if Tillich's concern does have a new vitality today, then it appears possible that something of value might be gleaned from his religious socialism.

Certainly any attempted slavish repristination of his work, which was of course bound spatially and temporally, would be a disservice to him and to the present. In light of the unparalleled threats to humanity's future, any contribution his example might offer would be modest. Yet the historical distance between his and the contemporary world might be advantageous insofar as it offers needed perspective for current efforts to find a new relationship between Christianity and Marxist socialism. Tillich's many-year struggle with this problem does throw off some signals that can give direction to related efforts in a very different world today. His religious socialism is one model for this encounter that in itself is not sufficient but which one would hope will always be a vital part of the interaction of these two historical movements.

Tillich's attempt to place socialism in theological perspective can be described as a "proleptic" model for the encounter of Christianity and socialism. It is proleptic in that Tillich anticipated in his own life and thought the day when the two would coalesce, would mutually penetrate each other, in the creation of a new society. In view of this hoped-for future, he immersed himself in both historical currents. As demonstrated in Chapter 2 and throughout this study, the cardinal mark of his religious socialism is that he was an insider of both realities. He was, as he described himself, "one who tries to combine Christianity and dialectical materialism in his own mind, and for whom the antithesis between the two represents a dynamic element in his own thought."[128] He lived with this tension, even where it was unresolved, because he was convinced that the next period of history would be socialist in form and Christian in substance.

Tillich's proleptic model can be contrasted with other conceivable alternatives. It differs from a view from both sides that claims the two are inherently incompatible, since it envisions a new possibility. It does not demand self-surrender or surrender of the other for the sake of a present accommodation, for it is cognizant of deep-seated differences between the two. His proleptic model recognizes that it is dependent upon common praxis for its realization, but this common praxis also means serious consideration of the theoretical aspects of both traditions.[129] Tillich's model is a step beyond "dialogue," if by this is meant conversation between two separate entities, since he is not a detached observer of one and a defender of the other but an active participant in shaping both within the horizon of the meaningful, socialist society. His model is not that of opposition, accommodation, practice (alone), or dialogue, but of anticipation.

Tillich's experience indicates that a proleptic stance is without doubt precarious. Because it stands at direct variance with existing ideas and interests, the resistance from both sides is powerful. Because it is an example of the spirit running far ahead of reality, it is in constant danger of losing touch with actual possibilities. In its eagerness to synthesize, it is tempted to tone down the distinctiveness of each and to overlook important differences. And if, as happened with Tillich, history moves in another direction than anticipated, then its vision can easily be dismissed as wishful pipedreaming.[130]

In spite of the intrinsic risks, however, Tillich's proleptic model is not without its benefits. Even if its immediate political impact was small, its existence as a creative, yes, esoteric minority was a concrete negation of the negative, a challenge to the uncritical alliance of altar and market, and a reminder of the failure thus far of the socialist promise. It is a model that "points the way" to at least one qualitatively different alternative.[131] Tillich's anticipatory model opens up a favorable opportunity to discover previously unnoticed "affinities" between Christian faith and socialist theory. It is also a helpful example of a theologian, prompted by the demands and expectations of an oppressed group and its theoretical expression, who probed further in the Judeo-Christian tradition. If history's verification process had moved or would move in a different direction, then it has established some sign-posts for this largely uncharted course.

Throughout this study it has been seen how Tillich sought to find new positive relationships between Christianity and socialism, much of it done on the basis of his understanding of eschatology. The following selection summarizes well Tillich's uniting of the two through his eschatological doctrine:

> In the struggle *against* a demonized society and *for* a meaningful society, religious socialism discerns a necessary expression for the expectation of the kingdom of God. But it repudiates the identification of socialism with the kingdom of God just as it rejects religious indifference towards constructive tasks within the world. It regards the unity of the socialist

dialectic, a unity of expectation and demand of that
which is to come, as a conceptual unity and at the
same time as a concrete and contemporary transformation of the Christian eschatological tension. Yet it
is aware of the uncertainty of every concrete realization from the intended unconditional fulfillment.
Therefore, it does not succumb to the profound disil-
lusionment that necessarily accompanies any uncritical (*ungebrochenen*) concrete expectation of the end.[132]

Large parts of Chapters 3 and 5 especially were an elaboration of this quotation, as was the last section of this chapter.
One notices once again how the key terms--demonized, meaningful,
kingdom of God, expectation, demand, socialist dialectic, tension, realization--have religious and socialist meaning, and
yet the two are not the same. This dialectical unity is a major
feature of Tillich's proleptic model. In asking further what
might be learned from this model, certain essential characteristics of it can be singled out. Tillich's theological interpretation of socialism resulted in a model that is concrete,
critical, comprehensive, and constructive.

First, Tillich's religious socialism is *concrete*. By understanding socialism as the expression of the proletariat, Tillich tied his theory to a particular historical movement and
stood in solidarity with the oppressed. He saw the class split
as the decisive structural reality of the present and considered
the proletarian situation as the norm for determining the validity of religious and socialist ideas and practices. At this
decisive point Tillich's socialism is closer to Marxist socialism than to intellectualistic, idealistic, or ethical socialism.

Because of this concrete connection, the possibility of
socialism stood or fell with the proletariat, and when this
class no longer seemed to offer an alternative to capitalism,
Tillich along with other socialists had to ask what had happened to their chosen agent of change and to analyze anew their
situation. With the changed situation after 1933, Tillich came
slowly to modify the decisive role he had given to the proletariat. In 1943 he was unable to identify "the favoured place"
with "a special sociological group," but was "inclined to believe that the broken people in all groups are the favoured
place in our present historical situation."[133] In 1945, in
what represented a major shift in his thinking, he found the
Christian churches as the historical group through which the

answer to the world situation had to be given.[134] Although he still supported some socialist-type political policies, he was no longer a socialist in his original sense of the word.

Does this mean that Tillich's Marxist analysis of his time and place was wrong? Did he misread the signs of the times? Was his deciphering of the reality of the kingdom of socio-political affairs in error? Or was his discernment only premature? A final judgment of these questions might have to wait until the eschaton; in any case, however, Tillich's experience illustrates the difficulties in making concrete theological-political decisions in the provisional reality of history. In the attempt to have ideas become historically embodied in the search for a new future, Tillich had little choice but to risk a link with a socio-political group. He was quite willing to identify with the proletariat. Such an inescapable venture makes the deciding dependent upon the necessities and contingencies, the complexities and the ironies of history, a factor that should prompt modesty for the claims for any such decision. Tillich's own socialist decision involved a careful balancing of dependence upon and independence from the proletariat, but even he did not escape the quandary given by new developments. The dilemma is a continuing one for Christians and socialists alike, and its answer must not be a dogmatic one. The early Tillich underestimated the flexibility of capitalism, but his insistence that the bourgeois world is primarily shaped through its economic structure might not be outdated. His contention that capitalism is demonic has not yet been proven wrong. Perhaps the question raised by the issue of concreteness can be phrased in language given by Tillich: Where is the social locus of expectation?

In another light, however, Tillich's religious socialism is lacking in concreteness. While he was concrete in his analysis of the present and as specific about the hoped-for-future as could be expected, he did not say enough about what went on in between. He was relatively silent on the strategy for change, perhaps because in his view of the division of labor he believed that this was a task for the politician and not for the theologian.[135] More importantly, Tillich did not give much concrete help for evaluating the human costs of the process of change.[136] Herbert McCabe has written, "Every moral problem of the slightest interest is a problem about who is to get hurt."[137] Tillich wrote little directly on who should or should not get hurt and what could be done to minimize "hurting" during the process of change. Some helpful principles might be available in his thought, but they are undeveloped in relation to the possible and probable brutality of any far-reaching change.[138]

Secondly, Tillich's proleptic model is *critical*. He adopted as his own the socialist protest against bourgeois society and the pre-bourgeois remnants used to support it and united them with his own critical perception of an age caught in the cage of self-sufficient finitude. He knew well how to utilize the critical component of dialectical thinking, and in bringing this into relationship with the Protestant principle of paradoxical thinking, his critical awareness was given an added dimension. His attack on the demonic character of capitalism and on the bourgeois ideology of harmony demonstrates his critical rational and prophetic stance. Here is one point where religious socialism is something more than socialism.

Tillich also turned his critical principle toward socialism itself. Religious socialism, he wrote, is a *"Kampfgemeinschaft"* within socialism that is loyal to both "political socialism" and "genuine Marxism." As a group struggling from within socialism it "wants to be nothing but the crisis and the unrest within the socialist life and worldview. It would not occur to us to say that we see no opposition between Christian and socialist morals. We see this opposition very deeply and very painfully. . . ."[139] The tension of a theological interpretation of socialism expressed itself in a radical and profound criticism of socialism, but one which was at the same time an affirmation of the socialist struggle.[140]

Tillich's fundamental criticism of socialism was directed at its failure to perceive itself in relation to the Unconditional. In socialism "the Unconditional is not grasped in its positive and negative powers."[141] If Lutheranism neglected the horizontal in favor of the vertical, socialism did the opposite.[142] Tillich's treatment of the "conflicts" of socialism in *The Socialist Decision* and especially of the utopian element there and in other places is an excellent sampling of what his internal criticism meant. He consistently challenged socialism's inability to break loose from bourgeois attitudes (e.g., its rejection of transcendence) and its tendency to idolatry (e.g., the unscientific faith in Marxist science and uncritical party loyalty).

For the proleptic model, the vocation of the Christian in a socialist movement is to be its "crisis and unrest" of which Tillich's critical attitude is a lively taste. It needs, however, to be combined with an awareness that the theologian is also under the judgment and grace of God. The religious socialist (and other types of political theologians) can do nothing worse than use the holy for political ends. At this crucial juncture, Tillich is worthy of emulation, for he was very aware that the mysterious reality he called gracious was not to be manipulated.

Thirdly, Tillich's socialism is *comprehensive*. His theory should be regarded as experimental, as an attempt to create bridges which, however, needed testing, or, as he put it as late as 1930, "religious socialism stands at the beginning of its development."[143] Tillich had a sense of the provisional character of his work; nevertheless, the breadth of religious socialism, especially when seen as the work of a circle, is indeed impressive. Its work, commented Tillich, is "by no means one-sided in its orientation, either politically or economically," for it sees the scope of problems as "universal."[144] This self-description is borne out in his religious socialist writings, especially *The Socialist Decision,* where he touched on economic, political, social, cultural, religious, and intellectual areas of life not only in relation to socialism but also in relation to political romanticism and the bourgeoisie. His comprehensive project included discussion of man, society, history, technology, nature, and God.

A great deal of the content of his comprehensive conceptual constructions opened up new ways of looking at questions involving socialism and Christianity. His insights into the religious, prophetic character of socialism, his transfiguration of ideology and utopia, his perception of the creative-destructive nature of bourgeois capitalism, his discovery of truth in materialism on the basis of a conception of man as a unity of the vital and spiritual, and his re-interpretation of historical dialectic as a unity of freedom and necessity are important contributions to the ongoing historical encounter. His description of expectation and the meaning he gave to it as an anthropological, prophetic, and political principle are perhaps the highpoint of his inclusive approach to socialism. With his religious socialism he showed that socialism is a question that goes beyond the proletarian situation.

Tillich's comprehensiveness, which was always in tension with his concreteness, allowed him to incorporate new concerns into his socialist theory, as, for example, his interest in establishing a new attitude toward nature. With his embracing vision he was a constant opponent of narrowness and dogmatism. His insistence on the importance of asking questions about the meaning of life, transcendence, and vitality, for example, meant that his socialist theory was congenial only to certain types of socialists, socialists who recognized that Marxist theory did not have all the answers. His word to many socialists of his day is one that deserves repetition: "You cut too much out of life."

Finally, Tillich's theological interpretation of socialism is *constructive*. Because he believed that the Yes is prior to the No, that judgment depends upon the awareness of grace, the accent of his writings was on formation or creation.[145] Thinking the answers which both had given in the past inadequate to the present, Tillich constructed anew socialist theory and Christian social thought. In his uniting of these two realities, he created a new theological-political conception, and in his proleptic model he anticipated the coming of a socialism and a Christianity that is profoundly different from anything that has gone under these names previously.

To transform socialism meant to bring it into explicit relationship with the Unconditional, with God. Tillich was adamant that for socialism to resolve its own inner dilemmas and to be a new reality in relation to capitalism, it had to see itself in reference to transcendence. What this meant for socialism has been a major topic in this study. Among other things it would involve the rise of new symbols to express the finally-meant of life.[146] There is, however, some ambiguity in Tillich's appeal, an ambiguity related to the personal response to religious socialism. What is involved for the socialist in making explicit the faith working in socialism? Is the line between unbelieving realism and believing realism thick or thin? What does the change from the one to the other mean? Is it a big step or a little one? Is it what the New Testament called metanoia? Or is the change in this area blurry?[147] Clear-cut answers to these questions do not appear in his writings.

The *telos* of his religious socialism was the building of a new social order, a qualitatively new post-bourgeois society. Tillich's eschatological vision spawned the hope of a new period of Christianity and a new period of social and economic justice. The crowning image of his proleptic model is the theonomous socialist society toward which action is to be directed. With this image Tillich affirmed human autonomy and called for more just socio-political structures, but with it he was also stating that change is more than achieving a new balance of power or a new social arrangement. He placed the question of meaning in the center of societal construction, and, like Augustine, he believed that the good society is ultimately dependent upon God. Dare the distant and disciplined hope of the Christian be anything less than the just and the meaningful society? Perhaps this is Tillich's enduring challenge to those who seek a new relationship between Christianity and socialism.

In summary, Tillich, in anticipating the coming of a new unity of religious substance and socialist structure, appropriated, criticized, and transformed both traditions. He proleptically embodied that for which he strove. The result is a theological interpretation of socialism that is concrete, critical, comprehensive, and constructive.

Conceivably Camara's appeal ia an anachronism that has come a century too late; conceivably the barriers between Christianity and Marxism are too great; conceivably the relationship of Christ and Marx is a side issue to the real and immense problems the contemporary age faces. If one or all of these are the case, then Tillich's religious socialism is at best an interesting and harmless aesthetic diversion. But it might also be possible that Camara has pointed to a vital and unsolved question, particularly acute in Latin America, but one he apparently believes should also be the concern of North Americans. Tillich once called the kairos "the socialist hour," and he was disappointed. But if the scope of the kairos is broadened to include the whole of the twentieth century, then, it might be argued, Tillich's phrase is an apt description of our time. If our age is indeed "the socialist hour," then Christians have a responsibility to attend to Marx and all he represents, seeking in common action and theory with socialists to actualize the best of both traditions and transform the demonic structures of the present. If this is a task for this time, then there is in Tillich's proleptic religious socialism a precursor from which much can be learned.

The Later Years, 1933-1965

Tillich's religious socialist hopes were crushed by Hitler. With the victory of National Socialism and the emigration of Tillich to America, the period of his life studied in this dissertation comes to an end. What happened to Tillich and his relationship to socialism after 1933? In order to answer this question and to place the early years in the perspective of his whole life, I will in this concluding section begin where Chapter 2 ended and in the briefest fashion describe Tillich's theological-political concerns after his departure from Germany. His later years fall into two distinct parts, 1933-1945 and 1945-1965.

Almost immediately upon his arrival in the United States, Tillich began to interpret for his new audience the developments in Germany, to oppose publicly Hitler's regime, and to aid and work with other emigres fleeing the new tyranny. In articles and lectures he warned about the dangerously demonic and pagan character of National Socialism and attacked its antisemitism.[148] He explained the meaning of religious socialism and described its failure: "The gulf between the secular orthodoxy of the Marxist political movements and the religious and ecclesiastical orthodoxy of the Lutheran tradition could not be bridged. Marxist orthodoxy rejected the religious interpretation of its ideas."[149] He continued to probe the relationship between Marxism and prophetic religion, writing during these years some of his most significant essays on the theme.[150] His diary of his first return trip to the Continent in 1936 shows his intensive political involvement and his extensive network of socialist and theological friends.[151]

Tillich joined the Fellowship of Christian Socialists and met new kindred spirits. Reinhold Niebuhr welcomed his first English book, *The Interpretation of History,* with the recommendation that "no book has appeared in this country which has more right to become a textbook of radical Christians. . . ."[152] The ecumenical Conference on Church, Community and State at Oxford in 1937 gave support to his religious socialist ideas, adopting in its official report a statement on the economic order that Tillich had helped to write.[153] He also worked with his fellow emigrants on a variety of levels. As President of "Selfhelp for Emigres from Central Europe" from 1936 on, Tillich organized practical aid for those pouring out of Germany. He was a member of the board of the Institute for Social Research, now driven into exile.[154] In person and by letter he continued his conversations with his German socialist friends. A leader among the emigres, he sought to give political and intellectual unity to the diverse group, hoping, as he had for years, to find a new synthesis of prophetism, humanism, and socialism.[155] In 1944 Tillich became President of the "Council for a Democratic Germany," an international group of emigrants wanting to influence the future shape of Germany.[156]

When he returned from his overseas trip in 1936 Tillich was convinced that "Europe had missed her providential moment, her kairos (the right moment from the point of view of eternity) and tries in vain to escape the destructive consequences of this failure."[157] He saw the present task as one of "'preparing for the day after to-morrow.'"[158] Tomorrow meant the war and its destructive consequences, a possibility Tillich had foreseen in 1932 if National Socialism were triumphant. He spoke often during this time of the tragic and demonic in history, combating, like Niebuhr, an easy historical optimism.[159]

When war came, Tillich, now an American citizen, supported the Allies' war effort.[160] One important way he did so was in a series of political-religious talks that were broadcast to the German people over the Voice of America every week from early 1942 to May 1944.[161] In these remarkable speeches and in his other lectures and writings, he held out hope for a new beginning once Hitler had been defeated.[162] Europe had missed its moment, but it was to be given another chance after the disasters of war. He maintained his epochal perspective; indeed, he enlarged it: "The world war is part of a world revolution."[163] The kairos was delayed, not cancelled. Sober, but undespairing, Tillich continued his political involvement and his kairos awareness until the war's end in 1945. But the war's end did

did not bring the possibility of one democratic, socialist Germany and a federated Europe, as he had hoped, but the division of Germany and the emergence of two antagonistic powers that controlled the fate of Germany. "The end of the Second World War with its metamorphosis into the Cold War meant the end of Tillich's concrete political engagement that since 1919 had made him famous as a religious socialist."[164] The kairos did not break in, and Tillich, deeply disappointed, turned his attention elsewhere.

Tillich's political period ended in 1945, having extended from the end of one war to the end of another. From 1945 until his death twenty years later, social and political questions played a subordinate role in his life and thought. While the situation after the First World War had activated his religious socialism, the aftermath of the Second World War led him to withdraw from the political arena. Now a second "break" occurred in his political-theological activity: the proclaimer of the kairos became the "guardian of the void."

In a discussion with Lowe, Horkheimer, and Pollock on January 28, 1945, Tillich spoke of his new disposition. Disappointed and exhausted, he had become more relativistic and sceptical in his attitude toward time.

> I was never a primitive utopianist and today I am no primitive absolutist. The catastrophe of the kairos hope has caused me to experience the absolute more than the political.
> I then believed it possible to bring about a fundamental change in Christian theology with the categories of religious socialism; today my hope is limited to giving to the Americans a developed theology, which they have never had. In 1920 it was different; then I wanted to inaugurate a new period of Christianity.
> Neither in thinking nor in acting can I be the old. In both I have reverted from the conversion situation of Paul into a somewhat sceptical situation of Saul.[165]

Tillich articulated a pivotal change in his mood and intentions. He set a new course for himself, a more modest one, without a kairos consciousness. In completing his *Systematic Theology* he did accomplish his modified goal. Lowe was right that day: ". . . dass Gott will, dass Tillich seine Dogmatik schreibt. . . ."[166]

A year later, in January 1946, in a lecture at the University of Chicago, Tillich for the first time publicly interpreted the present era as a "void." The theme, "Religion and Secular Culture," harkened back to his first lecture, "On the Idea of a Theology of Culture," but the sense of doom and defeat contrasted sharply with his earlier belief that a period of radical transformation was approaching.[167]

> While after the first World War the mood of a new beginning prevailed, after the second World War a mood of the end prevails. A present theology of culture is, above all, a theology of the end of culture, not in general terms but in a concrete analysis of the inner void of our cultural expressions. Little is left in our present civilization which does not indicate to a sensitive mind the presence of this vacuum, this lack of ultimacy and substantial power in language and education, in politics and philosophy, in the development of personalities, and in the life of communities.[168]

This void, he added, might become a "sacred void" if one expressed it and adopted an attitude of waiting, refusing to fill the vacuum with premature solutions.[169] The self-sufficient bourgeois era had not come to an end, and the task, as Tillich now saw it, was to demonstrate its emptiness without the confidence that an alternative is "at hand."

The void was the sign that hung over Tillich's later period, qualifying and transforming his work.[170] The ontological, priestly strain of his thinking overshadowed the eschatological, prophetic thrust of his religious socialism. The emphasis on the vertical modified his earlier concessions to the horizontal, the historical, and the utopian. Existentialism and psychoanalysis filled the space which socialism, now an almost forgotten concern, once occupied. He continued to use such concepts as theonomy and demonic, but now they no longer represented a unity of the religious and the political dimensions, and so they floated in the air. He spoke now of the apolitical "courage to be" and no longer of the concrete "socialist decision."[171] The contradictions he had once seen in modern society became now a general and universal threat to personhood for all modern people,[172] and the angst and meaninglessness of segments of the overclass became his point of departure instead of the oppression of the underclass. In place of heralding the coming of a new social order, he dwelt upon more domesticated themes such as "the lost dimension in modern society."[173] He became an apologist for the flight to the moon, but unlike his pervious critical social analysis he was unattentive to the looming dangers of the military-governmental-intellectual-industrial complex that sponsored it.[174] In spite of his achievements in his last twenty years, something significant was absent. The prophetic, the political, the socialist elements were now largely a memory and no longer a living passion. Tillich was aware of this. In interpreting his new destiny as a void, he was, among other things, calling attention to the vacuum in his own work.

Tillich was not of course totally unconcerned and uninvolved with political affairs, and his attitudes during the post-war years can be labeled those of a liberal democrat.[175] He stated what was then his approach to politics perhaps most clearly in a farewell speech in May 1955 to the New York Christian Action group. Tillich had been a member of this group and its predecessors (including the Fellowship of Christian Socialists) since the 1930's. He explained the evolution of the group's thinking, from the old ideas of religious socialism to its current position. "I was the most conservative of the group, changing most slowly, and Dr. Niebuhr was the most progressive."[176] He outlined the differences between the earlier and later point of view:

> a) We did not seek a radical transformation of a system, a revolution, but rather changes within the system which as a whole was not to be changed.
> b) We did not calculate in terms of historical necessities, even in dialectical terms, but rather saw problems as they arose without an underlying and overall interpretation of history.
> c) We had no sketch of a total world view, a description of a coming economy in all realms of life. This produces a less passionate temper, more political wisdom, and more concrete action.[177]

Tillich along with his cohorts had adopted a pragmatic, gradualist attitude toward the political questions of the day. In spite of the sharp differences, he did see continuities between this approach and his earlier one: both were a participation in the fight for the fragmentary actualization of the kingdom of God in history; both held onto the insight that individual and social healing were interdependent, and both sought to reveal the demonic powers in their historical situation. But now, he stated, "instead of prophets of the Kairos we have become guardians of the void, to keep demonic forces from entering it and to strengthen every divine force which might enter it."[178]

The task of the guardian of the void, he said at the end of his talk, is "to keep the prophetic spirit in the church alive and in society meaningful. This is wish and hope connected with respect to our own work of the past with quite an amount of resignation. 'Do it better.'"[179]

Tillich political attitudes were liberal and pragmatic but with one qualification, the sense of the "'negative kairos,'" the void.[180] His interpretation of the era as a void is in itself a critique of the political situation. The period of bourgeois capitalism and liberal democracy was not the end of history, but an interim arrangement, inescapable for a time, but one which faced a terminus in the indefinite future. Pragmatic, piece-meal engineering was needed for the moment but its relative value was recognized. To be a guardian of the void also implied the recognition that the Communist states had betrayed the socialist expectation. For Tillich the post-war years were a time of waiting, in which, to be sure, there were responsibilities to be shared, but the prophetic spirit would be heard again and announce the coming of a new era, one that he hoped would be structured according to justice and filled with the meaning-giving power of the Christian tradition. There was for him no going "'beyond religious socialism.'"[181]

CHAPTER 6

NOTES

[1] "Christentum und Sozialismus (II)," *GW*, II, p. 33. For an example of the continuity of Tillich's goal compare the 1938 essay, "Die politische und geistige Aufgabe der deutschen Emigration," *GW*, XIII, pp. 200-16, where Tillich is seeking a synthesis of the prophetic, humanistic, and socialist traditions.

[2] "Der junge Hegel und das Schicksal Deutschlands," *GW*, XII, pp. 126, 125.

[3] *RV*, p. 22. Note that here Tillich used "social" instead of "political" as he would do in *SD*. The two terms were used in a general way and seem to have the same meaning. Tillich's statement here is strong evidence that in interpreting the early Tillich one cannot bypass the practical concern he had for uniting the political and the religious dimensions.

[4] "Um was es geht," p. 119. Tillich's statement here is a reply to Hirsch's charge that Tillich's criticism of him had been a political and not a theological one.

[5] "Answer," p. 11.

[6] "PPPS," *PE*, p. 162; cf. German version, p. 7. Tillich's religious socialism should be considered as an expression of the missionary impulse of the Christian faith, or, as he called it, religious socialism is an apologetic effort. Cf. *OB*, pp. 60-64.

[7] "Um was es geht," pp. 118-19. While it appears to me that Tillich's prophetic attitude and kairos doctrine do embody a Chalcedonian solution, it is unusual that Tillich spoke here of divine *action*. In what sense does the Unconditional act?

[8] "Answer," p. 10; cf. "Kirchenfrage," *GW*, II, p. 13. The latter has the added "und der sozialistischen insbesondere."

[9] Ibid. "Kirchenfrage" in the more normal language of Tillich said at this point "the unconditionality of the religious principle that is independent of every definite cultural form . . .," *GW*, II, p. 13. This is a point where Tillich differed significantly from a Marxist interpretation of religion. In 1935 he wrote that the differences between Christian and Marxist anthropology could be reduced "to the opposition between transcendence and immanence. . . . By far the most important is the contrast between the Christian and the Marxist appreciation of the individual and his inward existence. The transcendental foundation offers Christianity the possibility of dissociating to a certain extent the inward existence of the individual from among [sic] the structural framework of the objective contradiction. This is the ground of the possibility of the care of individuals and of mysticism within Christianity." In Marxism, he continued, this is impossible. "The Christian and Marxist View of Man," p. 16. Clearly this is an either/or question for Tillich.

[10] Ibid. "Kirchenfrage" stated that the religious principle became "*concrete,* that it gained expression in definite forms of cultural life." Instead of pure inwardness Tillich here spoke of "universality." *GW,* II, p. 13.

[11] Ibid. "Kirchenfrage" saw the movement "from the Unconditional to the conditioned." *GW,* II, p. 14.

[12] Ibid. "Kirchenfrage" replaced "mutual penetration" (*wechselseitiger Durchdringung*) with "became one" (*ist es eins geworden*). *GW,* II, p. 14. In his appeal for a new relationship between Christianity and socialism Tillich often used the phrase of "becoming one." This should be understood after the model of "mutual penetration" and the examples he cited at this point. Tillich recognized that Christianity had always existed in relationship to social structures and therefore its "choice" was not that of connecting itself with no structure or with a structure but to which one. No order could claim to be the final Christian society, but Christianity was not free from the necessity of being tied to a particular social arrangement.

[13] Ibid. "Kirchenfrage," *GW,* II, p. 14.

[14] Ibid., pp. 10-11. "Kirchenfrage," *GW,* II, p. 14.

[15] "Basic Principles," *Pol. Exp.,* pp. 63-64.

[16] Ibid., pp. 64-65. Cf. "Church and Culture," *IH,* pp. 219-41.

[17] As a theologian of culture Tillich had some difficulty in explaining the existence of a separate sphere of religion. In 1919 he gave a psychological explanation. "Th. of Cul.," *WR?,* p. 175. As seen above, its existence is due to the presence of the demonic. As I have noted, Tillich's political commitment made him feel more and more alienated from the church. Although he never made the connection, one gains the impression that the proletariat comes close to taking over some of the role of the church in his theology (e.g., the locus of revelation).

[18] "RS (II)," *Pol. Exp.,* p. 57.

[19] *Christ and Culture* (New York: Harper Torchbooks, 1951), esp. Chs. 5 and 6. Cf. Carl J. Armbruster, *The Vision of Paul Tillich* (New York: Sheed and Ward, 1967), pp. 282-304. Armbruster created a new classification, "Christ the Depth of Culture," for Tillich. Armbruster, whose primary concern was with the later writings, also thought "Tillich is closest to the conversionist type." P. 288. He found, however, "certain nuances" which made him different from the conversionists, mainly, that Tillich "would probably see the taint of progressivism" in them. P. 288-89. This would perhaps be true for Maurice but not for the general type. Moreover, it is not clear what Armbruster gained with creating a new type. Depth is one of several ways of speaking of paradox. In light of his Lutheran background, Tillich is, I think, more adequately described as one standing on the boundary between "Christ and Culture in Paradox" and "Christ the Transformer of Culture." In his early writings the conversionist theme is very evident.

[20] Ibid., pp. 206-18. For Tillich's interpretation of Augustine see "Die Staatslehre Augustins nach de civitate dei," *GW,* XII, pp. 81-96. Originally published in *Theologische*

Blaetter, IV (1925), pp. 77-86. Tillich thought that in spite of all his pessimism, Augustine had laid the groundwork for a new, holy communal life. For those struggling for a future in which the unity of society would be grounded in unconditional being, in God, then, he concluded, there can scarcely be another leader than Augustine. P. 96. Cf. "The Totalitarian State and the Claims of the Church," *Social Research,* I, 4 (November, 1934), p. 422: "The failure of the religious socialist movement, which attempted to widen the horizon of Lutheranism by going back to genuine Christian and particularly Augustinian traditiona, is also largely attributable to this Lutheran separation between private and political morality."

[21] Cf. *OB,* p. 74. See above, Ch. 2, Secs. 1 and 3.

[22] See Karl Barth, *Eine Schweizer Stimee, 1938-1945* (Zollikon-Zurich: Evangelischer Verlag, 1948); William H. Lazareth, "Luther's 'Two Kingdoms' Ethic Reconsidered," *Christian Social Ethics in a Changing World,* ed. by John C. Bennett (New York: Association Press, 1966), pp. 119-31; Heinrich Bornkamm, *Luther's Doctrine of the Two Kingdoms,* trans. by Karl Hertz (Philadelphia: Fortress Press, 1966).

[23] Cf. Tillich "The Religious Situation in Germany To-day," *Religion in Life,* VII, 2 (Spring 1934), pp. 170-71.

[24] The following is not a discussion of all aspects of the complex and controversial two-kingdoms theory. Later, in an atmosphere that blamed Luther for National Socialism, Tillich defended Luther and his social ethic, especially at the point of Luther's understandings of *opus alienum* and *opus proprium.* See "Love's 'Strange Work,'" *The Protestant,* IV, 3 (December 1942 - January 1942), pp. 70-75. Also, *The Recovery of the Prophetic Tradition in the Reformation* (unpublished manuscript, 1950), p. 28. For Tillich's relation to Luther see Ch. 3, fn. 86. Tillich's interpretation of the Lutheran social ethic no doubt relied on Troeltsch. He welcomed the Luther Renaissance, but he criticized it for its lack of impact in the socio-political arena. One should remember that above all Tillich was criticizing the Lutheran ethic as he encountered it in Germany in the Weimar period. For a discussion of the social ethic of some prominent Lutheran theologians during this time see Hans Tiefel, "The German Lutheran Church and the Rise of National Socialism," *Church History,* Vol. 41, No. 3 (September 1972), pp. 326-36.

[25] "Zehn Thesen," *GW,* XIII, p. 178.

[26] "Cl. St.," *GW,* II, p. 190.

[27] "PPPS," p. 30; cf. *PE,* p. 179.

[28] "Christianity and Modern Society," *Pol. Exp.,* p. 7.

[29] "The Totalitarian State," pp. 421-22.

[30] "RS (I)," *GW,* II, p. 157; "RS (II)," *Pol. Exp.,* p. 53; "Answer," p. 9.

[31] "Christianity and Modern Society," *Pol. Exp.,* pp. 7-8.

[32] "PPPS," pp. 25-33; cf. *PE,* pp. 176-81.

[33] *GW,* XIII, p. 179. Cf. pp. 186-87.

[34] Ibid.

[35] Ibid., p. 177.

[36] "Protestantismus und politische Romantik," *GW*, II, p. 214.

[37] Ibid., pp. 214-15.

[38] Ibid., pp. 216-17.

[39] Tillich held on to the bourgeois principle as a "*critical principle*" and a "*corrective*." *SD, GW*, II, p. 271. He rejected the possibility of an absolute natural law but thought a relative natural law might have validity. *SD, GW*, II, fn. 21, p. 347. See esp. *RV*, fn 18, p. 305.

[40] *GW*, XIII, p. 178. When Arthur Cochrane in reference to these theses wrote that "at that time, Tillich viewed the situation as a struggle between socialism and Nazism," he obscured the theological character of Tillich's stance. *The Church's Confession under Hitler*, p. 79.

[41] Tillich's criticism of Hirsch was not so much a direct attack on his political judgments, with which he strongly disagreed but which he recognized as biographically codetermined, as it was an assault on his theological support for these judgments, which exempted the events of 1933 and 1934 and the National Socialist movement from the critical perspective of the kingdom. This is entirely consistent with his position described in the text. Cf. "Um was es geht," p. 119.

[42] "The Religious Situation in Germany To-day," *Religion in Life*, pp. 163-73. See Cochrane's book for a study of the Church Struggle. In this article Tillich referred to the resistance as "the most exciting event in the present history of the church, because in it the profoundest problem of contemporary church history has become visible. This problem is the problem of secularism." P. 172. Here and elsewhere Tillich interpreted the rise of National Socialism as the rise of a new paganism, which was out to destroy both Christianity and humanism. This paganism was a result of the emptiness of secularism, to which old demons rushed in.

[43] Ibid., pp. 163-66.

[44] Ibid., p. 166. Cf. "Totalitarian State," p. 422.

[45] "Die Theologie des Kairos," p. 327.

[46] Ibid. Cf. pp. 263-64.

[47] "Um was es geht," p. 119.

[48] *Social Teachings*, II, pp. 1012-13.

[49] "Jesus Christus und die soziale Bewegung," *Der Freie Aargoner*, VI, 153 (December 23, 1911), p. 1.

[50] For Barth's relationship to socialism see West, Chs. 5 and 6. Also, for a "revisionist" view see Friedrich-Wilhelm Marquardt *Theologie und Sozialismus* (Muenchen: Chr. Kaiser Verlag, 1972). Also Helmut Gollwitzer, *Reich Gottes und Sozialismus bei Karl Barth* (Muenchen: Chr. Kaiser, 1972). See also, Ch. 2, fn. 88, p. 41.

[51] "Karl Barth," *GW*, XII, p. 187. Originally published in *Vossische Zeitung*, No. 32, 1926. This article provides a convenient summary of Tillich's view of Barth at mid-decade.

[52] Review of Emanuel Hirsch, *Die Reich-Gottes Begriffe des neuren europaeschen Denkens, Theologische Blaetter*, I (1922), p. 43.

[53] "The Conquest of the Concept of Religion in the Philosophy of Religion," *WR?*, p. 123.

[54] "The Paradoxical Nature of the 'Positive Paradox,'" *The Beginnings of Dialectic Theology*, p. 142.

[55] "Zur Einfuehrung," *RV*, pp. 20-21.

[56] *OB*, p. 41.

[57] "What is Wrong with the 'Dialectic' Theology?," *The Journal of Religion*, XV, 2 (April 1935), p. 143.

[58] *RV*, fn. 30; *RV*, p. 21; "The Religious Situation in Germany Today," pp. 170-71; *OB*, p. 76.

[59] "Religion und Sozialismus," *Sozialistische Monatschefte*, XXVIII (May 15, 1922), pp. 446-47.

[60] *GW*, XIII, pp. 212-18. Loew, who had participated in the Kairos Circle and who had left it under the influence of Barth, had criticized Tillich in his article.

[61] Ibid., pp. 213-18. Tillich's early theological position cannot properly be classified as situationalist. For a discussion of Tillich as a modified natural law thinker, see George A. Lindbeck, "Natural Law in the Thought of Paul Tillich," *Natural Law Forum*, VII (1962), pp. 84-96.

[62] *Fragments Grave and Gay*, ed. with a Foreword and Epilogue by Martin Rumscheidt, trans. by Eric Mosbacher (London: The Fontana Library, 1971), p. 120.

[63] Ibid., pp. 120-21. The German word *Mitmenschlichkeit*, given in the English translation, has been omitted and retranslated as "co-humanity" instead of "brotherliness."

[64] Ibid., p. 122.

[65] *Church Dogmatics*, I, 1 (1932), pp. 82-83.

[66] Part of Tillich's letter is found in Breipohl, *Religioeser Sozialismus*, p. 220. Unfortunately it is a very brief selection. A much larger selection from Barth's letter is found in Ernst Wolf, "Politischer Gottesdienst," *Blaetter fuer deutsche und internationale Politik*, XI, 4 (1966), pp. 289-90. I was unable to locate the full text of either letter. This exchange took place after the Enabling Act of March 23. See Holborn, pp. 729-30; Bracher, p. 210.

[67] Breipohl, p. 220.

[68] Ibid. Breipohl's interpretation of this letter that Tillich was prepared for "partial co-operation (*Mitarbeit*)" with National Socialism and that therefore Tillich's suspension probably had little to do with his principled opposition to National Socialism is a view that is consistent with her presuppositions but is not in accord with Tillich's writings or actions, as described in the text. See especially Ch. 2, Sec. 6. Pp. 75-77.

[69] Wolf, p. 290.

[70] From the beginning Tillich insisted that the Christian who embraces socialism must also embrace the principles on which it is built. "Christentum und Sozialismus (I)," *GW,* II, p. 21. Tillich here outlined these principles as autonomy, rule of reason, this-worldliness, and humanity. PP. 22-24. One wonders if Barth was objecting to such ideas, if trust or respect for them was outside his interpretation of the exclusiveness of the Christian confessions.

[71] Barth ended his letter with these sharp words: "Therefore as before I will only censure you for the fact that also your presupposition (without esoteric socialism) does not stand in a sound (*ordentlich*) theology." Ibid., p. 219. As I am interpreting it, this presupposition refers to Tillich's understanding of universal revelation. For a study of Tillich's theology from a Barthian perspective see Alexander J. McKelway, *The Systematic Theology of Paul Tillich* (Richmond, Virginia: John Knox, 1964). The tension between the particular and the universal within the Christian faith is well-illustrated by these two theologians.

[72] Ibid., p. 290.

[73] Ibid., p. 289.

[74] On "plausibility structure," see Peter L. Berger, *A Rumor of Angels* (Garden City, N. Y., Doubleday and Company, Inc., 1969), pp. 42-43.

[75] Wolf, p. 290.

[76] Ibid.

[77] Ibid., p. 289.

[78] One is reminded of Max Weber's distinction between an "ethic of absolute ends" and "an ethic of responsibility." "Politics as Vocation," *From Max Weber,* trans., ed., and with an Introduction by H. H. Gerth and C. Wright Mills (New York: Oxford University Press, 1938), pp. 77-128. Both Tillich and Barth agreed that one had to combine the two ethics but they differed in their discernment of the situation and whether or not an ethic of absolute ends was required in this case.

[79] Earlier, in his review of Loew's article, Tillich had responded to a similar criticism: "It has almost become a dogma that the universal is the place to which we flee in order to escape the unconditional seriousness of our standing as sinner and responsible before God." Tillich replied that this could be true although it did not have to be. *GW,* XII, p. 214.

[80] The individual often seemed to disappear into an ontological possibility. This, of course, is a very broad definition of what esoteric might mean.

[81] Cf. Reinhold Niebuhr, "The Contribution of Paul Tillich," *Religion in Life,* VI (Autumn 1937), p. 581. "His terms may be abstract, but his thought is not. It deals in terms of rigorous realism with the very stuff of life."

[82] Barth had to leave his position at the University of Bonn in 1935.

[83] *My Travel Diary,* p. 118.

[84] "What is Wrong with the 'Dialectic' Theology?" This article is Tillich's most complete discussion of Barth.

[85] Ibid., p. 144.

[86] Ibid.

[87] "Ein Wendepunkt in Karl Barths Denken, zu seinem Buch: 'Die Kirche und die politische Frage,'" *GW*, XII, pp. 324-26. Originally appeared as "Karl Barth's Turning Point," *Christendom*, VI, 1 (1940), pp. 129-31.

[88] Ibid., p. 324.

[89] Ibid., pp. 325-26.

[90] Cf. *SD, GW*, II, fn. 23, p. 256. Here in commenting on Spengler's *The Decline of the West,* which had helped set the immediate post-war mood, Tillich wrote that "the rise of a second paganism in Christian form, combined with the depopulation and pauperization of Europe through self-annihilating wars, is a possibility that is closer to us today than it was when this book was having its greatest success."

[91] Cf. *Rel. Sit.*, p. 175. Tillich's statement here could include both Barth and himself: "Many of the religious movements which make the conception of a turn in time their chief symbol, have been indirectly influenced by Spengler's European pessimism--though they have converted it into an optimistic expectation of the end."

[92] "Die Theologie des Kairos," p. 319. In this context Tillich considered Hirsch's interpretation as that of the "'German hour.'"

[93] Ibid.

[94] Ibid.

[95] In his review of Hirsch's *Die Reich-Gottes* in 1922, Tillich accepted Hirsch's statement that "'the kingdom of God is the element of unrest in the history of the modern teaching of the state,'" and added, "The kingdom of God idea, that is, the realization of the Unconditional in the life of society, is not only the inciting element of the West but actually the basis of every doctrine of society." P. 43.

[96] "Die Theologie des Kairos," p. 312.

[97] Ibid. Cf. Hopper, pp. 78-80.

[98] Cf. Bonhoeffer, *Letters and Papers from Prison*, p. 166. Andre Dumas has written that Bonhoeffer had one concern: "to hold onto the world around him, since God is found in the concrete. This means making christological reality the center of one's very being. . . ." *Dietrich Bonhoeffer Theologian of Reality,* trans. by Robert McAfee Brown (New York: The Macmillan Company, 1971), p. 16. See also, pp. 274-76.

[99] In an interview in the 1960's Tillich was asked if there had been "an improvement in the attitude and practice of the Churches" since his early writings. He replied, "Yes, very much so," and in reference to the German Lutheran churches, he explained, "The Lutheran Churches were leaning very much in the direction of a transcendentalism, which believes that the Kingdom of God consists in a static heaven which is above time and

into which the individual enters. The question for them was not "How is the Kingdom of God working in time and space?: as we ask in the Our Father--"Thy Kingdom come"--but: "How can *I* come to the Kingdom as it is in heaven?" Today there is a change in Lutheran thinking. Lutheranism has become aware . . . that you cannot simply speak of the individual who wants to go to heaven. The Kingdom of God means more than this. It means something for the transformation of society. And so, there is a better understanding." "An Interview with Paul Tillich," with an Introduction by Lorenzo Avila, O.F.M., *Priestly Studies*, 30 (1965), p. 6.

[100] "Eschatology and History," *IH*, p. 280.

[101] "Albrecht Ritschl. Zu seinem hundertsen Geburtstag," *GW*, XII, p. 157. Originally published in *Theologische Blaetter*, I (1922), pp. 49-54. Tillich was contrasting his own understanding of the kingdom with that of Ritschl's, whose view he described as "the idea of the moral kingdom of reason in the Kantian sense."

[102] "Eschatology and History," *IH*, p. 278.

[103] The question raised by the authors of *The Common Catechism* in the context of discussing "God in History" is pertinent here: "Does what is new take place (as the 'dialectical' theologians maintained) in a call addressed to the individual believer, who then allows himself to be called away from the world and its sinful structures? Or, on the other hand, does this new element occur as a prophetic transcendence of, or passing above and beyond, the socialist movement in the struggle to renew society, as the young Paul Tillich insisted in his religious socialism?" (New York: A Crossroad Book, 1975), p. 8.

[104] "Kairos," *PE*, p. 35.

[105] Ibid., p. 39.

[106] "Eschatology and History," *IH*, p. 280. Cf. Carl E. Braaten, "Eschatology and Ontology in Conflict: A Study of Paul Tillich's Theology," *Christ and Counter-Christ* (Philadelphia: Fortress Press, 1972), p. 64. The following criticism is in part dependent upon this essay.

[107] Ibid., pp. 276-77.

[108]

[109] For a discussion of various types of eschatology see Carl E. Braaten, *History and Hermeneutics* (Philadelphia: The Westminster Press, 1966), pp. 160-74. Also Juergen Moltmann, *Theology of Hope* (New York: Harper and Row, Publishers, 1967), pp. 37-94.

[110] *SD*, *GW*, II, p. 239.

[111] Ibid., pp. 241-42. See above, Ch. 3, pp. 123-25.

[112] Tillich later wrote that "the balance" of "romantic and revolutionary" motives "has remained the basic problem of my thought and of my life ever since [my childhood]." Kegley and Bretall, p. 9. One crucial area where this is expressed is in the conflict of ontology and eschatology.

[113] "Christianity and Modern Society," *Pol. Exp.*, p. 3.

[114] "Church and Culture," *IH*, p. 234.

[115] "Kairos," *PE*, p. 42. Cf. Ch. 5, pp. 239-40.

[116] I often had the impression that Tillich, contrary to his intention, allowed the particularity of things to be swallowed up in ontological categories. The contingent is not permitted to be contingent, but is rather made a representative of one of three basic religious attitudes in which historical differences and distances are too easily bridged. Tillich's typological view of historical reality is very helpful and incisive, but if it is the basis of one's approach to history, something is lost.

[117] "Menschheit," *GW*, XIII, pp. 176-77. Originally published in *Mensch und Staat*, 1931. Somewhat surprisingly, Tillich developed this theme around the message of Pentecost, which, he interpreted, meant that "before the *one* rule, which is 'not of this world,' stands the *one* humanity."

[118] Cf. "The meaning of history is transcendent, is the ultimate, not the accidental and doubtful result of a development." "Eschatology and History," *IH*, p. 274.

[119] "The Interpretation of History and the Idea of Christ," *IH*, pp. 249-51.

[120] Cf. Wolfhart Pannenberg, *Jesus--God and Man*, trans. by Lewis L. Wilkens and Duane A. Priebe (Philadelphia: The Westminster Press, 1968), pp. 388-90.

[121] "The Interpretation of History and the Idea of Christ," *IH*, p. 256.

[122] Rarely if ever did Tillich use the metaphor of depth in *SD*. For discussions of the future and transcendence see Juergen Moltmann, "The Future as a New Paradigm of Transcendence." *Concurrence*, I, 4 (Fall 1969), pp. 334-45; Russell B. Norris, *God, Marx, and the Future* (Philadelphia: Fortress Press, 1974).

[123] Tillich distinguished three meanings of kairos: unique, general, and special. "Kairos," *PE*, pp. 46-47. In his letter to Hirsch Tillich admitted he had not sufficiently pursued the relation of the revelation in the Christ (unique kairos) to what happens in the (special) kairos, and there he tried to clarify the issue, arguing that the cross is the exclusive revelation of the last criterion of life and the kairos represented the place of "the incidence of a new revelation-correlation." "Die Theologie des Kairos," p. 318. Cf. Hopper, pp. 85-87. The question in the text is similar, but it asks about the relationship of the kairos and the eschaton.

[124] Masse und Geist, *GW*, II, p. 80. The German is "*zukuenftigen Absoluten*."

[125] "Goethe und die Idee der Klassik," *GW*, XII, p. 124. Originally published in *Hegel und Goethe. Zwei Gedenkreden* (Tubingen: Hohr, 1932).

[126] Cf. "Taken together, the writings of Tillich on this theme [Protestantism and Marxism] are more elaborate and systematic than anything else available." Adams, "Introduction," *Pol. Exp.*, p. xix.

[127] "Zur Psychologie des Sozialismus," *GW,* XII, p. 240. Ch. 5, pp. 214-15.

[128] "The Attack of Dialectical Materialism on Christianity," *World's Youth,* XIV, 2 (1938), p. 148. Although this was written in 1938, it had applied to Tillich for at least the previous fifteen years.

[129] Tillich recognized that "the unity of Christianity and dialectical materialism can be created only by a unity of common experience, and perhaps only by common martyrdom." Ibid., p. 157. He knew from his experience in the Berlin and *Neue Blaetter* circles that shared praxis--critically informed action--had the priority. One should remember that without question Tillich's forte was his conceptual ability.

[130] Tillich was aware of this possibility, especially in *SD,* where the decision was either socialism or barbarism.

[131] "Glaeubiger Realismus I," *GW,* IV, p. 86. Tillich here distinguished four attitudes in politics: 1) the politics of chance, of being bound to the powers of mere existence; 2) unbeliefful real politics, the sceptical, but deep politician; 3) utopian politics, the momentum that wants to realize an Unconditional; 4) the politics that points the way (*hinweisende*).

[132] "RS (II)," *Pol. Exp.,* p. 50.

[133] "Man and Society in Religious Socialism," *Christianity and Society,* VIII, 4 (Fall 1943), p. 21.

[134] *The World Situation* (Philadelphia: Facet Books, Fortress Press, 1965), p. 49. First published as a chapter in the symposium *The Christian Answer,* ed. by Henry P. Van Dusen (Charles Scribner's Sons, 1945).

[135] Adams has written that for an American context Tillich's work did not pay sufficient attention to voluntary associations, common law tradition, and the parliamentary tradition as means of change. "Paul Tillich's Dialectical Social Analysis," pp. 18-20. There was no discussion in Tillich about "palliatives" and "creative incrementalism," for example, which Denis Goulet has sought to distinguish. "World Hunger: Putting Development Ethics to the Test," *Christianity and Crisis,* Vol. 36, No. 9 (May 26, 1975), pp. 125-32.

[136] Reinhold Niebuhr's *Moral Man and Immoral Society,* written at approximately the same time as *SD,* offers an interesting contrast at this point since Niebuhr did explore the cost of change through such means as revolution and non-violence. Tillich never considered the possibilities of non-violence. *Moral Man and Immoral Society* (New York: Charles Scribner's Sons, 1960), Chs. 7-10.

[137] *What is Ethics All About?* (Washington: Corpus Books, 1969), p. 33.

[138] Possible explanations for this omission might be a sense that one could do little in face of the necessities of history. Perhaps it also expresses his antinomian tendency. In any case, he showed little concern for the concrete process of change.

[139] "Christentum, Sozialismus und Nationalismus," *GW,* XIII, p. 162, 165.

159See, for example, "The Kingdom of God and History"; The Meaning of Our Present Historical Existence," The Hazen Conference on Student Guidance and Counseling (Haddem, Conn.: Edward W. Hazen Foundation, 1938), pp. 19-29; "History as the Problem of Our Period," *The Review of Religion*, III, 3 (March 1939), pp. 255-64.

160"I Am an American," *Protestant Digest*, III, 12 (June-July 1941), pp. 24-26. "War Aims. I. Why War Aims?" *Protestant Digest*, III, 12 (June-July 1941), pp. 33-38. "War Aims. II. What War Aims?" *Protestant Digest*, IV, 1 (August-September 1941), pp. 13-18. "War Aims. III. Whose War Aims?" *The Protestant*, IV, 2 (October-November 1941), pp. 24-29.

161Schaefer-Kretzler, ed., *An Meine Deutschen Freunde*.

162Ibid., esp. pp. 69-86. "Spiritual Problems of Postwar Reconstruction," *PE*, pp. 261-69. Originally appeared in *Christianity and Crisis*, II (1942).

163"Storms of Our Times," *PE*, p. 239. Originally published in *Anglican Theological Review*, XXV, 1 (1943). Cf. "Spiritual Problems of Postwar Reconstruction," p. 262.

164Schaefer-Kretzler, p. 11.

165"Theorie und Praxis," p. 2.

166Ibid., p. 7.

167*PE*, pp. 55-65. Originally appeared in *Journal of Religion*, XXVI, 2 (1946). Cf. "Beyond Religious Socialism," *Christian Century*, XLVI, 24 (June 15, 1949), pp. 732-33.

168Ibid., p. 60.

169Ibid.

170Ibid., p. 65.

171*The Courage To Be* (New Haven: Yale University Press, 1959). First published in 1952.

172"The Person in a Technical Society," *Christian Faith and Social Action*, ed. and with an Introduction by John A. Hutchison (New York: Charles Scribner's Sons, 1953), pp. 137-54. Cf. "Ein Gruss von Paul Tillich," *Christ und Sozialist* (1961). A letter from Tillich Sept. 10, 1961.

173"The Lost Dimension of Religion," *Saturday Evening Post*, 30, 50 (June 14, 1958), pp. 29, 76, 78-79. Cf. Bloch;s comments on Tillich's "lost dimension," *Werk und Wirken Paul Tillichs*, p. 44.

174"The Effects of Space Exploration on Man's Condition and Nature," *The Future of Religions*, ed. by Jerald C. Brauer (New York: Harper and Row, Publishers, 1966), pp. 39-51.

175"Marxism and Christian Socialism," *PE*, pp. 259-60. First published in *Christianity and Society*, VII, 2 (1941). Cf. comments on President Roosevelt, Schaefer-Kretzler, ed., *An meine deutschen Freunde*, p. 58. In 1960 Tillich publicly supported John F. Kennedy for president and was invited to his inaugural ceremony. *From Time to Time*, p. 201.

[140] *Rel. Sit.*, p. 115.

[141] "Kairos," *PE*, p. 49. For a brief but excellent of his criticisms of socialism see pp. 49-50.

[142] "Cl. St.," *GW*, II, p. 190.

[143] "RS (II)," *Pol. Exp.*, p. 57.

[144] Ibid., p. 56.

[145] An example of this is the titles he gave to the sions of his article "Socialism": "Socialism as Ventu cialism as the Foundation for Formation (*Gestaltung*)," ism as the Power of Formation," and "Socialism as the Formation." *GW*, II, pp. 139-50. The emphasis on *Gest* clear throughout his religious socialist writings.

[146] *SD*, *GW*, II, pp. 349-54. Cf. *OB*, pp. 62-64.

[147] These questions drive into the area which Til cussed under the rubric of the "latent church" and it ship to the "manifest church," especially in relation the leaders and followers of a mass movement. For Ti development of the "latent church" concept see "Kirch humanistische Gesellschaft," *GW*, IX, pp. 59-61.

[148] Cf., for example, "The Religious Situation i To-day"; "The Totalitarian State and the Claims of t "The Meaning of Anti-Semitism," *Radical Religion*, IV 1938), pp. 34-36.

[149] "The Religious Situation in Germany To-day,"

[150] Cf. "The Christian and Marxist View of Man" tack of Dialectical Materialism."

[151] *My Travel Diary: 1936*.

[152] "The Interpretation of History by Paul Til *Religion*, II, 1 (Winter 1936), p. 41.

[153] "III, Report of the Section on Church, Com State in Relation to the Economic Order," from *The ference Report* is reprinted in *Christian Ethics*, e Beach and H. Richard Niebuhr, Second Edition (New Ronald Press Company, 1973), pp. 481-98. Tillich' fore the conference in July 1973 was entitled "The God and History," *The Kingdom of God and History*, et. al. (Chicago: Willett, Clark and Company, 193 41. Cf. "Author's Introduction," *PE*, p. xix.

[154] Jay, *The Dialectical Imagination*, fn. 87,

[155] "Die politische und geistige Aufgabe der Emigration," *GW*, XIII, pp. 200-20, 215.

[156] For a description of this organization a role in it, see Karin Schaefer-Kretzler, "Einlei *Deutschen Freunde*, pp. 16-18.

[157] "An Historical Diagnosis: Impression of Trip," *Radical Religion*, II, 1 (Winter 1936), p

[158] Ibid., p. 17.

[176]"Past and Present Reflections on Christianity and Society," transcript of Dr. Paul Tillich's notes for his remarks to the New York Christian Action retreat, May 1955, New York City, with minor changes. (Unpublished), p. 1.

[177]Ibid., p. 2.

[178]Ibid., pp. 2-3.

[179]Ibid., p. 4.

[180]Ibid., p. 2.

[181]Kegley and Bretall, p. 13.

BIBLIOGRAPHY

I. Primary Sources

For a complete listing of Tillich's works see Renate Albrecht (ed.), *Bibliographie und Text geschichte zu den Gesammelten Werken von Paul Tillich, GW,* XIV (1975), pp. 135-230.

Most of Tillich's writings can be found in Paul Tillich, *Gesammelte Werke,* Vols. I-XIII, ed. by Renate Albrecht (Stuttgart: Evangelisches Verlagswerk, 1959-1972). The German articles and books that are reproduced in *GW* will be indicated below.

The following four English anthologies contain translations of Tillich articles from 1919 to 1933. The English translations will be indicated below.

The Interpretation of History. Trans. by N. A. Rasetski and Elsa L. Talmey. New York: Charles Scribner's Sons, 1936.

Political Expectation. Ed. and with an Introduction by James Luther Adams. New York: Harper and Row, 1971.

The Protestant Era. Trans. and with a concluding Essay by James Luther Adams. Chicago: University of Chicago Press, 1948.

What is Religion? Trans. and with an Introduction by James Luther Adams. New York: Harper and Row, 1969.

A. Tillich's Works, 1919-1933 (listed chronologically)

1919

"Christentum und Sozialismus. Bericht an das Konsistorium der Mark Brandenburg." Manuscript from 1919. Published in *GW,* XIII, pp. 154-60. E. T. by James Luther Adams, "Answer to an Inquiry of the Protestant Consistory of Brandenburg," *Metanoia,* III, 3 (September 1971), pp. 10-12, 9, 16.

Der Sozialismus als Kirchenfrage. With Carl Richard Wegener. Berlin: Gracht, 1919. Also in *GW,* II, pp. 13-20.

"Ueber die Idee einer Theologie der Kultur," *Religionsphilosophie der Kultur. Zwei Entwuerfe von Gustav Radbruch und Paul Tillich.* Berlin: Reuther and Reichard, 1919, pp. 27-52. Also in *GW,* IX, pp. 13-31. E. T., "On the Idea of a Theology of Culture," *WR?,* pp. 155-81.

"Christentum und Sozialismus," *Das Neue Deutschland,* VIII (December 1919), pp. 106-10. Also in *GW,* II, pp. 21-28.

"Friedrich Thimme and Ernst Rolffs: *Revolution und Kirche,*" *Das neue Deutschland,* VII (July 1919), pp. 394-97. Also in *GW,* XII, pp. 194-99.

1920

"Christentum und Sozialismus," *Freideutsche Jugend,* VI (1920), pp. 167-70. Also in *GW,* II, pp. 29-33.

"Die Jugend und die Religion," *Die freideutsche Jugendbewegung: Ursprung und Zufunft.* Ed. by Adolf Grabowsky and Walter Koch. Gotha: Perthes, 1920, pp. 8-13.

1922

Masse und Geist: Studien zur Philosophie der Masse. Berlin und Frankfurt a. M.: Verlag der Arbeitsgemeinschaft, 1922. Also in *GW,* XII, pp. 200-03.

"Albrecht Ritschl: Zu seinem hundertsten Geburtstag," *Theologische Blaetter,* I, 3 (March 1922), pp. 49-54. Also in *GW,* XII, pp. 151-58.

"Religioese Krisis," *Vivos Vico,* II, 11 (April-May 1922), pp. 616-21. Also in *GW,* XII, pp. 200-03.

"Kairos," *Die Tat,* XIV, 5 (August 1922), pp. 330-50. Also in *GW,* VI, pp. 9-28. E. T. in *PE,* pp. 32-51.

"Die Ueberwindung des Religionsbegriffs in der Religionsphilosophie," *Kant-Studien,* XXVII (1922), pp. 446-69. Also in *GW,* I, pp. 367-88. E. T. "The Conquest of the Concept of Religion in the Philosophy of Religion," *WR?,* pp. 122-54.

"Zur Klaerung der religioesen Grundhaltung," *Blaetter fuer religioesen Sozialismus,* III, 12 (December 1922), pp. 46-48.

"Emanuel Hirsch: Die Reich-Gottes-Begriffe des neuren europaeischen Denkens," *Theologische Blaetter,* I (1922), pp. 42-43.

"Rudolf Stammler: Lehrbuch der Rechtsphilosophie," *Theologische Literaturzeitung,* XLVII (1922), pp. 417-20. Also in *GW,* XII, pp. 200-03.

1923

Das System der Wissenschaften nach Gegenstaendigen und Methoden. Ein Entwurf. Goettingen: Vanderhoeck und Ruprecht, 1923. Also in *GW,* I, pp. 111-293.

"Ernst Troeltsch," *Vossische Zeitung,* No. 58 (February 3, 1923), pp. 2-3. Also in *GW,* XII, pp. 175-78.

"Grundlinien des religioesen Sozialismus; Ein systematischer Entwurf," *Blaetter fuer religioesen Sozialismus,* IV, 8/10 (1923), pp. 1-24. Also in *GW,* II, pp. 91-119. E. T., "Basic Principles of Religious Socialism," *Pol. Exp.,* pp. 58-88.

"Kritisches und Positives Paradox. Eine Auseinandersetzung mit Karl Barth und Friedrich Gogarten," *Theologische Blaetter,* II, 11 (November 1923), pp. 263-69. Also in *GW,* VII, pp. 216-25. E. T., "Critical and Positive Paradox: A

Discussion with Karl Barth and Friedrich Gogarten," *The Beginnings of Dialectic Theology*. Ed. by James M. Robinson. Richmond, Virginia: John Knox Press, 1968, pp. 134-41.

"Antwort," *Theologische Blaetter*, II, 12 (December 1923), pp. 296-99. Also in *GW*, VII, pp. 240-43. E. T., "Answer to Karl Barth," in Robinson, pp. 155-58.

"Heinrich Eildermann: Urkommunismus und Urreligion," *Archiv fuer Sozialwissenschaft und Sozialpolitik*, L (1923), pp. 247-48.

"Ernst Lohmeyer: Soziale Fragen im Urchristentum," *Archiv fuer Sozialwissenschaft und Sozialpolitik*, L (1923), p. 250.

1924

Kirche und Kultur. Tuebingen: Mohr, 1924. Also in *GW*, IX, pp. 32-46. E. T., "Church and Culture," *IH*, pp. 219-24.

"Rechtfertigung und Zweifel," *Vortraege der Theologischen Konferenz zu Giessen*, No. 39 (1924), pp. 19-32. Also in *GW*, VIII, pp. 85-100.

"Erwiderung," *Wingolfs-Blaetter*, XIII (1924), p. 27.

"Christentum, Sozialismus und Nationalismus," *Wingolfs-Blaetter*, LIII (1924), pp. 78-80. Also in *GW*, XIII, pp. 161-66.

"Jugendbewegung und Religion," *Werkland*, IV (1924), pp. 61-64. Also in *GW*, XIII, pp. 130-33.

"Antwort (auf Mennicke: 'Zu Tillichs Systematik')," *Blaetter fuer Religioesen Sozialismus*, V, 5/6 (May-June), pp. 18-22.

"Die religioese und philosophische Weiterbildung des Sozialismus," *Blaetter fuer religioesen Sozialismus*, V (1924), pp. 26-30. Also in *GW*, II, pp. 121-31.

"Ernst Troeltsch: Versuch einer geistesgeschichtlichen Wuerdigung," *Kant-Studien*, XXIX (1924), pp. 351-58. Also in *GW*, XII, pp. 166-74.

"Ernst Troeltsch: *Der Historismus und seine Probleme*," *Theologische Literaturzeitung*, XLIX (1924), pp. 25-30. Also in *GW*, XII, pp. 204-11. E. T., *Journal for the Scientific Study of Religion*, I, L (October 1961), pp. 109-14.

"Ernst Troeltsch: *Der Historismus und seine Ueberwindung*," *Theologische Literaturzeitung*, XLIX, 11 (1924), pp. 234-35.

1925

"Religionsphilosophie," in Max Dessoir (ed.), *Die Philosophie in ihren Einzelgebieten*, II, pp. 769-835. Also in *GW*, I, pp. 295-364. E. T., "The Philosophy of Religion," *WR?*, pp. 27-121.

"Die Staatslehre Augustine nach *De civitate Dei*," *Theologische Blaetter*, IV, 4 (April 1925), pp. 77-86. Also in *GW*, XII, pp. 81-96.

1926

Die religioese Lage der Gegenwart. Berlin: Ullstein, 1926.
Also in *GW*, X, pp. 9-93. E. T. by H. Richard Niebuhr,
The Religious Situation. Cleveland: Meridian Books, 1956.

Das Daemonische. Eine Beitrag zur Sinndeutung der Geschichte.
Tuebingen: Mohr, 1926. Also in *GW*, VI, pp. 42-71. E. T.,
"The Demonic," *IH*, pp. 77-122.

"Kairos: Ideen zur Geisteslage der Gegenwart," in *Kairos, Zur
Geisteslage und Geisteswendung.* Paul Tillich (ed.). Darmstadt: Reichl, 1926, pp. 1-21. Also in *GW*, VI, pp. 29-41.

"Kairos und Logos: Eine Untersuchung zur Metaphysik des Erkennens," in *Kairos*, pp. 23-75. Also in *GW*, VI, pp. 43-76.
E. T., "Kairos and Logos," *IH*, pp. 123-75.

"Die gesitige Welt im Jahre 1926," in *Reichls Buecherbuch,* 17th
Year (1926). Darmstadt: Reichl, 1926, pp. 6-14. Also in
GW, X, pp. 94-99.

"Denker der Zeit: Karl Barth," *Vossiche Zeitung,* No. 32 (1926).
Also in *GW*, XII, pp. 187-93.

"Der Begriff des Daemonischen und seine Bedeutung fuer die systematische Theologie," *Theologische Blaetter,* V, 2 (February 1926), pp. 32-35. Also in *GW*, VII, pp. 285-91.

"Wilhelm Loew: Zum Problem der evangelischen Sozialethik,"
Blaetter fuer religioese Sozialismus, VII (July-August 1926), pp. 73-79. Also in *GW*, XII, pp. 212-18.

1927

"Die Ueberwindung des Persoenlichkeitsideals," *Logos,* XVI, 1
(March 1927), pp. 68-85. Also in *GW*, III, pp. 83-100.
E. T., "The Idea and the Ideal of Personality," *PE*, pp.
115-35.

"Glaeubiger Realismus," in *Theologenrunbrief fuer den Bund Deutscher Jugendvereine,* II (November 1927), pp. 3-13. Also
in *GW*, IV, pp. 77-87.

"Logos und Mythos der Technik," *Logos,* XVI, 3 (November 1927),
pp. 356-65. Also in *GW*, IX, pp. 297-306.

"Die Idee der Offenbarung," *Zeitschrift fuer Theologie und
Kirche,* VIII, 6 (December 1927), pp. 403-12. Also in *GW*,
VIII, pp. 31-39.

"Eschatologie und Geschichte," *Christliche Welt,* XLI, 22 (November 1927), pp. 1034-42. Also in *GW*, VI, pp. 72-82. E. T.,
"Eschatology and History," *IH*, pp. 266-84.

"Christentum und Idealismus. Zum Verstaendnis der Diskussionslage," *Theologische Blaetter,* VI (1927), pp. 29-40. Also
in *GW*, XII, pp. 219-38.

"Hendrik de Man: *Psychologie des Sozialismus*," *Blaetter fuer religioesen Sozialismus*, VIII (1927), pp. 21-25. Also in *GW*, XII, pp. 239-43.

1928

"Der soziale Pfarrer" (Diskussionsrede), *Die Verhandlungen des 35. Evangelisch-Sozialen Kongresses in Dresden.* Goettingen: Vandenhoeck und Ruprecht, 1928, pp. 74-77.

"Das religioese Symbol," *Blaetter fuer deutsche Philosophie*, I, 4 (January 1928), pp. 277-91. E. T. by James Luther Adams, "The Religious Symbol," *Journal of Liberal Religion*, II, 1 (Summer 1940), pp. 13-33. Also in *GW*, V, pp. 196-212.

"Das Christentum und die Moderne," *Schule und Wissenschaft*, II (1928), pp. 121-31, 170-77. Also in *GW*, XIII, pp. 113-30.

"Die technische Stadt als Symbol," *Dresdner Neueste Nachrichten*, No. 115 (May 17, 1928), pp. 1-5. Also in *GW*, IX, pp. 307-11.

"Ueber glaeubigen Realismus," *Theologische Blaetter*, VII, 5 (May 1928), pp. 109-18. Also in *GW*, IV, pp. 88-106. E. T., "Realism and Faith," *PE*, pp. 66-82.

"Die Bedeutung der Gesellschaftslage fuer das Geistesleben," *Philosophie und Leben*, IV, 6 (June 1928), pp. 153-58. Also in *GW*, II, pp. 133-38.

"Das Christentum und die Moderne Gesellschaft," *The Student World*, XXI (1928), pp. 282-90. Also in *GW*, X, pp. 100-07. E. T., "Christianity and Modern Society," *Pol. Exp.*, pp. 1-9.

1929

Religioese Verwirklichung. Berlin: Furche, 1930.

"Zur Einfuehrung"

"1. Die protestantische Verkuendigung und der Mensch der Gegenwart." Also in *GW*, VII, pp. 70-83. E. T., "The Protestant Message and the Man of Today," *PE*, pp. 192-205.

"2. Protestantische Gestaltung." Also in *GW*, VII, pp. 54-69. E. T., "The Formative Power of Protestantism," *PE*, pp. 206-21.

"5. Christologie und Geschichtsdeutung." Also in *GW*, VI, pp. 83-96. "The Interpretation of History and the Idea of Christ," *IH*, pp. 242-65.

"7. Natur und Sakrament." Also in *GW*, VII, pp. 105-23. E. T., "Nature and Sacrament," *PE*, pp. 94-112.

"9. Klassenkampf und religioeser Sozialismus." Also in *GW*, II, pp. 175-92. E. T. by James Luther Adams, "The Class Struggle and Religious Socialism." Unpublished manuscript.

"10. Der Staat als Erwartung und Forderung." Also in *GW*,
IX, pp. 123-38. E. T., "The State as Expectation
and Demand," *Pol. Exp.*, pp. 97-114.

"12. Lessing und die Idee einer Erziehung des Menschen-
geschlechts." Also in *GW*, XII, pp. 97-111.

"Anmerkungen"

"Der Protestantismus als kritisches und gestaltendes Prinzip,"
Kairos II: Protestantismus also Kritik und Gestaltung.
Ed. by Tillich. Darmstadt: Reichl, 1929, pp. 3-37. Also
in *GW*, VII, pp. 29-53. E. T., "Protestantism as a Critical and Creative Principle," *Pol. Exp.*, pp. 10-39.

Diskussionsrede. *Sozialismus aus dem Glauben. Verhandlungen
der sozialistischen Tagung in Heppenheim.* Zurich und
Leipzig: Rotapfel, 1929, pp. 101-04.

"Nichtkirchliche Religionen," in *Volkung Reich der Deutschen.*
B. Harms (ed.). Berlin: Reimar Hobbing, 1929, pp. 456-75.
Also in *GW*, V, pp. 13-31.

"Gegenwart und Religion," *Neuwerk,* XI, 1 (January 1929), pp.
2-11.

"Philosophie und Schicksal," *Kant-Studien,* XXXIV (1929), pp.
300-11. Also in *GW*, IV, pp. 23-35. E. T., "Philosophy
and Fate," *PE,* pp. 3-15.

"Karl Mannheim: *Ideologie und Utopie,*" *Die Gesellschaft,* VI,
10 (1929), pp 348-55. Also in *GW*, XII, pp. 255-61. E. T.
by James Luther Adams, "On Karl Mannheim's *Ideology and
Utopia.*" Unpublished manuscript.

1930

"Offenbarung," in *Die Religion in Geschichte und Gegenwart.*
Vol. 4. Hermann Gunkel und Leopold Zsharnack (eds.). 2.
Aurfl. Tuebingen: Mohr, 1930, pp. 1227-33. Also in *GW*,
VIII, pp. 40-46. E. T. by R. A. Wilson, "Revelation and
the Philosophy of Religion," in *Twentieth Century Theology
in the Making,* Vol. 1, ed. by Jaroslav Pelikan. London:
Collins, 1970, pp. 46-61.

"Sozialismus," *Neue Blaetter fuer den Sozialismus,* I, 1 (January 1930), pp. 1-12. Also in *GW*, II, pp. 139-50.

"Religioeser Sozialismus," *Neue Blaetter fuer den Sozialismus,*
I, 9 (September 1930), pp. 396-403. Also in *GW*, II, pp.
151-58.

"Adolf von Harnack" Speech at the occasion of Harnack's death,
June 10, 1930. First published in *GW*, XII, pp. 159-65.

"Die Geisteslage der Gegenwart: Rueckblick und Ausblick." Unpublished manuscript dating from approximately 1930. First
published in *GW*, X, pp. 108-20.

1931

Protestantisches Prinzip und proletarische Situation. Bonn: Friedrich Cohen, 1931. Also in *GW,* VII, pp. 84-104. E. T., "The Protestant Principle and the Proletarian Situation," *PE,* pp. 161-81.

"Sozialismus: II. Religioeser Sozialismus: in *RGG,* Vol. 5 (1931), pp. 637-48. Also in *GW,* II, pp. 159-74. E. T., "Religious Socialism," *Pol. Exp.,* pp. 40-57.

"Theonomie," in *RGG,* Vol. 5, pp. 1128-29.

"Das Wasser," in *Das Gottesjahr 1932.* Ed. by Wilhelm Staehlin. Kassel: Baerenreiter, 1931, pp. 65-68. E. T. in James Luther Adams, *Paul Tillich's Philosophy of Culture, Science, and Religion,* pp. 62-64.

"Mensch und Staat," "Blut gegen Geist," "Kunstpolitik," "Einheit des Widerspruches," "Daemonen," "Neu Schoepfung," "Utopie," "Drei Stadien," "Menschliche Moeglichkeiten," "Das Fragen," "Menschheit," in *Der Staat seid Ihr, Zeitschfrift fuer deutsche Politik,* I (1931), pp. 11, 26, 43, 56, 91, 107, 124, 139, 155, 171, 187-88. Also in part in *GW,* XII, pp. 167-77.

"Das Problem der Macht: Versuch einer Philosophischen Grundlegung," *Neue Blaetter fuer den Sozialismus,* II, 4 (April 1931), pp. 157-70. Also in *GW,* II, pp. 193-208. E. T., "The Problem of Power," *IH,* pp. 179-202.

"Kirche und humanistische Gesellschaft," *Neuwerk,* XIII, 1 (April-May 1931), pp. 4-18. Also in *GW,* IX, pp. 47-61.

"Zum Fall Eckert. Eine Stellungnahme," *Neue Blaetter fuer den Sozialismus,* II, 8 (August 1931), pp. 408-09. Also in *GW,* XIII, pp. 166-67.

"Die Doppelgestalt der Kirche," *Neuwerk,* XIII (1931), pp. 239-43. Also in *GW,* IX, pp. 77-81.

Unpublished manuscripts on socialism, early 1930's. B 2 (17); B 6 (28, 29, 30) in Tillich Archives, Harvard Divinity School.

1932

"Der junge Hegel und das Schicksal des Deutschland," in *Hegel und Goethe. Zwei Gedenkreden.* Tuebingen: Mohr, 1932. Also in *GW,* XII, pp. 125-51.

"Zehn Thesen," in *Die Kirche und das Dritte Reich: Fragen und Forderungen deutscher Theologen.* Ed. by Leopold Katz. Gotha: Klotz, 1932, pp. 126-28. Also in *GW,* XIII, pp. 177-79.

"Der Sozialismus und die geistige Lage der Gegenwart," *Neue Blaetter fuer den Sozialismus,* III, 1 (January 1932), pp. 14-16.

"Protestantismus und politische Romantik," *Neue Blaetter fuer den Sozialismus*, III, 8 (August 1932), pp. 413-22. Also in *GW*, pp. 209-18.

"Selbstanzeige," *Neue Blaetter fuer den Sozialismus*, III, 12 (December 1932), pp. 667-68.

"Christentum als Ideologie. Stellungnahme zur Regierungserklaerung des Kabinetts von Papen." Unpublished manuscript from 1932. First published in *GW*, XIII, pp. 179-81.

"Freiheit der Wissenschaft." Unpublished manuscript probably from 1932. First published in *GW*, XIII, pp. 150-53.

1933

Die sozialistische Entscheidung. Potsdam: Alfred Protte, 1933. Also in *GW*, II, pp. 219-365. E. T. being prepared by Franklin Sherman and Roy Enquist.

B. Tillich's Works, 1910-1918, 1934-1967

1910

Die Religionsgeschichtliche Konstruktion in Schellings Positiver Philosophie, Ihre Voraussetzungen und Principien. Breslau: Fleischmann, 1910. E. T., *The Construction of the History of Religion in Schelling's Positive Philosophy: Its Presuppositions and Principles*. Trans. and with an Introduction by Victor Nuovo. Lewisburg/Penn.: Bucknell University Press, 1974.

1912

Mystik und Schuldbewusstsein in Schellings Philosophischer Entwicklung. Guetersloh: Bertelsmann, 1912. Also in *GW*, I, pp. 13-108. *Mysticism and Guilt-Consciousness in Schelling's Philosophical Development*. Trans. and with an Introduction by Victor Nuovo. Lewisburg/Penn.: Bucknell University Press, 1974.

1913

"Kirchliche Apologetik." Unpublished manuscript. First published in *GW*, XIII, pp. 34-63

1914/15

"Bericht ueber die Taetigkeit als Feldgeistlicher an den Herrn Feldpropst des IV. Armeekorps." Unpublished manuscript from 1914/15. First published in *GW*, XIII, pp. 71-79.

1934

"The Religious Situation in Germany Today," *Religion in Life*, III, 2 (Spring 1934), pp. 163-73.

"Die Theologie des Kairos und die gegenwaertige geistige Lage. Offener Brief an Emanuel Hirsch," *Theologische Blaetter,* XIII, 11 (November 1934), pp. 305-28.

"The Totalitarian State and the Claims of the Church," *Social Research,* I, 4 (November 1934), pp. 405-33.

"Theodor Wiesengrund-Adorno: *Kierkegaard, Konstruktion des Aesthetischen,*" *Journal of Philosophy,* XXXI, 23 (November 1934), p. 640.

1935

"What is Wrong with the 'Dialectic' Theology?", *Journal of Religion,* XV, 2 (April 1935), pp. 127-45.

"Um was es geht. Antwort am Emanuel Hirsch," *Theologische Blaetter,* XIV, 5 (May 1935), pp. 117-19.

"Marx and the Prophetic Tradition," *Radical Religion,* I, 4 (Autumn 1935), pp. 21-29.

"The Christian and Marxist View of Man." Universal Christian Council for Life and Work. December 1935. Unpublished manuscript.

1936

My Travel Diary: 1936. Between Two Worlds. Ed. and with an Introduction by Jerald C. Brauer. New York: Harper and Row, Publishers, 1970.

"On the Boundary. An Autobiographical Sketch," *IH,* pp. 1-40. Retranslated as a separate book, Charles Scribner's Sons, New York, 1966.

"The Social Functions of the Churches in Europe and America," *Social Research,* III, 1 (February 1936), pp. 90-104.

"Christianity and Emigration," *Presbyterian Tribune,* LII, 3 (October 29, 1936), pp. 13-16.

"An Historical Diagnosis: Impression of a European Trip," *Radical Religion,* II, 1 (Winter 1936), pp. 11-17.

"Prophetische und marxistische Geschichtsdeutung." Manuscript from 1934-36. *GW,* VI, pp. 97-108.

1937

"The Church and Communism," *Religion in Life,* VI, 3 (Summer 1937), pp. 347-57.

"Mind and Migration," *Social Research,* IV, 2 (May 1937), pp. 295-305.

1938

"The Kingdom of God and History," *The Kingdom of God and History.*

Chicago, New York: Willett, Clark, 1938, pp. 107-41. Address before the World Conference on Church, Community and State, Oxford, England, July, 1937.

"The Attack of Dialectical Materialism on Christianity," *World's Youth,* XIV, 2 (1938), pp. 147-57.

"The Gospel and the State," *Crozer Quarterly,* XV, 4 (October 1938), pp. 251-61.

"The Meaning of Anti-Semitism," *Radical Religion,* IV, 1 (Winter 1938), pp. 34-36.

"Die politische und geistige Aufgabe der deutschen Emigration." Manuscript from June 1938. *GW,* XIII, pp. 200-16.

1939

"Germany is Still Alive," *Protestant Digest,* I, 3 (February 1939), pp. 45-46.

1940

"Freedom in the Period of Transformation," *Freedom: Its Meaning.* Ed. by Ruth Nanda Anshen. New York: Harcourt, Brace and Co., 1940, pp. 123-44.

"The Meaning of the Triumph of Nazism," *Christianity and Society,* V, 4 (Fall 1940), pp. 45-46. Resume by Charles Stinnette.

"Karl Barth: The Church and the Political Problem of our Day," *Christendom,* V, 1 (1940), pp. 129-31. Also in *GW,* XII, pp. 324-26.

1941

"Love's 'Strange Work,'" *The Protestant,* IV, 3 (December 1941-January 1942), pp. 70-75.

1942

"Marxism and Christian Socialism," *Christianity and Society,* VII, 2 (Spring 1942), pp. 13-18. Also in *PE,* pp. 253-60.

"Herbert Marcuse: *Reason and Revolution,*" *Studies in Philosophy and Social Science,* IX (1942), pp. 476-78.

1943

"Man and Society in Religious Socialism," *Christianity and Society,* VIII, 4 (Fall 1943), pp. 10-21.

"Tillich-to-Thomas Mann Letter (23 May 1943)," in *The Intellectual Legacy of Paul Tillich.* Ed. by James R. Lyons. Detroit: Wayne State University Press, 1969, pp. 101-07.

1944

An meine deutschen Freunde. Politische Reden. With an Introduction and Notes by Karin Schaefer-Kretzler. Stuttgart: Evangelisches Verlagswerk, 1973. Talks over "The Voice of America," March 31, 1942 to May 9, 1944.

1945

"The World Situation," in *The Christian Answer*. Ed. and with an Introduction by Henry P. Van Dusen. New York: Charles Scribner's Sons, 1945, pp. 1-44. Reprinted, *The World Situation*. Ed. and with an Introduction by Franklin Sherman. Philadelphia: Fortress Press, 1965.

"Theorie und Praxis." Unpublished discussion, Max Horkheimer, Adolph Lowe, Friedrich Pollock, and Paul Tillich, January 28, 1945. Tillich Archive, Goettingen, Germany.

1946

"Religion and Secular Culture," *Journal of Religion,* XXVI, 2 (1946), pp. 79-86. Also in *PE,* pp. 55-66.

1948

"Author's Introduction," *PE,* pp. ix-xxix.

"How Much Truth is in Karl Marx?," *Christian Century,* LXV, 36 (September 8, 1948), pp. 906-08.

1949

"The Present Theological Situation in the Light of the Continental European Development," *Theology Today,* VI, 3 (October 1949), pp. 299-310.

"Beyond Religious Socialism," *Christian Century,* LXVI, 24 (June 15, 1949), pp. 732-33.

"Existentialism and Religious Socialism," *Christianity and Society,* XV, 1 (Winter, 1949-50), pp. 8-11.

"John Bennett: *Christianity and Communism,*" *Union Seminary Quarterly Review,* IV, 2 (January 1949), pp. 41-42.

1950

"The Recovery of the Prophetic Tradition." Washington, D. C.: Henderson Services, 1950. Three lectures at the Washington Cathedral Library, November-December, 1950.

1951

Systematic Theology. Vol. 1. Chicago: University of Chicago Press, 1951.

"Politische Bedeutung der Utopie im Leben der Voelker.: Berlin: Weiss, 1951. E. T., "The Political Meaning of Utopia," in *Pol. Exp.,* pp. 125-80.

1952

"Autobiographical Reflections" and "Answer," *The Theology of Paul Tillich*. Ed. by Charles W. Kegley and Robert W. Bretall. New York: Macmillan, 1952.

The Courage to Be. New Haven: Yale University Press, 1952.

1953

Der Mensch im Christentum und im Marxismus. Duesseldorf: 1953. Also in *GW*, III, pp. 194-209.

"The Person in a Technical Society," *Christian Faith and Social Action*. A symposium ed. by John A. Hutchison. New York: Charles Scribner's Sons, 1953, pp. 137-54.

1954

Love, Power and Justice. New York: Oxford University Press, 1954.

1956

"Sozialismus, (IV) Neuere Richtungen, (4) Religioeser Sozialismus," *Handwoerterbuch der Staatswissenschaften*, Vol. IX. Ed. by Erwin V. Beckerath, et. al. Stuttgart: Gustav Fischer, 1956, pp. 507-08.

1957

Systematic Theology. Vol. 2. Chicago: University of Chicago Press, 1957.

1958

"The Lost Dimension of Religion," *Saturday Evening Post*, 230, No. 50 (June 14, 1958), pp. 29, 76, 78-79.

"Kairos," *A Handbook of Christian Theology*. Ed. by Marvin Halverson and Arthur A. Cohen. New York: Meridian Books, 1958, pp. 193-97.

1959

"Kairos--Theonomie--Das Daemonsiche. Ein Brief zu Eduard Heimanns Siebzigsten Geburtstag," *Zur Ordnung von Wirtschaft und Gesellschaft. Festausgabe fuer Eduard Heimann*. Tuebingen: Mohr, 1959, pp. 11-15. Also in *GW*, XII, pp. 310-15.

"The Struggle Between Time and Space," *Theology of Culture*. Ed. by Robert C. Kimball. New York: Oxford University Press, 1959, pp. 30-39.

"Between Utopianism and Escape from History," *Colgate Rochester Divinity School Bulletin*, XXXI, 2 (May 1959), pp. 32-40.

1960

"Hermann Schafft," *Hermann Schafft. Ein Lebenswerk*. Ed. by

Werner Kindt. Kassel: Staunda, 1960, pp. 11-16. Also in
GW, XIII, pp. 27-33.

"Marx's View of History. A Study in the History of the Philosophy of History," *Culture in History. Essays in Honor of Paul Radin.* Ed. by Stanley Diamond. New York: Columbia University Press, 1960, pp. 631-41.

"Christentum und Marxismus," *Politische Studien*, XI, 119 (March 1960), pp. 149-54. E. T., "Christianity and Marxism," *Pol. Exp.*, pp. 89-96.

"The Basic Ideas of Religious Socialism," *Bulletin: The International House of Japan, Inc.*, No. 6 (1960), pp. 11-15.

1961

"Ein Gruss von Paul Tillich," *Christ und Sozialist*, No. 4 (1961), p. 7.

1963

Systematic Theology, Vol. 3. Chicago: University of Chicago Press, 1963.

1964

"Interrogation of Paul Tillich." Conducted by William I. Reese. *Philosophical Interrogations.* Ed. by Sydney and Beatrice Rome. New York: Holt, Rinehart and Winston, 1964, pp. 355-409.

1965

Ultimate Concern. Tillich in Dialogue. Ed. by D. Mackenzie Brown. New York: Harper, 1965.

"An Interview with Paul Tillich." Conducted by Lorenzo Avila, O.F.M. *Priestly Studies*, XXXI, 3 (1965), pp. 2-15.

1966

"Rejoinder," *Journal of Religion*, Vol. 46, No. 1, Pt. II (January 1966), pp. 184-96.

1967

Perspectives on 19th and 20th Century Protestant Theology. Ed. by Carl E. Braaten. New York: Harper, 1967.

II. Secondary Sources

A. *On Tillich's Religious Socialism*

For a more complete listing of sources of Tillich's and others' religious socialism see the bibliographies in the two books by Breipohl and the one by Ulrich.

Adams, James Luther. "Christian Socialism," *Encyclopeadia Britannica*, 1965, V, pp. 639-40.

_____. "Introduction," *Political Expectation*. New York: Harper and Row, 1971, pp. vi-xx.

_____. "Paul Tillich's Dialectical Social Analysis." Paper read at the American Theological Society, Midwest Division, April 22, 1955. Mimeographed.

_____. "Tillich's Concept of the Protestant Era," *The Protestant Era*. Chicago: University of Chicago Press, 1948, pp. 273-316.

_____. "Tillich's Interpretation of History," *The Theology of Paul Tillich*. Ed. by Charles W. Kegley and Robert W. Bretall, New York: Macmillan, 1952, pp. 294-309.

Allwohn, Adolf. "Tagung der religioesen Sozialisten," *Theologische Blaetter*, VI, 4 (April, 1927), pp. 106-07.

Amelung, Eberhard. "Religious Socialism as an Ideology; A Study of the 'Kairos-circle' in Germany Between 1919-1933." Unpublished Doctor's dissertation, Harvard, 1962.

Balzer, Friedrich-Martin. "Zur Geschichte der religioes-sozialistischen Stroemungen in der Weimarer Republik," *Internationale Dialog Zeitschrift*, V, 1 (1972), pp. 37-41.

Barth, Karl. *Church Dogmatics*, I, 1. Trans. by G. T. Thomson. Edinburgh: T. and T. Clark, 1936.

Beyer, Hans. "Der 'religioese Sozialismus' in der Weimarer Republik," *Deutsche Zeitschrift fuer Philosophie*, VIII, 11/12 (1960), pp. 1464-83.

Bizer, Ernst. "Die Zeitschriften Religioesen Sozialismus," *Christliche Welt*, XLV, 15 (1931), pp. 716-19.

Blaetter fuer religioesen Sozialismus, I-VII, 1920-27. Ed. by Karl Mennicke.

Breipohl, Renate. *Religioeser Sozialismus und buergerliches Geschichtsbewusstsein zur Zeit der Weimarer Republik*. Zurich: Theologischer Verlag, 1971.

_____ (ed.) *Theologische Buecherei 46. Dokumente zum religioesen Sozialismus in Deutschland*. Muenchen: Chr. Kaiser Verlag, 1972.

Dehn, Guenther. *Die alte Zeit, die vorigen Jahre*. Muenchen: Chr. Kaiser Verlag, 1962.

Driver, Tom F. *"Political Expectation* and *My Travel Diary"* (review), *Union Seminary Quarterly Review*, XXVII, 3 (Spring 1972), pp. 179-81.

Fischer, James V. "Tillich's Political Expectation, a review," *The Unitarian Universalist Christian*, Vol. 26, Nos. 3-4 (Autumn/Winter 1971), pp. 8-12.

Fitch, Robert E. "The Social Philosophy of Paul Tillich," *Religion in Life,* XXVII (1958), pp. 247-56.

Fuchs, Emil. "Die erste imternationale Konferenz der religioesen Sozialisten," *Christliche Welt,* XXXVIII, 31/32 (1924), pp. 609-14.

Gehse, Fritz. "Protestantismus und Sozialismus bei Paul Tillich," *Christ und Sozialist,* No. 1 (1969), pp. 1-4.

Gerlach, Otte. "Der religioese Sozialismus in der Theologie und Philosophie Paul Tillichs," *Christ und Sozialist,* Nos. 2/3 (1955), pp. 2-7.

Gunz, Johanna. *Sozialismus und Religion im Deutschland der Nachkriegszeit.* Muenchen: Dunker und Humblot, 1933.

Heimann, Eduard. "Tillich's Doctrine of Religious Socialism," *The Theology of Paul Tillich,* pp. 312-25.

_____. "Paul Tillich 1886-1965," *Christ und Sozialist,* No. 4 (1965), pp. 1-2.

Kaiser, Kurt. *Materialien ueber den religioesen Sozialismus in Deutschland aus der Zeit von 1918-1933.* Doctor's dissertation, Basel, 1962.

Kantzenbach, Friedrich Wilhelm. "Fuenfzig Jahre religioeser Sozialismus in Deutschland 1918-1968," *Evangelische Kommentar,* XII (1968), pp. 710-11.

Koch, Walter. "Geistige Bewegung," *Sozialistische Monatshefte,* XXVI (June 28, 1920), pp. 531-33.

Kuchemann, Clark A. "Professor Tillich: Justice and the Economic Order," *The Journal of Religion,* XLVI, 1, pt. II (January 1966), pp. 165-83.

Lam, Elizabeth P. *The Place of Marx in Christian Thought. A Part of a Dissertation Submitted to the Faculty of the Divinity School for the Degree of Doctor of Philosophy.* Chicago: University of Chicago, 1939.

_____. "Tillich's Reconstruction of the Concept of Ideoloby," *Christianity and Society,* V, 5 (1940), pp. 11-15.

Leese, Kurt. *Die Religionskrisis des Abendlandes und die religioese Lage der Gegenwart.* Hamburg: Hoffmann und Campe Verlag, 1948.

Lowe, Adolph. "In Memoriam: Eduard Heimann, 1889-1967," *Social Research* XXXIV, 4 (Winter 1967), pp. 609-12.

_____. *The Price of Liberty. A German on Contemporary Britain.* Second ed., London: Leonard and Virginia Woolf, 1937.

_____. Personal Interviews. October 15, 1971 and May 24, 1972.

Marsch, Wolf-Dieter. "Theologie und Marxismus im religioesen Sozialismus," *Internationale Dialog Zeitschrift,* V, 1 (1972), pp. 6-23.

_____ and Gerhard Rein (eds.) *Werk und Wirken Paul Tillichs. Ein Gedankbuch.* Stuttgart: Evangelisches Verlagswerk, 1967.

Means, Paul Banwell. *Things That are Caesar's. The Genesis of the German Church Conflict.* New York: Round Table Press, Inc., 1935.

Meyer, Gerhard E. O. "The Religious Socialist in the World Crisis," *The Journal of Liberal Religion,* III, 3 (Winter, 1942), pp. 131-50; III, 4 (Spring 1942), pp. 195-216.

Midgley, Louis C. "Ultimate Concern and Politics: A Critical Examination of Paul Tillich's Political Theology," *The Western Political Quarterly,* XX, 1 (March 1967), pp. 31-49.

Muhler, E. "Christlich-soziale Bewegung," *Staatslexikon,* 5th ed., I, pp. 1264-70.

Neue Blaetter fuer den Sozialismus, I-IV, 1930-1933. Ed. by Eduard Heimann, Fritz Klatt, August Rathmann, and Paul Tillich. Potsdam.

Niebuhr, Reinhold, *"The Interpretation of History* by Paul Tillich," (review), *Radical Religion,* II, 1 (Winter 1936), pp. 41-42.

Osterroth, Franz. "Der Hofgeismarkreis der Jungsozialisten," *Archiv fuer Sozialgeschichte,* IV (1964), pp. 525-69.

Rathmann, August. "Glaeubiger Realismus," *Politischer Rundbrief des Hofgeismarkreises der Jungsozialisten,* No. 5 (January 1926), pp. 26-32.

_____. "Christentum und Sozialismus," *VZ,* No. 172 (Sonnabend, July 27, 1963), Sonderseite.

_____. "Ethischer oder dialektischer Sozialismus?" Unpublished manuscript, September 1971.

_____. "Sozialistische Gestaltung aus christliche Verantwortung," *VZ,* No. 159 (July 11, 1964), Sonderseite.

_____. "Tillich als religioeser Sozialismus," *GW,* XIII, pp. 564-68. Longer version available as unpublished manuscript.

_____. Personal interview. July 17, 1973.

Rendtorff, Trutz. *Christentum zwischen Revolution und Restauration.* Muenchen: Claudius Verlag, 1970.

Rolinck, Eberhard. "Paul Tillich und der religioese Sozialismus," *Aufbruch von links.* Ed. by Otto Betz and Ludger Zinke, Muenchen: Verlag J. Pfeiffer, 1969, pp. 121-38.

Scheider-Flume, Gunda. "Kritische Theologie contra theologisch-politischen Offenbarungsglauben," *Evangelische Theologie*, XXXIII, 2 (March/April 1973), pp. 114-37.

Schwendtfeger, Erich. "Die politische Theorie in der Theologie Paul Tillichs." Doctor's dissertation, Marburg, 1969.

Shinn, Roger L. *Christianity and the Problem of History*. New York: Charles Scribner's Sons, 1953.

Soecknick, Gerda. *Religioeser Sozialismus der neueren Zeit unter besonderer Beruecksichtigung Deutschlands*. Jena: Gustav Fischer, 1926.

Sozialismus aus dem Glauben. Verhandlungen der sozialistischen Tagung in Heppenheim. Zuerich und Leipzig: Rotapfel, 1929.

Staehli, Martin. "Materialistische Grundlegung des Christentums," *Internationale Dialog Zeitschrift*, V, 1 (1972), pp. 23-37.

Strohm, Theodor. *Kirche und Demokratischer Sozialismus*. Muenchen: Chr. Kaiser Verlag, 1968.

_____. *Theologie im Schatten politischer Romantik*. Muenchen: Chr. Kaiser Verlag, 1970.

Stumme, John R. "*Ontologie, Theologie, gesellschaftliche Praxis*" (review of book by Thomas Ulrich), *Lutheran World*, II, 2 (1973), p. 210.

Ulrich, Thomas. *Ontologie, Theologie, gesellschaftliche Praxis Studien zum religioesen Sozialismus Paul Tillichs und Carl Mennicke*. Zurich: Theologisches Verlag, 1971.

Wnedland, Heinz-Dietrich. "Der religioese Sozialismus bei Paul Tillich," *Der Kirche in der revolutionaeren Gesellschaft*. Guetersloh: Guetersloher Verlagshaus Gerd Mohn, 1967, pp. 208-35.

West, Charles C. *Communism and the Theologians*. New York: Macmillan Company, 1958.

Wolfinger, Hans-Dieter. *Der unvollendete Sozialismus*. Hamburg: Furche-Verlag, 1970.

B. Selected Material on Tillich's Life and Thought

For a complete bibliography on works about Tillich written before 1945 see the book by Adams. For bibliographies on later writings about Tillich see Osborne and Tait.

Adams, James Luther. *Paul Tillich's Philosophy of Culture, Science and Religion*. New York: Harper and Row, 1965.

_____. "Paul Tillich on Luther," *Interpreters of Luther*. Ed. by Jaroslav Pelikan. Philadelphia: Fortress Press, 1968, pp. 304-34.

Amelung, Eberhard. *Die Gestalt der Liebe.* Guetersloh: Gerd Mohn, 1972.

Armbruster, Carl J. *The Vision of Paul Tillich.* New York: Sheed and Ward, 1967.

Braaten, Carl E. "Eschatology and Ontology in Conflict: A Study of Paul Tillich's Tehology," *Christ and Counter-Christ.* Philadelphia: Fortress Press, 1972, pp. 54-66.

_____. "Paul Tillich as a Lutheran Theologian," *Chicago Lutheran Theological Seminary Record,* Vol. 67, No. 3 (August 1962), pp. 34-42.

Eberhardt, Hermann. "'Ethik des Reiches Gottes'--Die grundlegende Funktion des Reich-Tottes fuer die Sozialethik bei Paul Tillich," *Sozialethik im Umbruch der Gesellschaft.* Ed. by Heinz-Dietrich Wendland. Goettingen: Vandenhueck und Ruprecht, 1969, pp. 198-212.

Gardner, Romaine Laverne. "Theonomous Ethics. A Study in the Relationship Between Ethics and Ontology in the Thought of Paul Tillich." Unpublished Doctor's dissertation, Columbia University, 1966.

Hopper, David. *Tillich: A Theological Portrait.* Philadelphia and New York: J. B. Lippincott Co., 1968.

Kegley, Charles W., and Robert W. Bretall (eds.) *The Theology of Paul Tillich.* New York: The Macmillan Company, 1952.

Leibrecht, Walter. "The Life and Mind of Paul Tillich," *Religion and Culture: Essays in Honor of Paul Tillich.* Ed. by Walter Leibrecht. New York: Harper and Brothers, 1959, pp. 3-27.

Lindbeck, George A. "Natural Law in the Thought of Paul Tillich," *Natural Law Forum,* VII (1962), pp. 84-96.

Lyons, James R. (ed.) *The Intellectual Legacy of Paul Tillich.* Detroit: Wayne State Press, 1969.

Mahan, Wayne W. *Tillich's System.* San Antonio, Texas: Trinity University Press, 1974.

Mahlmann, Theodor. "Eschatologie und Utopie im geschichtsphilosophischen Denken Paul Tillichs," *Neue Zeitschrift fuer systematische Theologie und Religionsphilosophie,* VII (1965), pp. 339-70.

May, Rollo. *Paulus: Reminiscences of a Friendship.* New York: Harper and Row, 1973.

McKelway, Alexander J. *The Systematic Theology of Paul Tillich. A Review and Analysis.* Richmond, Virginia: John Knox Press, 1964.

Niebuhr, Reinhold. "The Contribution of Paul Tillich," *Religion in Life,* VI (Autumn 1937), pp. 574-81.

Osborne, Kenan B. *New Being. A Study on the Relationship Between Conditioned and Unconditioned Being According to Paul Tillich.* The Hague: Martinus Hijhoff, 1969.

Pauck, Wilhelm. "Paul Tillich 1886-1965," *Theology Today,* XXIII, 1 (April 1966), pp. 1-11.

Paul, William Wright. "Paul Tillich's Interpretation of History." Unpublished Doctor's dissertation, Columbia University, 1959.

Pelikan, Jaroslav. "Ein Deutscher Lutherischer Theologe in Amerika, Paul Tillich und die dogmatische Tradition," *Gott ist am Werk.* Ed. by Heinz Brunotte and Erich Ruppel. Hamburg: Furche-Berlag, 1959, pp. 27-36.

Piper, Otto. *Recent Developments in German Protestantism.* London: Student Christian Movement Press, 1934.

Pitcher, William Alvin. "Theological Ethics in Paul Tillich and Emil Brunner. A Study in the Nature of Protestant Theological Ethics." Unpublished Doctor's dissertation, University of Chicago, 1955.

Robinson, James M. (ed.) *The Beginnings of Dialectic Theology,* Vol. 1. Trans. by Keith R. Crim and Louis De Grazia. Richmond, Virginia: John Knox Press, 1968.

Scharlemann, Robert P. "The Scope of Systematics: An Analysis of Tillich's Two Systems," *Journal of Religion,* 48 (1968), pp. 136-49.

Schedler, Kenneth. *Natur und Gnade. Das sakramentale Denken in der fruehen Theologie Paul Tillichs (1919-1935).* Stuttgart: Evangelisches Verlagswerk, 1970.

Shishido, Miles Motoynki. "Individual and Community in the Systems of Marx and Tillich." Unpublished Doctor's dissertation, University of Chicago, 1967.

Sommer, Guenter Frederick. "The Significance of the Late Philosophy of Schelling for the Formation and Interpretation of the Thought of Paul Tillich." Unpublished Doctor's dissertation, Duke University, 1960.

Tait, L. Gordon. *The Promise of Tillich.* New York: J. B. Lippincott, 1971.

Tillich, Hannah. *From Time to Time.* New York: Stein and Day, 1973.

Zahrnt, Heinz. *The Question of God; Protestant Theology in the Twentieth Century.* Trans. by R. A. Wilson. New York: Harcourt, Brace and World, 1969.

Zucker, Wolfgang M. "The Demonic: From Aeschylus to Tillich," *Theology Today* (1962), pp. 34-50.

C. *Other Related Material*

Acton, H. B. "Historical Materialism," *The Encyclopedia of Philosophy,* Vol. 4. New York: Macmillan Publishing Co., 1967, pp. 12-20.

Bachmann, E. Theodore. "The Church and the Rise of Modern Society, 1830-1914," *Christian Social Responsibility,* Vol. II, *The Lutheran Heritage.* Ed. by Harold C. Letts. Philadelphia: Muhlenberg Press, 1957, pp. 89-137.

Barth, Karl. *Fragments Grave and Gay.* London: The Fontana Library, 1971.

_____. "Jesus Christus und die soziale Bewegung," *Der Freie Aargoner,* VI, 153 (December 23, 1911), p. 1.

_____. *The Word of God and the Word of Man.* Trans. by Douglas Horton. New York: Harper and Row, 1957.

Beach, Waldo and H. Richard Niebuhr. *Christian Ethics.* Second ed. New York: The Ronald Press Company, 1973.

Bellah, Robert N. *The Broken Covenant.* New York: A Crossroad Book, 1975.

Berger, Peter L. *A Rumor of Angels.* Garden City, N. Y.: Doubleday and Co., 1969.

Berryman, Phillip E. "Latin American Liberation Theology," *Theological Studies,* Vol. 34, No. 3 (September 1973), pp. 357-95.

Blumhardt, Christoph. "Christoph Blumhardt's Letter to his Friends" (November 1899). Trans. by James A. Hinz. *Metonia,* III, 3 (September 1971).

Bonhoeffer, Dietrich. *Letters and Papers from Prison.* Ed. by Eberhard Bethge. Trans. by Reginald H. Fuller, New York: The Macmillan Co., 1953.

Borg, Daniel R. *"Volkskirche,* 'Christian State' and the Weimar Republic," *Church History,* XXXV, 2 (June 1966), pp. 186-206.

Bornkamm, Heinrich. *Luther's Doctrine of the Two Kingdoms.* Trans. by Karl Hertz. Philadelphia: Fortress Press, 1966.

Braaten, Carl E. *History and Hermeneutics.* Philadelphia: The Westminster Press, 1966.

Bracher, Karl Dietrich. *The German Dictatorship.* With an Introduction by Peter Gay. Trans. by Jean Steinberg. New York: Praeger Publishers, 1970.

Bransted, Ernest K. *Germany.* Englewood Cliffs, New Jersey: Prentice-Hall, 1972.

Bultmann, Rudolf. "Religion und Sozialismus," *Sozialistische Monatshefte,* XXVIII (May 15, 1922), pp. 442-47.

Camara, Dom Helder. "What Would St. Thomas Aquinas, the Aristotle Commentator, Do if Faced with Karl Marx?" Lecture given at the University of Chicago, October 29, 1974.

Christianson, Gerald. "J. H. Wichern and the Rise of the Lutheran Social Institution," *The Lutheran Quarterly,* XIX, 4 (November 1967), pp. 357-70.

Cochrane, Arthur C. *The Church's Confession under Hitler.* Philadelphia: The Westminster Press, 1962.

The Common Catechism. New York: A Crossroad Book, 1975.

de Man, Hendrik. *The Psychology of Socialism.* Trans. from the Second German edition by Eden and Cedar Paul. New York: Henry Holt and Co., 1928.

Dodge, Peter. *Beyond Marxism: The Faith and Works of Hendrik de Man.* The Hague: Martinus Nijhoff, 1966.

Drummond, Andrew Landale. *German Protestantism Since Luther.* London: The Epworth Press, 1951.

Dumas, Andre. *Dietrich Bonhoeffer Theologian of Reality.* Trans. by Robert McAfee Brown. New York: The Macmillan Co., 1971.

Dupre, Louis. *The Philosophical Foundations of Marxism.* New York: Harcourt, Brace and World, Inc., 1966.

Eagleson, John (ed.) *Christians and Socialism.* Maryknoll, N. Y.: Orbis Books, 1975.

Easton, Loyd D. and Kurt H. Guddat (eds.) *Writings of the Young Marx on philosophy and Society.* Garden City, N. Y.: Anchor Books, 1967.

Engels, Fredrick. *Socialism Utopian and Scientific. The Essential Left.* New York: Barnes and Noble, Inc., 1961, pp. 103-46.

Feuer, Lewis S. (ed.) *Marx and Engels Basic Writings on Politics and Philosophy.* Garden City, N. Y.: Anchor Books, 1959.

Frostin, Per. "Modern Marxist Critique of Religion--A Survey," *Lutheran World,* XX, 2 (1973), pp. 141-54.

Gay, Peter. *Weimar Culture. The Outsider as Insider.* New York: Harper and Row, 1970.

Gollwitzer, Helmut. *Reich Gottes und Sozialismus bei Karl Barth.* Muenchen: Chr. Kaiser, 1972.

Goulet, Denis. "World Hunger: Putting Development Ethics to the Test," *Christianity and Crisis,* Vol. 36, No. 9 (May 26, 1975), pp. 125-32.

Gutierrez, Gustavo. *A Theology of Liberation.* Trans. and ed. by Sister Caridad Inda and John Eagleson. Maryknoll, New York: Orbis Books, 1973.

Heimann, Eduard. "Der Sozialismus als sittliche Idee und die materialische Geschichtstheorie," *Archiv fuer Sozialwissenschaft und Sozialpolitik,* LII (1924), pp. 139-76.

Holborn, Hajo. *A History of Modern Germany 1840-1945.* New York: Alfred A. Knopf, 1969.

Hunt, Richard N. *German Social Democracy 1918-1933.* Chicago: Quadrangle Books, 1970.

Jay, Martin. *The Dialectical Imagination: A History of the Frankfurt School and the Institute of Social Research, 1923-1950.* Boston: Little, Brown and Co., 1973.

Kupisch, Karl. *Quellen zur Geschichte des deutschen Protestantismus (1871-1945).* Berlin: Musterschmidt-Verlag, 1960.

Landauer, Carl, in collaboration with Elizabeth Kridl Valkenier and Hilde Stein Landauer. *European Socialism. A History of Ideas and Movements from the Industrial Revolution to Hitler's Seizure of Power.* 2 Vols. Berkeley and Los Angeles: University of California Press, 1959.

Latourette, Kenneth Scott. *Christianity in a Revolutionary Age.* Vol. IV. *The Twentieth Century in Europe.* New York: Harper and Brothers, 1961.

Lazareth, William H. "Luther's 'Two kingdoms' Ethic Reconsidered," *Christian Social Ethics in a Changing World.* Ed. by John C. Bennett. New York: Association Press, 1966, pp. 119-31.

Macquarrie, John. *Twentieth Century Religious Thought.* New York: Harper and Row, Publishers, 1963.

Mannheim, Karl. *Ideology and Utopia.* Trans. by Louis Wirth and Edward Shils. New York: Harcourt, Brace and Co., 1936.

Marquardt, Friedrick-Wilhelm. *Theologie und Sozialismus--das Beispiel Karl Barths.* Muenchen: Chr. Kaiser, 1972.

Marty, Martin E. *The Modern Schism.* New York: Harper and Row, 1969.

Marx, Karl. *The Economic and Philosophic Manuscripts of 1844.* Ed. with Introduction by Kirk J. Struik. New York: International Publishers, 1964.

_____ and Frederick Engels. *The German Ideology.* Ed. with an Introduction by R. Pascal. New York: International Publishers, 1947.

Massanari, Ronald L. "Christian Socialism: Adolf Stoecker's Formulation of a Christian Perspective for Social Change for the Protestant Church in Nineteenth Century Germany," *The Lutheran Quarterly,* XXII (May 1970), pp. 185-98.

_____. "True or False Socialism: Adolf Stoecker's Critique of Marxism from a Christian Socialist Perspective," *Church History,* Vol. 41, No. 4 (December 1972), pp. 487-96.

McCabe, Herbert. *What is Ethics All About?* Washington: Corpus Books, 1969.

Moltmann, Juergen. "The Future as a New Paradigm of Transcendence," *Concurrence,* I, 4 (Fall 1969), pp. 334-45.

_____. "Theology as Eschatology," *The Future of Hope.* Ed. by Frederick Herzog. New York: Herder and Herder, 1970, pp. 1-50.

_____. *Theology of Hope.* New York: Harper and Row, 1967.

Niebuhr, H. Richard. *Christ and Culture.* New York: Harper and Brothers, 1951.

Niebuhr, Reinhold. *Moral Man and Immoral Society.* New York: Charles Scribner's Sons, 1960.

Norris, Russell B. *God, Marx, and the Future.* Philadelphia: Fortress Press, 1974.

Ogletree, Thomas W. (ed.) *Openings for Marxist-Christian Dialogue.* Nashville: Abingdon Press, 1968.

Oestreicher, Paul (ed.) *The Christian Marxist Dialogue.* London: The Macmillan Co., 1969.

Ortlieb, Heinz Dietrich (ed.) *Zur Ordnung von Wirtschaft und Gesellschaft. Festausgabe fuer Eduard Heimann zum 70, Geburtstage.* Tuebingen: J. C. B. Mohr, 1959.

Pannenberg, Wolfhart. *Basic Questions in Theology.* Vol. 1. Trans. by George H. Kehm. Philadelphia: Fortress Press, 1970.

_____. *Jesus--God and Man.* Trans. by Lewis L. Wilkens and Duane A. Priebe. Philadelphia: The Westminster Press, 1968.

_____. *What is Man?* Trans. by Duane A. Priebe. Philadelphia: Fortress Press, 1970.

Rendtorff, Trutz. *Church and Theology. The Systematic Function of the Church Concept in Modern Theology.* Trans. by Reginald H. Fuller. Philadelphia: The Westminster Press, 1971.

Shanahan, William O. *German Protestants Face the Social Question.* Vol. I. *The Conservative Phase, 1815-1871.* Notre Dame, Indiana: University of Notre Dame Press, 1954.

Stern, Fritz (Intro.) *The Path to Dictatorship 1918-1933. Ten Essays.* Trans. by John Conway. Garden City, New York: Anchor Books, 1966.

Stone, Ronald H. *Reinhold Niebuhr: Prophet to Politicians.* Nashville: Abingdon Press, 1972.

Tiefel, Hans. "The German Lutheran Church and the Rise of National Socialism," *Church History,* Vol. 41, No. 3 (September 1972), pp. 326-36.

Troeltsch, Ernst. *The Social Teaching of the Christian Churches.* 2 Vols. With an Intro. by H. Richard Niebuhr. Trans. by Olive Wyon. New York: Harper and Row, 1960.

Tucker, Robert. *Philosophy and Myth in Karl Marx.* Cambridge: University Press, 1964.

van der Bent, Ans. J. *The Christian Marxist Dialogue: An Annotated Bibliography.* Geneva: World Council of Churches, 1969.

Waxman, Chaim I. (ed.) *The End of Ideology Debate.* New York: A Clarion Book, 1968.

Weber, Max. "Politics as Vocation," *From Max Weber.* Trans., ed., with an Intro. by H. H. Gerth and C. Wright Mills. New York: The University of Oxford Press, 1958, pp. 77-128.

Wolf, Ernst. "Politischer Gottesdienst," *Blaetter fuer deutsche und internationale Politik,* XI, 4 (1966), pp. 289-301.

PRECIS

This study explores the dialectical relationship of Christian and socialist concepts in Paul Tillich's thought during his German, socialist period, 1918 to 1933. It argues that the central concern of his "religious socialism" was to interpret, criticize, and transform Marxist socialism and Protestant Christianity from a prophetic theological perspective. He placed socialism in theological perspective in anticipation of a new historical era that would be structured according to socialist principles and empowered with the meaning-giving substance of the Christian tradition.

Tillich's theological-political efforts are first set within their historical context (Chapter 2). His movement from a conservative background to socialism, his relation to the church and theology during Weimar years, and his involvement as a critical theorist within the socialist movement are traced. The events, the people, and the ideas important to him are introduced.

The systematic analysis of Tillich's thinking begins in Chapter 3 with a discussion of "The Meaning of Socialism." He understood socialism to be the expression of the proletarian situation, a religious phenomenon, and a prophetic and autonomous movement. It is shown that Tillich derived his theological perspective from his understanding of justification and eschatology. Special note is made of his interpretation of "expectation," the symbol of socialism, the basic attitude of the prophets, and the normative posture of man. Finally, it is noted, Tillich considered socialism to be a "living movement" open to transformation.

Tillich's encounter with Marxist theory is then considered. Chapter 4 discusses his critical affirmation and development of historical materialism. Tillich accepted Marx's claim that the "socially producing man" is the subject of history, but he rejected the philosophical basis of a narrow economism. He found that Marx viewed man as a unity of being and consciousness, and he endorsed the Marxist analysis of the capitalist age. Tillich adopted the concept of ideology and related to the Protestant principle. In Chapter 5 Tillich's concept of historical dialectic is analyzed. For him historical dialectic is a critical and revolutionary theory of change that views social movement as one of tension and conflict. It is a theory that unites transcendental destiny and historical responsibility in the proletariat and envisions a new society but not the ultimate social order. Tillich elaborated the meaning of dialectic with the concept of expectation, and he sought to reinterpret the utopian element in Marxism. In these two chapters Tillich's agreement and disagreement with Marxist theory, as well as his efforts to reshape it, become clear.

Attention turns directly to Tillich's theological perspective in the final chapter. His dialectical principles for understanding the relationship between the divine and the human and between religion and politics are presented and appraised. Tillich's position is then compared to those of Karl Barth and his own Lutheran tradition. His eschatological stance is singled out for special consideration and criticism. Finally, in a summary section, Tillich's way of relating Christianity and socialism is characterized as a "proleptic model" and is seen to be a position that is concrete, critical, comprehensive, and constructive. The value and the limits of this model are suggested. The dissertation concludes with a short survey of Tillich's relationship to socialism after 1933.

VITA

I was born November 6, 1942, the eighth child of Esther K. (Engelsted) and Lawrence A. Stumme, and was named John Richard. My father, a Lutheran pastor, was Administrator of the Muscatine (Iowa) Lutheran Homes, a home for children and the aging. I attended Zion Lutheran Grade School and Muscatine High School. From 1960 to 1962 I was a student at Wartburg College, Waverly, Iowa, and in the fall of 1962 I transferred to the University of Iowa, Iowa City. I received my Bachelor of Arts degree from the University of Iowa in 1964 and was graduated With Honors and With Distinction. I was made a member of Phi Beta Kappa. I worked for a year at Holy Family Lutheran Church, an inner-city congregation in Chicago, and then enrolled at Lutheran School of Theology in Chicago in 1965. My year of internship was spent on Chicago's West side at Bethel Lutheran Church and the Christian Action Ministry. After receiving my Master of Divinity degree from LSTC in 1969, I began a doctoral degree program in Christian Ethics at Union Theological Seminary in New York. I was a resident at Union for three years, and then in 1972 I went to Germany with the help of a scholarship from the Lutheran World Federation to continue work on my dissertation. In Germany I studied for a year at the Kirchliche Hochschule, Berlin, and the Freie Universitaet, Berlin. Beginning in the fall of 1973 I taught at St. Olaf College, Northfield, Minnesota, where I was an Assistant Professor. Since August, 1977, I have been at ISEDET, the Union Theological Seminary in Buenos Aires, Argentina, where I teach systematic theology and ethics. On June 5, 1966, I was married to Sandra Sue Snair. We are the parents of two sons, Simeon Martin, born January 6, 1972, and Abram John, born June 28, 1975.

3 1542 00137 1131

WITHDRAWN

230
T577zst

830195

DATE DUE			

Haas Library
Muhlenberg College
Allentown, Pennsylvania